Mastering Technical Sales

The Sales Engineer's Handbook

Second Edition

For a listing of recent titles in the *Artech House Technology Management Library,* turn to the back of this book.

Mastering Technical Sales

The Sales Engineer's Handbook

Second Edition

John Care
Aron Bohlig

**ARTECH
HOUSE**

BOSTON | LONDON
artechhouse.com

Library of Congress Cataloging-in-Publication Data
A catalog record for this book is available from the U.S. Library of Congress.

British Library Cataloguing in Publication Data
A catalogue record for this book is available from the British Library.

ISBN: 978-1-59693-339-2

Cover design by Igor Valdman

© 2008 ARTECH HOUSE, INC.
685 Canton Street
Norwood, MA 02062

10 9 8 7 6 5 4 3 2 1

Contents

Acknowledgments

It would be impossible to mention everyone who contributed toward the ideas and concepts expressed within this book. We are all shaped by the work environment, as well as by those individuals who are around us on a day-to-day basis and those who transiently touch our careers.

First, thanks to our editorial team of Mark Walsh, Barbara Lovenvirth, and our mystery reviewer.

I would like to thank each and every manager I have ever worked with—notably Alice Kessler, Mark Armenante, Ted Yarnell, Wendell Meeks, Dick Trovato, Tim Miller, Gene Holcombe, and Eric Popiel. I have also had the pleasure of working with some of the finest salespeople in the world, who, whether they knew it or not, taught me much of what is in this book. So, a big thank-you goes out to Linda Weber, Mike Lombardo, Stephanie Porter, Bruce Duchene, Ralph Gordon, Young Sohn, Frank Fallon, Mike Mickle, Katie Bruno, Bill Beckley, Andy Cacossa, Marc Schnabolk (twice!), Brian George, Anthony Stella, Rick DeMare, Andrew Travis, Alan Gurock, and Elizabeth Arnsdorf.

This book is about the personal experience of being a sales engineer (SE), so much of which was taken from my SE teams and peers at Oracle, Sybase, Vantive, and Business Objects. In particular, each of the following taught me something about effective management: Joel Kapit, Nancy Lindsey, Elsie Weiler, David Lesniak, Steve Rubich, Gary Sing, Scott Leisten, Carlos Nouche, John Chiavelli, Vic Morvillo, Brian Baillod, Todd Tharpe, Chris Tippett, and Richard Foster.

Proving that good ideas can come from the marketing department, Eric Carrasquilla, Teri Palanca, John Kreisa, and Emily Mui helped out with some invaluable insights into the SE psyche. Many individuals contributed ideas or reviewed specific content. Thanks to Sid Amster and John Vairo for their constant encouragement, Jim Vouloumanos and Mike Shilling for infrastructure, Derek Crawford, Mike Lohr, and Phil Cooper for their feedback on webcasts and presentations, and Peter Cohan for *Great Demo!*

Credit also needs to be given to my parents, who taught me the value of hard work and that if you don't have a dream, it will never come true, as well as to my children, Amanda and Matthew, who I know believe that very same thing.

Finally, my heartfelt gratitude goes out to my wife, Allison, who remains convinced that I will someday write the great American novel.

John Care
Newtown, Pennsylvania
August 2008

Thank you to past and current managers and mentors who have inspired me and encouraged a drive for excellence in all endeavors: Lyle Bohlig, John Pearson, Dan Akers, Todd Carter, Kris Klein, Zach Maurus, David Popowitz, Don Smith, and Bob Spinner.

I would also like to thank those who helped out with early reviews of chapters, engaged in content discussions, or provided ongoing support and feedback: Jason McKarge, Scott Anscheutz, Bob Spinner, Dave Yarnold, Carol Chase, Lisa Tucci, Dwight DePalmer, Sandy Ward, Eric Allart, Mark Puckett, Rodney Goodger, Jonathan Farmer, and Don Smith.

Thanks as well to a large group of people whom I had the pleasure of working with and seeing in action. Your exploits can be found in the text, so don't be surprised if the some of this sounds familiar: Tim Miller, Matt Panning, Alex Saleh, Brett Cain, Derek Sampson, Simon Beavis, Nick Earl, Dave Henshall, Joe Jouhal, Mark Christiani, Jon Parkes, David Quantrell, David Baldry, Bruno Labidoire, Steven Kresko, Nick Riitano, Jay Tyler, John D'Amour, Matt Roloff, Barry Holley, and Nelson Veiga.

And a triple-special thanks to my wife, Sheryl, and children, Signe and Halle. Thanks for the patience while I was ticking away at the computer late at night or early in the morning. You are the best.

Aron Bohlig
San Francisco, California
August 2008

Introduction: Why Study "Technical Sales"?

Small opportunities are often the beginning of great enterprises.

Demosthenes

If you are reading this book, you are probably either directly responsible for selling high-tech products or are in a supporting group such as training or marketing. Since the initial publication of this book, we have learned from our discussions in the sales community that these techniques are relevant for companies addressing a wide spectrum of industries, including software, hardware, networking, storage, security, professional services, financial technology, information services, outsourced services, capital equipment, medical equipment and devices, aircraft components, defense, and others. We have found that this content is applicable to any complex sales environment where there are two sets of buyers: a business buyer and a technology or domain expert gatekeeper.

This second edition was designed to bring the original content up to date and keep it fresh. Since the original publication, the art of sales has remained relatively constant, but there have been industry changes, such as the emergence of software-as-a-service (SaaS), changes in typical organizational structures, the acceptance of the webcast as a presentation technology, and so on. In addition, we have certainly learned more since then as well and want to pass this information on to you. So, you will discover that we have significantly revamped and rewritten numerous chapters, including some new case studies, as well as added five new chapters dealing with two different aspects of demonstrations, utilizing a CRM/SFA system, the new hybrid technical-sales specialist position, and management metrics for running the sales-engineering organization.

In any case, congratulations; the techniques detailed in this book have contributed to the success of many technical-sales professionals, and we are confident they will improve your sales results as well. This book was specifically written to help decode the "black art" of selling complex, high-value products. These types of products are unique in their need to have a technical professional—a sales consultant or sales engineer—involved in the sale. Our systematic approaches can enable any level of sales or marketing person to improve his or her capability to deliver service to the customer and improve sales as a result.

The trade-book press is glutted with volumes on how to sell, so why do we think another one is necessary? Most books today focus on "old-school selling," an approach that is more than 100 years old and is pretty well documented. Those books are great for the Willy Lomans of the world who are focused on turning a quick buck with high-pressure sales. There are also some excellent books that describe *sales methodologies*, or processes to follow to improve your sales. These books are generally focused on establishing and cultivating relationships with key executives.

What's missing is an equal focus on improving the methods and skills of those who engage in the technology side of the sales equation. This is a new aspect of selling that has become increasingly important during the last few decades as technology-based products and services have become an important component of the global economy. It is no longer sufficient to have a basic background in a field and some nice brochures. In some cases, customers we have dealt with have run product evaluations with teams of 20 people, of which 5 or 6 have PhDs in system architecture or a similar field. So, today's high-tech salesperson needs to do the job of yesterday, relationship selling, while maintaining an extremely high level of technical proficiency in their products—certainly a tall order. The good news is that this profession pays extremely well, and if you are good, you will always be able to find a job.

It is worth taking a minute to consider why sales engineers are so highly paid. This role is still evolving, as evidenced by the variety of terms for the position: sales consultant (SC), sales engineer (SE), solutions architect (SA), and many other permutations. As mentioned, the skills required are diverse and frequently difficult to find in a single individual. This means that good SEs are a rare breed. But why do companies pay so dearly for this unusual skill set? The answer is something we call the *product/market gap*. This gap refers to the fact that by the time a high-tech product gets to market, it is fundamentally dated. This may mean that the product is too slow or doesn't have the full suite of features currently demanded by the market. It is your job to sell these products that poorly match the market need to the customers who constitute that market. In some cases, your products will perfectly reflect the current needs of the market, but usually only for a short period. This product/market gap is driven, on the one hand, by media and analysts who are always demanding more of vendors and, on the other, by the executives in your company who want to expand the use of your product beyond your traditional customers. The good news is that when this happens, an exciting frontier is born, one where there is money to be made and excitement to be had.

So, this book is intended to help you:

1. Make money;

2. Improve your skills;

3. Keep your sanity.

This book is set up in a modular fashion so you can order those priorities as you see fit. Each chapter is each meant to serve as a lesson in a particular facet of the job. Each should be short enough that you can easily read it and apply its lessons to your skills and needs in a single evening or during a single plane flight. It is our hope that you can use this book to great effect while traveling. Some chapters include material that is paraphrased from other chapters to provide context, but in general each chapter can be read individually.

How should you get started? Later in this chapter, we recommend specific chapters to start with, depending on your role and level of experience. If you are new to sales, you may want to start from the beginning or at least cover the first few chapters. Once you complete Chapter 2, "An Overview of the Sales Process," try to pick a chapter relevant to problems you are currently facing in a sales cycle.

While reading the material, keep in mind that each technique must be customized to your particular situation. In sales, the best practice is always the one that wins the deal. Quoting verbatim from this book is unlikely to win you points with a difficult sales rep, but the practices we have documented should give you sufficient background to reach a mutually beneficial solution. You will find that the chapters are broken into three parts, each targeting a progressively more experienced reader. Within each chapter, we also give specific advice based on the reader's seniority and assumed level of skill.

The chapter format is simple but designed to help you best leverage the material. Review the list of goals provided at the beginning of each chapter and use that as a framework to digest the material that follows. If you are not new to sales, pencil in other goals you may have. Then proceed through the material. Once you reach the "Skill Building" portion of a chapter, read the appropriate section. Now take a few minutes to reflect on your personalized goals and see if you have sufficient information on how to reach those goals. If not, do you now have a good enough understanding of the problem to pursue the solution? Our hope is that using this approach, a very high proportion of common sales and career issues can be explored. We firmly believe that if you apply the material in this book, you will experience better win rates, higher quota achievement, and greater personal satisfaction. You will also have better tools to manage your career and your personal brand. In addition, on finishing this book, you should gain additional insight into what makes your prospects and your coworkers "tick." This understanding should help you interact with them more effectively to your mutual benefit.

We now take a look at various types of sales engineers and suggest the chapters of specific interest based on level of expertise.

New SE

> *Major benefits:* You will learn how to develop your skills in sales and technology. You will also be exposed to advanced sales concepts, techniques, and strategies before you are forced to use them in the field.

> *Target chapters:* "An Overview of the Sales Process" (Chapter 2), "The Dash to Demo" (Chapter 8), and "Getting Started" (Chapter 14). The

book you are holding represents hundreds of years of cumulative sales experience; we wish we had had such a reference when we began.

Experienced SE

▸ *Major benefits:* You will gain an improved understanding of interactions across the sales team, reduced stress levels, and increased effectiveness through team selling. You will also read about tactical improvements and hear suggestions for how to raise your visibility and improve your chances for promotion. You will learn to apply structured techniques to concepts about which you have had an intuitive understanding. When you come across such an idea, take the time to reflect on how your experience relates to what you have read. Try to use the frameworks we have provided to systematize the best practices you have previously employed with what we have documented. The result will be a personalized approach that will improve the consistency of your output, leading to higher sales.

▸ *Target chapters:* "The *U* in Technical Sales" (Chapter 17) and "Time Management for SEs" (Chapter 26).

Sales Manager or Sales Trainer

▸ *Major benefits:* How do you add value to the sales force today? Too many people in your position do not continuously challenge themselves by applying that metric to every strategic decision or component of course work. This book covers both management issues and suggestions for systematizing tactical excellence in your team. We also provide insight into often overlooked issues such as technical-sales organization structures and political issues within the sales organization. Our hope is that you will find this book to be an excellent framework or supplement for your training plan.

▸ *Target chapters:* "Organizational Structure" (Chapter 23), "Building the Infrastructure" (Chapter 24), and "Managing by the Metrics" (Chapter 27).

Sales Representative

▸ *Major benefits:* Although many of the topics we cover are concerned with technical-sales issues, many chapters will assist the sales representative as well. Not only will you benefit from the tactical skills we discuss, but you can improve your communication and level of understanding within your sales team. Spend 10 to 15 hours reading the suggested chapters and then give the book to your sales engineer. You will be better able to jointly sell and service your customers.

▸ *Target chapters:* "Needs Analysis and Discovery" (Chapter 5), "The Dash to Demo" (Chapter 8), "Evaluation Strategies" (Chapter 11), and "Competitive Tactics" (Chapter 19).

Marketing and Product Management

▸ *Major benefits:* This book will provide you with a perspective on where you should best invest your resources to help the sales force. Your fast path to success is to read the sales process overview chapter, Chapter 2. Then ask a salesperson how much time she spends in each sales stage. Find the bottlenecks or time sinks, read the appropriate chapters, and begin improving your support in those key areas.

▸ *Target chapters:* "An Overview of the Sales Process" (Chapter 2), "The Hybrid Sales Specialist Position" (Chapter 22), and others depending on current needs.

Technical Consultant

▸ *Major benefits:* As a technical consultant, you will benefit in two ways from this book. First, some of the concepts and processes are directly applicable to the sales cycles you will be engaging in or supporting. Second, you will frequently have to deal with vendor sales teams. This book will help you better understand how those teams operate and how you can get the most out of them for your client.

▸ *Target chapters:* "An Overview of the Sales Process" (Chapter 2) and "Evaluation Strategies" (Chapter 11).

If you still have questions, go to: http://www. masteringtechnicalsales.com, and we will be happy to respond to your inquiry.

Chapter Goals

Understand different phases of the sales process.

Know which groups are responsible for specific steps in the sales process.

Provide an overview of the key contributions expected of the SE at different points in the process.

An Overview of the Sales Process

If everything's under control, you're going too slow.

Mario Andretti

Much information about sales processes and methodologies has been published, all of which focuses on bringing structure to a sale but provides little guidance to the SE. This chapter briefly examines the major phases involved in the introduction of a new product, its introduction via a direct sales force, and its subsequent purchase by a customer. Table 2.1 lists the steps in the sales life cycle. For each stage in the sales process, there is a subsequent chapter (Chapters 3 through 13) that provides more detail. The reality is that the sales process is usually much more fluid than what is presented here. Use this overview to identify areas where you have the least experience and consider starting with those chapters first.

7

Table 2.1
Sales Life Cycle

Step	New Product Introduction	Chapter
1	Market definition	
2	Marketing campaign	
	Sales Process	
3	Lead qualification	3
4	Request for proposal (RFP) (optional)	4
5	Needs analysis, discovery, and customer engagement	5,6
6	Presentation, demonstration, and proposal	7–10
7	Evaluation (optional)	11
8	Negotiation and closing	12
	Postsales Support	
9	Account management and add-on sales	13

Definition of the Market

Long before a salesperson even thinks about selling a product, a marketing manager or an executive comes up with a bright idea for a new product or service. In theory, the person who thinks up the offering has been interacting closely with potential customers and has defined a product that will satisfy a real market need. You would be shocked and dismayed by how often this is not the case. This phase is intimately related to the definition of your lead qualification criteria (Chapter 3). The marketing department will have one or more *target customer profiles* that will define the initial set of customers on which the sales force will call.

Marketing Campaigns

Now someone responsible for *demand generation* builds a campaign to reach potential purchasers of your product and make them aware of what you have to offer. The marketing team will likely employ a variety of approaches to reach these customers. We will consider a few different approaches and focus on how each will impact your situation in the sales cycle.

Customer Events

New products are often previewed at international, national, or regional customer events. Whether brief evening sessions or full, multiday boondoggles, these are effective ways of receiving direct feedback regarding the value proposition from existing customers. This feedback is highly subject to "sampling errors," where the views of the purchasers of the old product are assumed to be similar to those of the nominal purchasers of the new product. This can be particularly problematic if the new product appeals to a different type of business buyer or decision maker, but the early feedback can be very helpful nonetheless.

Trade Shows and Seminars

Frequently, a company will host an exhibition at a trade show. The result will usually be several hundred (or thousand) moderately qualified leads. Based on our experience, usually a handful of very well-qualified leads may result (perhaps 5% of the total). As you may know, attending a trade show is often an excuse for training or a "junket" on the part of junior customer attendees. As a result, most leads from trade shows will not be high enough in quality to make it to your sales team. However, trade shows can be particularly helpful for new product introductions, enabling marketers to receive immediate feedback regarding forthcoming product releases directly from potential customers. Ideally, this is one of the first steps performed in a marketing campaign in order to help refine the marketing message for the "low-touch" forms of marketing such as mailers, where the message cannot be customized on the fly.

Mailing Lists and Outbound Calling Campaigns

The mailing list and calling campaign represent the old-fashioned style of sales approach. Mail campaigns, both hardcopy and electronic, are the modern equivalent of the traveling door-to-door salesman. The ratio of useless names and numbers to real leads is probably on the order of 100 to 1. Usually, a customer is sent materials describing your solution. If they respond, a telemarketer will then follow up to begin the sales cycle. As we will discuss later, these types of leads are difficult to generate and qualify. Be sure to be gentle when working with your telemarketing team on these leads.

Partners

A partner (system integrator, distributor, or value-added reseller) may bring you into a deal. These types of deals have advantages and disadvantages.

One positive aspect is that there is probably a qualified deal to be pursued; otherwise, the partner would not be taking the time to engage with you. One negative aspect is that you will usually not have direct access to the customer, and you will probably be brought in at the last moment possible for any customer deliverable.

Lead Qualification

Lead qualification has two major components. The first is the preliminary qualification performed by your telemarketing support person. This type of qualification is usually intended to validate the prospect's budget and probability of purchase and to identify the key people your sales team should contact. If the project is big enough and seems likely to go forward, the lead will be "handed off" to your sales representative. The sales representative is then responsible for developing an account plan to try to secure the prospect as a customer.

As part of this process, you and the sales representative will perform the second phase of lead qualification. In this phase, the salesperson will revalidate the customer's budget and timeline, and you will be responsible for validating the customer's technical requirements. If the prospect looks like it has a budget, is likely to buy, and has a technical environment compatible with your product's requirements, then you progress to the next phase of the sales cycle.

Request for Proposal

At this point, you should be clearing your schedule in preparation for generating a significant amount of paperwork. The niceties have been completed, and the prospect is going to request details surrounding your company, products, and whatever other criteria are important so that a decision can be made. These documents can be anywhere from 10 to several hundred pages long. A very thin request for proposal (RFP) is a good indicator that you are dealing with a project team that has not gone through this process previously. A very thick RFP usually means that the customer has hired a consultant who is trying to prove his value by adding additional detail and complexity to the process.

In cases where you are a key vendor for your customer, you may be able to avoid the initiation of an RFP process. If this is the case, try to find out what criteria are used to establish when an RFP is required. Most large companies have very strict guidelines regarding when competitive bids need to be issued and when established vendors can be used. By understanding these criteria, you can avoid accidentally inviting competitors to bid on your customers' projects.

If your company is a major player in your market, you will also frequently receive unsolicited RFPs. This usually means that either a competitor or a systems integrator has already sold the concept of the product to the prospect, and the prospect is trying to ensure that they have a look at the best products on the market. This situation is a very difficult one in which to compete because this unknowing third-party competitor will already have had access to the prospect's key contact personnel and will have set expectations that may exceed your capabilities.

Needs Analysis, Discovery, and First Customer Engagement

Frequently, a prospect will issue an RFP to a large number of vendors (five or more) and then put together a "short list" of the vendors whose products they wish to pursue. If your company is on this list, you will be permitted to ask questions of the prospect. This phase is usually called *discovery* or *needs analysis*. This is a critical phase because it is during your discovery that you will learn enough about your customer to put together a personalized solution. This is also your first real opportunity to interact with the customer. Your ability to identify pain points and respond with a compelling value proposition is a true measure of your skill as an SE.

Presentation, Demonstration, and Proposal

This part of the process consists of three phases: the presentation, the demonstration, and the proposal.

Presentation
Once you have completed your discovery session, you will be expected to present your findings. These presentations will typically be in response to your customer's request to detail different aspects of your solution. You should also certainly take the initiative and be sure that you present any additional selling points you identified during discovery. In the presentation chapter (Chapter 7), we provide insight into ways you can improve your presentation delivery.

Demonstration

If you are a new SE, you will probably see the demonstration as the most challenging part of the sales process. Depending on your client's needs and the quality of your product, this may very well be the case. The truth is that giving a demonstration is easy. Giving a good demonstration that meaningfully communicates the value of your solution is very, very difficult. Many SEs never rise above merely listing off the features of their products. If you are not beyond this phase yet, this book will help you learn how to put together a presentation that uses product demonstrations as the proof points for your key messages. In the end, your ability to choose the correct messages—and then substantiate them—will determine whether your proposal is superior to your competitor's.

Proposal

Some customers may make yet another cut, further reducing the number of vendors allowed to make a proposal. The proposal is meant to reflect the solution that you are recommending based on your interaction with the customer. The proposal will also usually include pricing and different legal terminology describing the way your company does business. Many sales teams spend relatively little effort on the proposal, knowing that the evaluation is complete by this point. You will still usually be required to put together a document describing the products you are recommending as well as any details describing other dependencies on the customer, such as other products they may need to have in place.

Evaluation (Optional)

Some customers will insist on being able to "pilot" or evaluate your product in advance of a purchase. Many companies have advanced, self-administering pilot kits. Increasingly, evaluation materials are available directly for download from a company's Web site. Most complex hardware and software products will require some level of human support to make sure that the customer is able to make the best use of your software. These projects can typically be one of the most challenging areas in technical sales.

Negotiations: Close or Lose—Getting the Deal

At this point, your job is done, and it is up to the salesperson to earn her money. You may be brought in for last minute clarification of technical points, but most of the focus is on the financial and legal terms of the contract. So, cross your fingers and try to relax.

Postsales Support and Ongoing Account Management

After purchasing your solution, a company will have to implement and then maintain it on an ongoing basis. Your sales team should continue to be involved with the customer. You will personally benefit from developing the relationship and the opportunity to use the customer as a reference. Over time, you will also have the opportunity to sell add-on products to the customer. By continuing to support the customer, you will improve the probability that these sales will continue. Usually, these types of sales require less effort on your part, which makes them very attractive.

Summary

This chapter provides an overview of a typical sales cycle. If you look at Table 2.2, which summarizes the key stages, you will notice that most of your activities are grouped toward the middle of the sales cycle. You should review this table and try to identify any other patterns of activity related to your business. Prioritize your reading of this book's chapters based on where you spend the most time during your sales process.

Table 2.2
Sales Stages and Key Tasks for the SE

Step	Stage	Key Tasks for the SE
1	Definition of the market	Relax.
2	Marketing campaigns	Relax.
a	Mailing lists and so forth	Relax.
b	Partners	Proactively establish relationships with partners. Understand how partners expect you to support them so you can do so effectively.
c	Trade shows and seminars	Relax. Perhaps enjoy a junket.
3	Lead qualification	Validate technical environment.
4	RFP	Wham! Get ready to answer hundreds of questions. This is a very time-intensive step.

Table 2.2 (continued)

Step	Stage	Key Tasks for the SE
5	Needs analysis, discovery, and engagement	Moderate activity: conduct background reading, interviews, and business analyses.
6	Presentation, demonstration, and proposal	Heavy activity is required for all the steps in this phase.
a	Presentation	Synthesize your analysis into a presentation of your business value.
b	Demonstration	Demonstrate the solution that delivers your value proposition.
c	Proposal	Develop a written proposal that can be used as part of a financial proposal to the customer.
7	Evaluation	Intense activity: there is significant preparation, and a lot of time is spent with the customer.
8	Negotiation: Close or Lose	Relax once again.
9	Postsales support	Minimal activity is required.
a	Support	Some support will usually be required. Focus on maintaining your relationship.
b	Sell add-on products	This is your primary activity during this period.

Skill Building

New SE	Focus on understanding how the sales process works in your company so you can better balance your time across different sales efforts. As you will discover, certain steps in every sales process tend to be very effort intensive. By recognizing when these steps are likely to occur, you can better balance your schedule and stagger meetings or deliverables.
Experienced SE	There isn't a lot you can gain by having an extremely in-depth understanding of the sales process. You can try to deepen your understanding in order to better understand future job opportunities if you are interested in marketing or one of the other supporting functions. Frankly, you are better off avoiding becoming entangled in the first phases of the sales process as they will largely reduce your selling time without resulting in tangible sales results.
SE Manager	Understand the sales cycle to help effectively allocate work across your team (see new SE above). You should understand the sales process well enough to know when one of the supporting functions isn't delivering as you would expect. This will enable you to give constructive feedback to the different groups and to escalate critical issues to management.

Chapter Goals

Comprehend the concept of *lead quality* as it relates to your solution.

Understand the different roles and motivations in the lead qualification process.

Recognize qualification alternatives based on various methods of acquiring leads.

Lead Qualification

> These are the new leads. These are the Glengarry leads. And to you they're gold.
>
> *David Mamet, Glengarry Glen Ross*

A solid lead is worth more than gold, and too many bad leads can cost you your job. *Lead qualification* is the process by which the sales team will try to make the initial evaluation to determine whether or not you are likely to close a sale. An irony of the sales process is that the least experienced member of the sales team, the telemarketer, usually handles lead qualification. The telemarketer will evaluate the lead and give it a ranking based on the customer's likelihood of purchasing the product, but not necessarily from your company.

If this is someone else's job, why do you need to know about the process? Many SEs adopt this attitude. Unless you already have the support of experienced sales staff, this inattentiveness will result in wasted time and a poor win rate, as attested to by the case study below.

CASE STUDY: WHEN A POOR FIT IS NO FIT AT ALL

> Our sales team spent more than 18 months working with a French apparel manufacturer trying to land a big deal. It was an extremely competitive situation in which we expended a lot of time meeting with the customer, understanding their needs, and putting together multiple proposals to meet those needs. We also spent a lot of time prototyping potential solutions at our own expense. The customer had some high-priced consultants working on the deal, so we assumed that they were serious. After this extremely painful sales process, the customer decided that no solution on the market met enough of their needs and subsequently decided to suspend their process for 12 months. The worst thing was that we knew how poor of a fit and how expensive our solution would be for the customer, but we kept after the deal anyway.

This example highlights one of the most common challenges sales teams face when they encounter a project that has already developed its requirements. Once the customer's expectations are set, you will have a much more difficult time convincing them that your solution meets their requirements. The example shows a situation where consultants set the expectation independently of any particular offering. If another vendor was responsible for setting the expectations, there's little hope you will be able to win the deal.

On the other hand, if you get involved with every lead that crosses your telemarketers' desks, you will have no time to focus on real opportunities. The reality is that, while telemarketing is responsible for this function, leads will come from multiple sources. In some cases, you will have well-qualified leads and will be able to quickly proceed to the next stage. In other cases, the lead will be poorly qualified, and you and your sales team will end up doing much of this preliminary work. In this chapter, we focus on improving the efficiency and effectiveness of the lead qualification process. We provide guidance on how to customize the process and improve your efficiency by better integrating qualification activities across the sales team. Note that we have split this chapter into two sections. If you are an individual contributor, read until you come to the word "stop," then jump to the summary. The remainder of the chapter is useful for managers or for senior individual contributors who are helping to improve lead qualification processes. In the second part of the chapter, we describe the three most likely circumstances under which a lead will enter your pipeline.

You Can Get Leads Too

You will often have the opportunity to get leads yourself. If you are working at a trade show, have sold a similar product previously, or have a friend with connections, then you already have leads. In a major-account environment, where you may only be dealing with three or four customers, lead generation is actually, officially or not, part of your job function.

In general, the best thing to do in these situations is to qualify and work the leads in conjunction with your sales rep, but without involving your telemarketer, because if the telemarketer is supporting you, he or she will have to enter the lead into the list of corporate prospects, and it might be assigned to a different sales team. In practice, this is unlikely but not uncommon. Most sales reps will be sufficiently savvy to know how to successfully manage this type of situation.

If you have identified a lead, you should first inquire about whether any bonuses are associated with lead generation. Many organizations provide incentives for employees to send valid leads to the telemarketing organization. Frequently, you must complete a minimal amount of paperwork. Be sure to complete the formalities as soon as possible so no one else can come forward with the lead before you claim credit for it.

Lead Quality

Now let's discuss the different possible ratings of a lead and how the leads are rated through the use of different questions.

Lead Ratings

To begin with, it is important to understand that not all leads are created equal. All leads can be categorized based on their characteristics. These categories are an attempt to qualify the value of the lead to your company. *Value* usually refers to the probability of purchase and to the total value of the purchase. The lead rating is a very artificial concept, but it is useful for you to understand it so you can participate in sales strategy discussions with your sales representative.

The lead rating may be used by your marketing organization to distribute the leads or merely used for tracking purposes. For example, a marketing organization might try to make sure that all sales teams have a similar chance of success by giving each team an equal number of high-quality leads. Obviously, if a single team got all of the best leads, it would be far more likely to hit its quota.

Different marketing organizations use different methods of ranking leads, but they are usually based on a set of letters or numbers with some inherent order. Common examples are *A*, *B*, *C*, or 30/60/90/120, or perhaps initials that represent a qualitative commentary: *L* for "likely," *U* for "unlikely," and so on. Now let's discuss what makes a lead "good."

Qualification Criteria

The following discussion looks at some of the most common qualification criteria. In recent years, variations of these questions have commonly begun to show up on Web sites, e-mail, or mail-in reply cards for products and services. These are examples of marketing organizations trying to turn you into a lead for their product. Your company is probably going through a very similar process. Try to think of some other good criteria for your company and for your sales team. Table 3.1 lists common questions that might be used by a telemarketing group.

We now look at the budget, time frame, and fit in greater detail.

Table 3.1
Typical Lead Qualification Questions

Questions Posed by Telemarketer
Budget
Do you have a budget for this project?
Can you tell me what the total budget is for the project? This helps us determine which level of solution may be appropriate for you.
Time frame
When do you expect the purchase to be completed?
Need
Do you have a corporate standard in the following areas?
Database platform
Server operating system
Client operating system
Are there any consulting firms assisting you with your evaluation or with other related projects?
Do you have anyone in your company who has worked with our products previously?
What other products are you considering?
Are there any existing solutions we will have to factor into our solution?
Do you plan to implement this yourself or will you be using external resources?

Hint:

Often, the prospect will be reticent about providing some of the information discussed next. A stubborn prospect may need to be reminded that their own sales organization goes through exactly the same process to qualify a lead and that by providing whatever information is available, they will enable you to provide the best service for their unique requirements.

Budget

One of the most important questions related to sales opportunities is, do they have a budget? The situation of a prospect without a budget will usually indicate that it is unlikely that the prospect has the ability to make a purchase, even if they decide that your solution fully meets their needs. As such, this is a critical piece of data to have. If your prospect does not have a budget, then you need to know when they expect to have one. Frequently, you will run into IT groups who want to investigate new products but whose investigations will not turn directly into a project. The issue is knowing whether your prospect is "just looking" or really performing research as the initial step in a project. Frequently, your sales rep will use this question as an opportunity to meet the customer's senior management to confirm that there really is a project and that there really will be a budget.

Some sales reps are uncomfortable probing too deeply into the specifics of an organization's budget. Some prospects feel that if they tell you what their budget is, your price will be equivalent to the number they give you. A question like the following one is a good way to approach the issue: "Can you tell me what your estimate is for total internal resources and total cost associated with the project?"

If your customer is still uncomfortable providing that information, the sales rep will probably provide them with a budgetary quote. In practice, you may be able to get access to budget information when the rep cannot. Posed by the technical consultant, the budget question is valid. You will need to know that information to help structure the proposal.

Knowing what the budget is will also help determine if the customer is truly in the market for a solution like yours. If their number is too low, they are probably looking for a solution with fewer features. If their budget is higher than normal, the prospect may be looking at higher-end solutions or expecting to have significant systems-integration costs. In either case, the information will directly impact whether you stay in the deal as well as your sales strategy. A low budget may also signify a customer's desire for an initial pilot or even a misestimation of the total cost of the project.

Time Frame

Another critical factor in determining the worth of a lead is the customer's purchase time frame. If your customer is planning on making a purchase within 3 months, they will likely expect very quick turnaround on their requests. You should be very willing to support them in the project because you are very close to a potential commission. Usually, the farther out the purchase time frame is, the lower the rating of the lead. From your company's perspective, the prospect could change their corporate priorities, could go out of business, or could find another reason to spend their money elsewhere in that time. Obviously, from the perspective of the sales organization, you want a purchase to take place as quickly as possible.

Asking about the time frame for the project is usually a very simple task: inquiring "What is your expected time of purchase?" will usually result in a direct answer. If it doesn't, consider that a significant red flag. A more valuable line of questioning revolves around what happens if the purchase doesn't take place. Try asking, "Do you have any milestones that are driving this purchase date?" This will give you a sense of what the real time frame will be. Accounting departments will frequently drive their companies to delay significant purchases until they are really needed. Knowing about any compelling events will help your sales team as they conduct their strategy sessions.

Fit: Do the Prospect's Needs Match Your Solution?

The criteria discussed so far establish the possibility that a purchase decision will take place in a reasonable time frame. Now you must consider whether or not your solution represents the best possible option for the customer. This is the most subjective part of a lead rating, and it is usually handled by establishing a set of questions meant to determine the prospect's relative priorities for different components of your system.

We can give you no simple questions to get to the heart of this issue, but your company should provide training in this area. A good strategy is to ask the customer what the business justification for the project is. Once you know what the business justification is, you will have a better idea of what questions you can ask to determine the "fit" for your solution.

In general, pose your questions in a way that will indicate a customer's preference for your solution compared to the alternatives. If the customer generally prefers the alternative option, you will know you have a lot of work ahead of you to change this preconception.

Acute Organizational Pain Can Trump Budget, Time Frame, and Fit

The existence of a formal project designed to select and implement a product is usually a feature of relatively mature markets. At times, you may find yourself selling a product that is at an early stage, where there are few guidelines for purchasers to make decisions. In other cases, the organization may develop a sudden, and unbudgeted, need for your product. You should remain open to finding these opportunities, but they can be harder to qualify—meaning you will have to spend more time working with your prospect to determine if there is a true need for your solution, as well as the ability to pay for it.

CASE STUDY: WHEN A MISSION CRITICAL SYSTEM GOES DOWN, BUDGETS CAN BE UP FOR GRABS

> One of us once had a client whose primary revenue-generating transaction-processing system hit a severe capacity constraint. Performance ground to a halt, and customers began defecting to competitors due to system errors and other quality-of-service issues. The client would have written a check for several million dollars on the spot to resolve the issue and prevent the loss of revenue and client accounts. Unfortunately, it took several months of expensive diagnostic consulting and lost revenue before the problem could be fully addressed.

Effective Lead Qualification

Competitive Implications of Technical Qualification Criteria

Most qualification questions have to do with customer budget, project team, or other financial or organizational indicators of purchase probability. You will also become aware of technical factors that serve as indicators of your competitiveness in a sales situation. Most of these factors relate to existing relationships your prospect has with other vendors or service providers. For example, if your product competes with a product from IBM and the customer already has a computer from IBM or perhaps has professional-services staff from IBM on site, then they may be heavily disposed to work with IBM.

The question then is, does this existing technical predisposition affect the quality of the lead? In many cases, it will. If the factor is a positive, build it into your value proposition. If the technical issue is a negative, ask the prospect up front if this is a "deal breaker" issue. If your product does not work in French and the customer has an office in Paris, you may not be able to win the deal no matter how much effort you put into the sales cycle.

Making the Decision to Say No

Your sales representative often will not have the in-depth product background to know when your competitors have outmatched you. This may make it difficult for the sales representative to perform the evaluation necessary to truly qualify the lead. In cases such as these, it is best to write a one- or two-page document describing your major relative competitive strengths and weaknesses and what it would take to prove to the customer that you would be the superior solution. Then, review this analysis with the sales representative. The decision to disqualify a lead will have to be a mutual one. By preparing a succinct but careful analysis, you will make it easier for the rep to understand your logic.

As an SE, you need to discuss this situation carefully with your manager after an initial conversation with the sales rep. Very few reps like to walk away completely from a potential deal and will usually attempt to sell you (after all, that is their job) on why the sales team should proceed with the opportunity. If you support multiple sales representatives, then it becomes an issue of prioritization that you can manage upward by delegating the eventual decision to your superior. When supporting a single rep, you can simply ask, which other lead/opportunity should I drop to pick this one up?

Defending Your Position When the Sales Rep Disagrees

If you feel strongly that a lead is not worth pursuing, you should absolutely say so. If necessary, discuss the issue with your manager. However, be prepared. At the end of the day, it is the rep's job to make those decisions, so you may get dragged along against your will. Remember to try to be flexible. Many technical consultants have a tendency to feel slighted when the sales representative makes a decision with which the consultant does not agree. The most difficult decisions arise in cases when a large proportion of the work that needs to be completed after a lead is deemed qualified falls on the SE. Examples would be the areas of requests for proposal (RFPs), requests for information (RFIs), or deep onsite discovery sessions.

Low-Cost Fallback Strategies

By now, you have probably reached the unpleasant conclusion that although you have opportunities to benefit from improvements to the lead qualification process, you will still generally be subject to the whim of your sales representative. This is true, but it is the nature of the relationship. It is worth taking the time to identify fallback strategies for those times when your sales team receives more qualified leads than you can realistically pursue. Chapter 26, "Time Management for SEs," covers this topic in more detail. A mature sales team will occasionally pass up good leads if their schedule will not allow them to spend sufficient time with the customer. By taking on more than you can handle, you will only dilute your efforts across all of your deals.

> | STOP | This concludes the basic material on lead qualification. The balance of the chapter will be valuable if you are a manager or if you are responsible for implementing or improving the lead qualification process in your division. If neither of these criteria describes your role, we recommend skipping to the chapter summary at this point.

Internal Roles in the Lead Qualification Process

Take a moment to think about your sales team and how you work together. Are there overlaps in the information you are capturing? Are there certain activities that one member in the group has the skill to perform more effectively? These questions are relevant at any point in the sales process, but especially in lead qualification. The decision to go forward with a lead represents a commitment of time and resources across the sales team. We now consider each of the internal roles and how they participate in the lead qualification process.

Sales Representative

The sales rep is responsible for the final decision on whether or not to pursue a lead. The salesperson will be responsible for defending this decision to management. She will often decide to pursue poorly qualified leads if a sufficient number of well-qualified leads are not available. If done for a long period, this can indicate that either your company's financial prospects are poor or the sales rep's prospects are poor, neither of which bodes well for you. Some sales reps will focus on one or two extremely large deals at a time. This form of "big-game hunting" can be very rewarding or financially disastrous. It is important for you to be comfortable with your rep's philosophy with regard to lead qualification and pursuit. This philosophy has a direct impact on your pay and the hours you must work to receive it.

Hint: The Rule of 200

Perform this simple piece of mathematics. Take your personal quota (or the combined quota of the reps you support) and divide by 200. That is the amount of expected revenue per day your activities need to justify.

Telemarketer/Lead Development

The telemarketer is responsible for capturing basic data about the prospect's organization, need for your products, and ability to purchase those products. Unfortunately, telemarketers are frequently compensated based on the number of leads they turn over rather than strictly on the closure rate of the leads they hand off to your sales team. This can result in a decrease in lead quality as the telemarketer tries to achieve his quota by passing on leads that are either not qualified or have been qualified when they should have instead been rejected.

If the telemarketer works with a group of sales representatives rather than a single sales rep, internal political issues may be associated with which sales rep gets a certain lead. If the telemarketer has any discretion regarding where a lead gets routed, he may make an effort to send good leads to his friends in the field. Most lead distribution systems are built to prevent this possibility, but being sales, such things do happen. It is certainly in your best interest to know if this is a possibility. If it is, make sure you cultivate a strong relationship with the telemarketer.

Sales Management

Sales management rarely gets involved in the lead qualification process. They may be responsible for distributing leads or for making sure that each sales rep gets his or her fair share of incoming leads of a relatively equal quality. Management will only get involved if a political squabble arises related to equitable lead distribution or if you have chosen to reject a lead. Frequently, if you decline to participate in a project, the customer will try to contact your sales manager to find out why. This highlights the need for your sales team to have very well-defined reasons for not pursuing leads. Sales management usually sees their involvement in lead qualification activity as necessary but as a low value-add activity.

SE

Traditionally, the SE has a minimal role. As an SE, you may be asked to verify that the customer's legacy environment has systems that are compatible with the products you are trying to sell. It is important that you expand your role to make sure your needs are accounted for in the lead qualification process. The telemarketer will have access to many of the people who will have the information you need for subsequent phases of your sales process. By simply developing a good relationship with your telemarketers, you can usually get them to do some of this additional work while they are performing the basic lead qualification task.

Care and Feeding of the Telemarketing Team

Before you drift off daydreaming about offloading too much of your discovery session onto the telemarketers, remember that they probably will not understand a detailed answer on many technical topics. What's more, the telemarketer is really going above and beyond the call of duty by helping you out, so you should be appreciative of any additional work performed.

Try to keep the qualification questions to two basic types: technical qualification and customer profile information. Work with your sales rep and the telemarketer to identify trends in your sales successes. Good sales teams will often find that they have a very high close rate for certain types of deals or certain types of prospects. Often you will develop a personal strategy that is entirely independent of that espoused by your sales and marketing organization.

Lead Qualification in Action: The Process with Three Common Scenarios

Now that you have an understanding of the goals and players, we will discuss three very common scenarios requiring lead qualification. Each scenario is fundamentally similar but has unique characteristics that will require you to vary your approach.

Solicited Leads

Generally, a response to a marketing campaign, a hit on your Web site, or perhaps a business card dropped off at your company's kiosk at a trade show will generate a solicited lead. Often, your marketing department will offer incentives to entice potential leads to give you their information. Unfortunately, this action results in a high percentage of respondents who just want a free T-shirt or coffee mug. Luckily, there are still several people between you and the prospect at this point.

The first of these people is your telemarketer. The telemarketer is responsible for taking the contact information provided and following up with the individual to determine his or her needs. The telemarketer will then develop the initial account profile, prepare appropriate contact profiles, and compile some amount of lead qualification information. This new lead is then assigned either to a territory or directly to your sales rep. If the lead is assigned to a territory, the manager of that territory will then assign the lead to a sales team.

Unsolicited Leads

In many industries, the majority of leads result from telemarketers and salespeople actively trying to generate interest in your company's products. In this case, the telemarketer may begin with a list of company names that meet certain criteria, usually based on the size of the corporation, geographical location, and probable need for your company's products. The telemarketer must then try to identify the appropriate personnel at the company who may be interested in your products and who control the buying decision. The next step is to try to convince those potential buyers that they have a need that your product meets. Either the telemarketer or the sales rep performs this step, depending on the level of access you have in the prospect's organization.

This initial sales pitch is usually a long and time-consuming process. The sales representative will probably send letters, e-mail out product information, and try to present to the potential customer—all in the hopes of arousing an interest in your product line. At this point, your sales team will have no idea whether or not the customer will be able to get a budget to pay for your product.

It is important to realize the amount of work that goes into these types of leads. Usually, if a telemarketer or sales representative has gone to that level of effort, it is worth your while to follow through, even if you don't believe the prospect is a good fit for your products. This is based both on the amount of time your organization has already invested in the prospect, as well as the emotional involvement the telemarketer or salesperson is likely to have with the potential customer. Additionally, your sales organization has already imposed on the customer to a certain degree, and it is a matter of professional courtesy to deliver on the expectation set by the sales representative or telemarketer.

Current Projects or Recommended Leads

The best-qualified lead is usually one where the customer has already established a project to pursue a product like yours. These leads are frequently the result of a recommendation on the part of an industry analyst who covers your solution. A project indicates recognition of the need as well as a certain commitment in human resources (the project team). If the project also includes external consultants brought on to help with the evaluation, this is an additional indication that the prospect is serious. This sign does not mean that you should not apply a rigorous lead qualification process. Just because the prospect has a need and some level of budget does not mean that your product, or any product, will meet the customer's requirements.

These projects often manifest themselves as RFPs, which are sent to someone in your organization. The RFP process is covered in detail in Chapter 4, but for qualification purposes, it is usually up to your sales team to determine if you think you can put forth a competitive bid for an RFP.

Summary

Lead qualification is an advanced topic for the SE because it is largely the responsibility of the sales rep and telemarketing team. By understanding the process you can accomplish the following:

- ▸ Know the right questions to ask prospects to qualify them.
- ▸ Give appropriate feedback to your sales rep and telemarketing team.
- ▸ Improve your understanding of the customer's business needs.

By developing a joint strategy for qualifying leads, your sales team can improve its ability to focus on good leads. Qualification should be a constant activity throughout the sales process; smart salespeople are continually looking for indications that their time is better spent elsewhere. Following these disciplines will improve your probability of closing sales and will help eliminate low-probability deals from your pipeline.

Skill Building

New SE	Work to understand the qualification criteria the telemarketers use. These should directly reflect the value proposition and solution strategy you are using in your demonstrations and presentations. Understand the three different scenarios by which you may receive a lead. Consider how different sources of leads may impact your sales strategy.
Experienced SE	Further develop your relationship with the telemarketing team. Focus on understanding the process from their perspective and building a joint set of qualification criteria. Remember that the time you spend developing these relationships will pay off when the telemarketers gather technical information, allowing you to be better prepared for your initial meetings.
SE Manager	Help your SEs make the right connections with the telemarketing organization. Review the qualification criteria to make sure they accurately reflect the market on which your team is focused. If the criteria are off base, work with your senior team members and the telemarketing group to improve the questions. Help your SEs manage their relationships with their sales reps. If you see patterns of friction emerging, work to resolve the issue or reassign the SE.

Chapter Goals

Understand how to create
a response to a request
for proposal (RFP).

Learn how to create a
quantitative RFP scoring
system.

Be able to present and
follow up as needed on
an RFP.

The RFP Process

Reasonable men adapt themselves to their
environment; unreasonable men try to adapt
their environment to themselves. Thus all
progress is the result of the efforts of unreasonable men.

George Bernard Shaw

A standing joke among the SE community is
that RFP actually stands for "really fast
paperwork." An RFP, or its younger brother, the
request for information (RFI), should be viewed
as a two-edged sword. It is both an opportunity
to win business and an opportunity to waste
resources. In this chapter, we will examine how
to create an RFP, the go/no-go decision, how
to handle deadlines, strategies for avoiding an
RFP, completion of the RFP, presentation, and
follow-up.

Creation of an RFP

An RFP provides a company with the opportunity to describe its requirements with the

31

expectation that one or more vendors can satisfy those requirements. Ideally, these requirements will be wrapped within a business case, some economic data, and an extensive business and technical background, plus all the necessary legalities and purchasing requirements.

As a general rule, the more business data contained within an RFP, the more thought has gone into its construction. The business-to-technical ratio (BTR) is an indicator of which department created the RFP. The lower the BTR, measured in terms of business pages divided by technical pages (BTR < 1), the more likely the IT group created the RFP. An additional implication of a low BTR is that it signifies more work for the SE as compared to the salesperson.

Basic Rule of RFPs

If you are not involved in any aspect of creating the RFP, then you are likely to lose. An RFP, whether written internally or externally by a consultant, is always influenced by outside factors. Some initial contact and selling from at least one vendor or systems integrator will have impacted the requirements. This affords that vendor the luxury of setting the stage and laying out some additional requirements about which the RFP originator may never have thought.

Hint: Have Your List Ready

Always have some "rigged" RFP questions, which showcase a competitive advantage, ready to provide to the prospect on demand. You may even offer to supply these questions well before RFP issuance to save the customer time and effort.

Remember that creating an RFP is a long and arduous task. The customer RFP team often welcomes any strategies for shortening the process, such as providing boilerplate questions. Because external consulting organizations are generating an increasing number of RFPs, we cannot stress enough the importance of an effective partner-education program.

The downside of an externally created RFP is that the same organization is often contracted to evaluate the responses. This means that minimal access is provided into the prospect's end user base because the consultant acts, in the interest of vendor fairness, as the gatekeeper to the organization.

The Go/No-Go Decision

Whether an RFP slams onto the desk of a salesperson or glides gently into an electronic inbox, the sales team needs to decide either to compete or to decline to respond. Factors to consider include these:

 › Your involvement in the RFP design and construction;
 › Product fit;
 › Competitors (including internal);
 › Time frame;
 › Budget and approval process;
 › Partner/systems integrator (SI) involvement;
 › Resource constraints;
 › Executive pressure.

A professional RFP response consumes many resources, so either commit wholeheartedly to respond or decline. Simply bolting together some boilerplate shows a lack of respect on the part of the sales team for the prospect. This is one occasion when "good enough is good enough" is *not* sufficient. Although neither of us particularly cares for the RFP process, we can both state honestly that when we compete, it is professional, and it is to win.

Too many sales organizations fail to correlate RFP completion with winning deals. We are aware of one sales organization where the overall opportunity win rate was 50%; yet, the win rate for unsolicited RFPs was 5%. A financial-services organization once told us that their win rate, measured over 18 months on thousands of RFPs, was just under 7%. Drawing to an inside straight playing poker yields better odds! Naturally, exceptions arise; when dealing, for instance, with regulated industries, state and local governments, and so forth, completion of an RFP is an absolute requirement for contract award. However, it is safe to say that responding to RFPs is unlikely to help your sales team overachieve on their quotas.

Salespeople will be far more enthusiastic about committing to a response than the SE—and usually in inverse proportion to the volume of work required of them. Aside from basic qualification techniques, making the sales representative the project manager for the RFP is *your* qualifier. Assuming that your organization does not have an RFP response team but does have basic templates and boilerplate, asking the rep to "put some skin in the game" is a necessity. Otherwise, the SE organization will spend their time completing RFPs at zero apparent cost to the sales representative. We would suggest that the sales representative/project manager complete and publish a high-level project plan, with a target internal completion time of at least 24 hours before the external deadline.

A compete decision is often made based on available resources. If a rep has an empty pipeline or a new SE has just been hired, it is viewed as a training exercise. Although this is admirable on-the-job training, it leads to substandard work unless supervised by experienced managers and, therefore, consumes valuable resources.

As an SE, you should not be afraid to ask the hard questions about an RFP. Deciding to complete an RFP is a task that should be managed upward: get your manager's input and agreement on the best course of action. Being asked to respond to an unqualified RFP detracts from more valuable opportunities and, when carried to extremes under tight timelines, is demoralizing and also highly detrimental to your bank balance.

Internally Scoring the RFP

The go/no-go decision described in the preceding section can be quantified by applying a score to each incoming RFP. Using the same objective measurement system for each RFP affords numerous benefits to the presales organization. First, it takes some of the emotion out of deciding how to respond to an RFP; second, it allows for ongoing measurement of RFP success against a score; finally, it provides a method to prioritize between conflicting RFPs in the event of resource limitations.

The scorecard should be a simple, one-page, fill-in-the-blanks sheet that both the account executive and the sales consultant can complete easily once they have actually read the RFP. Assign points, both positive and negative, based on a variety of business, technical, and opportunity-specific factors. For example, an RFP from an existing customer may score five points, as opposed to that from a new customer, which may score zero. Should the existing customer be a positive reference for you, add another two points. Create a set of weightings based on key technical issues that are either wins or show stoppers for your solution. Also allow for the fact that some competitors are easier to beat than others.

After you have devised the scoring system, retrofit it against some historical RFP wins and losses over the past 6 to 12 months to judge its validity. Remember that this is not an absolute measure of the probability of success, but it is another data point upon which to make a decision. Also note that the score should not be viewed as a success rate but simply as a relative score for each RFP as measured against other RFPs. Once the scoring system is correctly calibrated, on a scale of 0 to 100, you will find very few wins with a score under 40 and very few losses with a score over 75. The decision points are how to handle those RFPs that fall into the grey area. However, when conducting a go/no-go RFP meeting, you will be in a position to prioritize between a 70 RFP and a 50 RFP.

CASE STUDY : THE ECONOMICS OF RFP RESPONSES

A 2-year study conducted by a large software company within one of its European areas concluded that they spent €2 million per year in direct time and materials to capture €9 million in revenue. However, the opportunity cost of the time was €18 million (meaning potential sales made if that time had been spent selling instead of responding), leading to a net loss of €11 million. Their RFP win rate was under 10% during the first year of measurement. After implementing a formalized RFP scoring and response system, they raised their win rate to 22%, simply by engaging in fewer RFP battles and improving the quality of those RFPs they did respond to. Compared to the previous year, they turned a €4.5 million "profit" within their RFP operations.

Appendix 4A shows an outline scorecard, and the resource section of the Web site provides a more functional scorecard.

Handling Deadlines

It is a sad fact of vendor life that an RFP that took 3 months or more to create often demands a response inside 10 days due to some artificial deadline. Fact of life number two is that the review, selection, and award timelines laid out in the average RFP are met less than 10% of the time. A spot-check we made of completed RFPs within their respective sales channels yielded an uninspiring 1-in-22 ratio in terms of prospects meeting their timelines.

When a deadline is unreasonable, the sales team should strategize and then call the prospect organization immediately to request an extension. Any reasonable request will usually be granted; a refusal is a good indicator that you may not be a serious contender for the business. Honesty is usually the best policy, with the possible exception of claiming that you are too busy. Being "too busy" implies to the prospect that you do not have enough time for them. Very often, an issue with training, vacation, or existing customer commitments makes finishing the RFP by the deadline a problem. It is crucial that the SE organization agree to meet any deadlines because they are usually on the critical path for RFP completion. An SE may already have an RFP to complete, be preparing for a demonstration, or have prospect discovery meetings set up. Getting a 1-week extension may make the difference between responding and declining to bid.

Hint: The Salesperson May Not Be the Best Person

Many companies automatically ask for an RFP extension, whether needed or not. Using the SE manager, instead of the sales manager, to make the call to the prospect typically yields a higher success rate for extra time.

A secondary tactic is to request more time to gather additional facts and details. Even though most RFP-issuing organizations will set up vendor conference calls and meetings, you will rarely get to meet the ultimate end users of the system or products you are selling. These meetings are also very stilted and awkward because all of the responding companies will be present, and no one wants to say anything that may give a clue as to strategy or direction.

Hint: Reward Me for Being Smart

As an SE, you may need to ask for additional data outside of the RFP. This could be economic, technical, or business information. You may also request a formal one-on-one meeting with the end users. Frequently, the prospect will reply that they would then have to provide that data to all vendors. Suggest that they provide that data or access only to those vendors who ask. In effect, you are saying, "Reward me for being smart."

Strategies for Avoiding an RFP

Despite all indications to the contrary, there are creative ways of avoiding an RFP. However, bear in mind that every single one of your competitors will be trying the same tactics. Numerous contractual and sales approaches lie outside of the SE organization. Two popular techniques that the SE organization can control are the *technical reference close* and the *limited trial/workshop close*. Both techniques involve considerable work and commitment both from the SE and the prospect, but they do give you control over the sales cycle.

The technical reference close can be used when you are certain that, based on the RFP, your product is a 100% fit for the client. Also you need to be executing a frontal competitive strategy and to be confident that you can provide more references than your competition. The approach is to state, "If I can show you two similar companies who had the same problems you do and have them tell you how we fixed them, can we short-circuit this process?" Then follow that up with, "Starting this project 6 months earlier will save you $1 million." At the very least, it will make the executive sponsor think twice about the process; the best case is that they will say yes. The real work in this approach comes in setting up the reference calls, possibly even site visits, and in coaching your references about likely questions and what to say.

The next level of effort is the limited trial/workshop approach. This technique involves installing your product for a fixed period, usually 30 days or less, subject to meeting certain success criteria. (More details about general trials are given in Chapter 11, which discusses technical-sales strategies.) This results in more effort than actually completing the RFP, but it (1) takes your competition out of the picture, (2) gets you inside the building, and (3) consumes valuable time that cannot be then spent with another vendor. Even if another vendor convinces the prospect to give them the same option, you have still reduced the playing field and are now going head to head against just one competitor.

The Alternate Response Tactic

You will undoubtedly receive some RFPs that will score poorly either because they are clearly outside of your sweet spot or are from a customer that issues one RFP a month and has failed to award you any recent business. Although in both instances it may be acceptable to "no bid," there is a compromise response to consider.

In the case of a poor product fit, where an alternative implementation or architecture exists that would suit your solution, you may generate an alternate response. In effect, this is a politely worded document that states, "Our solution set is not a good fit for your business problem with regard to the way you have asked us to solve it. However, if you would like to consider doing it this way instead (as we just implemented at <*other customer name*>), here is how we would do it for you." At the very least, such a response will always generate a conversation with the customer and, in many cases, has been a game-changing event that led to the withdrawal and eventual reissuance or expansion of an RFP.

In the instance of the RFP-happy customer, especially if considered strategic by the account executive, an alternate response may serve to reset the relationship and allow a drill-down into why so many previous RFP responses were rejected. Although initiating this tactic is outside of the responsibilities of the SE team, a well-defined set of metrics can be an early indicator of such a problem area and discussed during account reviews on an objective rather than subjective basis.

Completing the RFP

Once the decision to compete has been made, gather the sales team and any external resources together to plan the response. As stated earlier, making the sales representative the project manager ensures equal participation from all sides. Decide up front who will be responsible for tasks ranging from data gathering to collation and copying.

Hint: Setting the Standards

New sales organizations typically will not have access to any RFP boilerplate or standard responses. If this is the case, use any RFP to set the standard for RFP responses. Decide on font, headings, style, and format, and enforce their use. A sizable library of compatible RFP data will rapidly be built. Then track your success rate.

As the SE member of the RFP team, you will be responsible for all technical questions contained within the document. These may be complex architecture issues or simple "speeds and feeds," depending on the products and services you are proposing. We recommend that you print a copy of the RFP and use a highlighter to mark those sections you are responsible for. Note that "responsible for" means that it is your task to make sure that they are answered, not necessarily that you must answer them personally. Then feed your commitments back to the RFP team so that everyone knows what you have accepted accountability for. Our credo is that "the SE organization is the organization of last resort," so it is also in your interest to make sure that all the other items are also covered.

Many of the more mature SE organizations either have an internal RFP team or an electronic software package that can be used to answer most standard questions. Failing this, an RFP library should be created on which an SE can draw (see Chapter 24) for many of the standard responses to common questions. Unless this is your organization's very first RFP or it is for a brand-new product, you should have a wealth of prior literature to which you can refer.

At this point, review your section and begin to divide it into different categories. Many RFPs now contain their basic Q&A in a spreadsheet style format that makes this process considerably easier. Categorize each question based on who will answer it. A certain proportion will be your direct responsibility, while others may belong to marketing, product engineering, or a technical/domain specialist. Either you or your manager should contact any individuals outside the SE organization from whom you need help; explain the opportunity and timeline and emphasize that they are being asked to help on only a small number of questions. Should you need help from within the SE organization, but outside of your immediate branch or area, let your management team take care of securing that resource for you.

Numerous SE organizations view an RFP as allowing them to find the most creative way to say yes to each question. While we certainly encourage a liberal view of any product's capabilities, many RFP responses eventually form part of the contract when awarded, so proceed with caution. However, if you can start each answer with a yes or, if appropriate, a no, it makes the RFP easier to score from the prospect's point of view.

Where possible, refer your answer back to your technical or educational literature, but include the text in the response like this: "Yes, this feature has been available in our product since 2007 (ref: *System Guide Release 10*, p. 244)."

Referring to an outside document, unless it is copyrighted by another company, leads to much page flipping by whoever reads the RFP. You want to make reading your responses as easy and painless as possible. Present all your answers in a clear, legible form. Should a question ask for a list of features or functions, provide them in tabular or bulleted form as opposed to a simple comma-separated list. Where possible, include diagrams showing why your product meets that particular requirement.

Also include any competitive advantages you feel you may have. There is nothing wrong with pointing out your strengths, or even indirectly a competitor's weaknesses, in the text of an answer.

Presentation and Follow-Up

Even though most RFP responses are handled electronically, many requestors still require a physical hardcopy. The RFP should be bound, personalized, and printed in color, and it should project the impression of the professional organization that created it.

As much care should go into the creation of a cover letter and an executive summary as goes into the RFP itself. The executive summary will be read by more people, and doubtless in greater detail, than any RFP ever will be. Think of it as your marketing flyer for the prospect for the duration of the RFP evaluation and scoring. The cover letter and summary should point out, both in business and simple, technical terms, why your organization is uniquely qualified to receive the final contract award.

Also insist that a meeting be set up either to deliver the RFP response or to review it within 48 to 72 hours after receipt. Allowing the sales team to physically present the RFP allows for some real-time feedback and a quick psychological assessment to occur. It also provides an excuse to get inside the prospect's building and potentially set up some other meetings.

Hint: Follow Up Internally Too

Once the RFP response has been delivered, make sure that you follow up and thank all the people internally who helped you complete it. Once you have an update about the opportunity, that is, once you make the short list, notify your extended team to keep them in the loop. Should you need further resources for the deal, or even have another RFP to complete, a little thanks will go a long way, and if you consistently win RFPs, people will be more likely to respond to your requests for help.

Once the RFP is delivered, maintain contact with the prospect, providing a steady stream of copies of press releases, technical updates, and journal articles—anything, in fact, to keep your name in front of the people who will make decisions. As the SE, it is your responsibility to develop some rapport with the prospect's technicians who will be reviewing the RFP. Offering to personally explain some responses, add extra detail, or provide insight into future plans can all be "hooks" to set up a follow-up session.

Summary

Engage early and try to set the ground rules for the RFP process. Be prepared to contribute questions and additional material directed toward your competitive strengths. If the RFP arrived "out of the blue," be very careful about your decision to respond.

Try creative ways to avoid the RFP, but once the decision is made to respond, after quantitatively scoring the RFP for success, engage fully. Develop a good executive summary that highlights your value proposition. Push the account executive to project-manage the internal process, making sure you fully define your responsibilities. Seek some face time with the prospect after RFP delivery and finally make sure you thank everyone involved—internally and externally.

Skill Building

New SE	1. Set resource priorities with your manager.
	2. Be prepared with some "rigged" RFP questions.
	3. Learn how to access the RFP library.
	4. Review with your manager all external resources available to you.
Experienced SE or SE Manager	1. Question the qualification of the deal.
	2. Develop a call script in which you can ask for a time extension.
	3. Clearly define roles and responsibilities.
	4. Create an RFP scorecard to measure the likelihood of success.
	5. Attempt to have the salesperson project-manage the response.
	6. Develop a relationship with key technical staff within the prospect.
	7. Focus on the development of the executive summary. Use this as the initial input for your discovery and analysis process.

Appendix 4A

RFP Analysis One-Pager				
Opportunity name:			SCORE:	61.0
Opportunity Information				
Existing <Company> Customer?	y		Score +8	8
Existing <Company> Products?	y		Score +8	8
Do we have a prior, positive history with the client?	n		Score +/- 8	-8
Is this the replacement of an incumbent vendor?	n		Score -6	0
Have we met with this customer on this opportunity prior to this RFP?	y		Score +10	10
Has the customer established an ROI expectation?	y		Score +5	5
We know the business drivers, time frame, budget, approval process and high-level decision criteria in the client organization.			GRADE +/- 10	6
A consulting group is evaluating the response and our relationship with the consulting group is good. If no consulting group involved, enter "0".			GRADE +/- 10	5
We have influenced the RFX and we are "favored" vendor.			GRADE +/- 10	5
Response timelines understood and achievable?	y		Score -10	0
Is purchasing our main contact?	n		Score -7	0
Do we have an executive sponsor?			GRADE +/- 10	5
Do we have access to the right stakeholders/influencers?			GRADE +/- 4	2
Are there objectional legal terms & conditions?	n		Score - 8	0
Misc Weighting (e.g complimentry products)			Grade +/- 8	4
RFP Pages (Total)	200	**BTR**		
Business Description	50	0.56	Score BTR * 4	2
Technical Description	90			
T&C/Legal Stuff	20			
Neutral Filler	40			
Strategy				
Is a partner required to provide the complete solution?	n		Score -5	0
Evaluate our track record with the partner. (If no partner, enter "0".)			GRADE +/- 5	5
Is the partner a boutique shop? (If no partner, enter "n.")	n		Score +3	0
Is the partner a Big Five shop? (If no partner, enter "y.")	n		Score -2	0
Differentiators				
Customer is looking for a suite or multi-faceted vendor	y		Score 4	4
Single brand, more than 3 products?	y		Score +8	8
Multiple brands, more than 3 products?	y		Score +8	8
Stay Away				
Currently includes unsupported platforms, OS or databases	n		Score -6	0
Requires sophisticated ad-hoc reporting, not in native product	n		Score -6	0
Looking for SOA architecture	n		Score -6	0
Requires multiple references within this specific vertical	n		Score -6	0
Competition				
IBM	y		Score -7	-7
HP	y		Score -7	-7
SUN	n		Score -3	0
Oracle	y		Score -7	-7
CA	n		Score -2	0
SAP	n		Score -4	0
Microsoft	n		Score -5	0
Other :	n		Score -5	0
Other :	n		Score -3	0
Other :	n		Score -3	0
Other :	n		Score -3	0
Other :			GRADE 0 to -5	5
				61

"Grade" means you enter a subjective score between the indicated ranges
Use a capital "Y" for YES

Completed By
Sales:
Pre Sales:

Chapter Goals

Identify and understand the steps in the generic needs analysis process.

Be able to customize the generic discovery process to your product.

Understand how sales-people add value in the discovery process.

Needs Analysis and Discovery

Discovery consists of seeing what everybody has seen and thinking what nobody has thought.

Albert Szent-Gyorgyi

Performing an accurate needs assessment and analysis is one of the greatest opportunities for the SE to add value during the sales cycle. At this stage, you will be defining the business problem that will be resolved in your proposal, and you will begin to identify ways to differentiate the solution you offer. This is also your first opportunity to build a relationship with the customer project team.

Overview

During the needs analysis stage, you have three goals: (1) increase your personal credibility with the customer, (2) build your relationship and rapport with the customer team, and (3) develop an understanding of the problems

43

faced by the customer. Other chapters in this book provide general recommendations for enhancing your credibility and relationship building. This chapter is devoted to the third goal, unearthing and understanding why the customer needs your solution. It is important to impose a process on the discovery phase because many things need to happen in a short time. By reading this chapter and customizing the process we provide, you can improve the effectiveness and consistency of your needs analysis.

Why Discovery Is Critical

Some SEs underestimate just how important the discovery process is to the sales process. To appreciate its importance, think back to the last meeting at which you spoke with people from your marketing or engineering groups. If your experience was typical, you were probably impressed by the marketers and engineers, but you may have felt that perhaps they didn't really "get it." The truth is that many companies make their products without really understanding the needs of the customer. This lack of understanding may be reflected in every official company effort directed toward the customer. Take a minute to review the marketing collateral you have been given to help you sell your product. Ask yourself how well it speaks to the current business issues your customer is facing. The marketing and engineering groups often operate at a disadvantage because what they produce usually doesn't reach the customer for at least 3 to 6 months. This introduces a significant problem. The lag between the time when your corporate groups produce something and when it reaches your customer can result in out-of-date marketing messages. We call this the *product/market gap*. Even otherwise effective marketing messages are often too generic for a given customer to relate to. Combine the possibility that your product group didn't "get it" in the first place with the fact that the release is out of date, and your products may have lost much of their potential impact by the time they reach the customer.

On the other hand, you are with the customer in real time. The discovery phase is important because it is when you take the off-the-shelf messages and products and begin to construct a customized solution for the customer. The customization you are doing may be at the level of a PowerPoint presentation, or you may spend days designing custom software, hardware, or networking solutions. By taking the time to understand your customers' business needs, you are laying the foundation for selling them something they can understand and apply to their business. The fact that you are able to make a hefty commission for doing so is a testament to the value you are adding to your company.

During discovery, you are acting as a systems integrator on your customer's behalf, putting together a proposal for a cutting-edge solution, centered on your company's products. It is this value-added aspect that gives you the right to impose your own structure on the sales process at this point. As you review the steps discussed below, write in additional data or requirements relevant for your customers. Pay particular attention to any dependencies between steps. Such dependencies must be factored into your plan when scheduling appointments and resources during the needs analysis process. The rest of this chapter is broken into sections describing the seven primary steps in the discovery process.

The Seven-Step Needs Analysis Approach

Step 1: Identify Needed Information

Preparation Before Customer Engagement

Going into the needs analysis phase, you should identify the pieces of information necessary to generate a winning proposal for your customer. Building qualification criteria and a needs analysis template is really the job of marketing or your sales-operations group, but if no one else has done it, it may fall on your shoulders. Taking the time and initiative to apply this kind of process will definitely pay off in the results you experience.

The abbreviated sample shown in Table 5.1 focuses specifically on the support requirements for an enterprise software application. Note that even within this technical document, hidden qualification questions remain. Questions concerning whether support staff and related hardware or software have been included in the budget will give you important information about how well prepared the customer is for your project. If they have not considered the support and hardware infrastructure, it is unlikely that they are close to a purchase.

Engaging the Customer

Now that you have the basics in place, you are ready to engage the customer. At this point, the only formal information you have about the project may be the request for proposal (RFP). With a little creativity and an Internet connection, you should be able to come up with the following quickly:

Table 5.1
Technical Needs Analysis Template

Customer Name:
List relevant standards:
Database: Oracle/MS SQL Server/Sybase/Other:
Server OS:
Client OS:
Average peak-time network latency:
Server hardware:
Platform/OS:
Currently owned or planned purchase?
Will other applications be present on server?
Is the hardware, database, and other software budgeted?
Our software requires a -time administrator. Has this person been identified?
Our software requires certain programming skill sets. Do you have Java programmers on staff?

- Initial RFP;

- Any quotations or statistics provided by customer team members during your initial interactions;

- Financial records for public companies;

- Transcripts from company investor calls;

- Recent company press releases.

Try to locate, or at least identify, these documents before presenting your discovery plan to the customer. In addition to impressing them with your thoroughness, you may also help remind them of other potential sources of information. Table 5.2 shows a needs analysis worksheet that may help you organize your thoughts.

Table 5.2
Needs Analysis Worksheet

Task	Done	Notes/ Next Step
Define information requirements		
Gather existing information		
RFP:		
Design documents		
Data on operations		
Planned operational/financial goals for the next period		
Build the perfect pitch:		
Use the generic pitch from marketing		
Customize		
Validate with friendly customers and coach		
Interview key staff:		
Technical		
Business		
Other standards groups		
Observe current processes:		
Capture and incorporate internal jargon		
Gather at least two examples of how the current system doesn't meet employee or customer needs		
Synthesize information		
Prepare and present summary		

To complete this step, compare the data you have collected with the checklist of information you need. Prepare a list of any specific documents or elements of information you will need in order to progress as shown in Table 5.3. You will not have had the opportunity yet to schedule the appointments shown in this table, but you will be well prepared to set them up rapidly.

Table 5.3

Information Gathering Worksheet

Data Item Who/When—Sales Team	Who—Customer
Existing hardware, software SE–Meeting 4/12	IT
Architectural standards SE–Conference call 4/15	IT–Standards group
Three user interviews SE–Follow-up 4/14	User manager (S. Stone) will set up for us
Group goals for coming year Sales rep–Meeting TBD	IT director (B. Brown)

Hint: Navigating Through Internal Corporate Politics

You may discover that you are being blocked from speaking with the customer by your own internal corporate politics. This frequently happens when a salesperson insists that he or she has already met with and interviewed the customer, and you only need to listen to a debriefing. A second situation occurs when you are working within a very large corporation, and the major account representative is extremely possessive of account contacts and jealously guards access into the account. In both of these situations, you have an absolute professional right to speak with the prospect and should insist upon a meeting, even if it is brokered by the account representative. An alternative tactic is to ask for the technical contact at the account so that you can confirm Internet/firewall/logistical information for the upcoming presentation.

Step 2: Build the Perfect Pitch

Now that you have a rough idea of what the customer wants, begin putting together an initial view of the overall business issues and how you will respond to them. Think of this as a map you will use throughout the needs analysis process. By documenting the vision at this stage, you can begin reinforcing your selling points during every interaction with the customer. If you are new to the product you are selling, beginning with the perfect pitch is a particularly good approach. You can work with your manager or marketing team to produce a generic value proposition for this type of customer, then customize it as you go. This gives you the ability to come into the account with an industry-tested value proposition that will improve as you work with your customer. The goal is to have a presentation that captures all of their needs and represents your best possible solution to them.

The perfect sales pitch constitutes the subject of many other books; for the purposes of your discovery session, it should be a slide presentation with the following outline:

- Slide 1: Customer business problem:
  - State problem description.
  - Show brief financial analysis describing expected benefit of solution.
- Slide 2: Business processes and stakeholders:
  - Diagram business processes and identify stakeholders for each.
  - Expand on this as you gain more information.
- Slide 3: Solution definition—high-level walkthrough:
  - Provide executive summary describing proposed solution.
  - List key benefits.
  - Describe expected financial and operating impact (don't give numbers at this point).
  - Have one solution slide for each business-process slide (above).
- Slide 4: Technical summary:
  - Show high-level diagrams or description of technology, architecture, and standards of proposed solution.
- Slide 5: Similar customer examples:
  - Discuss other successful customers and validate why those customers are appropriate comparisons. This will both reinforce your position and potentially unearth additional information, helping you to understand how these customers see themselves as unusual.
- Slide 6: Rollout summary and milestones.

Note that there is no explicit "close" in this presentation. At this point, you do want to position yourself as the leading vendor; the goal of the presentation is information gathering and relationship building.

You can certainly change the structure of the presentation as you see fit. The key points are to present a well-defined business need that will justify the purchase of your solution, a solution to meet the need, and necessary evidence to prove that you can implement (and, ideally, have already implemented) the solution you are proposing to the customer.

When complete, your perfect pitch will be an invaluable tool during the discovery process. It should constitute no more than 6 to 10 slides and will serve as an excellent way for you to quickly review what you discovered during your customer interviews. In a later chapter, we will discuss how you can prepare and deliver a perfect pitch.

Hint: Keep Your Customer's Process in Mind

As you begin your discovery phase, consider the process from your customer's perspective. Their goal will be to reach an accurate and concrete decision as quickly as possible. The steps described in this chapter will result in the customer's receiving the best possible inputs into their decision in the shortest time possible.

Step 3: Explain the Needs Analysis Process

Often, your customer will not expect you to suggest a more in-depth needs analysis, and sometimes they will even question whether or not your additional investigation is a necessary process. In most cases, however, your customer will appreciate the additional due diligence, understanding that the quality of the output correlates to the quality of the input. If the customer does push back, you need to be prepared to insist on going through the discovery process in order to obtain the information needed to best respond to your customer's needs. If the customer is truly adamant that you won't have any opportunity to perform your needs analysis, then this may be a good reason to end the process there. The only exception is in the case of a formally run evaluation, where the only exchanges of information are in well-defined meetings or other communications. The reasoning behind this type of evaluation is to be sure that no vendor has more or less information than any other. It is a highly ethical way to run an evaluation, but it does limit your ability to improve your proposal based on your industry experience.

To make sure that your executive sponsor appreciates the additional value that your sales team is bringing, have your account executive give an overview of your discovery process early in the sales cycle. Share the plan you have developed, and ask if there are any other sources of information you should be aware of so that you can make the best recommendation possible. You should also maintain a one-page executive summary for use when you call on resources from your marketing or engineering departments. Table 5.4 provides a sample summary.

Table 5.4
Sample Solution Brief

Customer: Acme Industries

Account ID: 00001

Sales Team: Jane Smith and Jim Doe

Brief: Acme industries is a Fortune 1000 maker of custom building products, primarily windows and window fittings for high-rise buildings. They operate through a regional direct sales force.

Statement of Needs: Many of Acme's products are entirely custom, but come from regional inventory storage locations. Acme hopes the solution will help them in three general ways:
1. Improve margin by selling more on-hand inventory
2. Improve visibility into future orders
3. Lower transportation costs

Specific Benefits:
Lower time to delivery by 2 days
Decrease necessary inventory of generic products by 30%
Quote higher margin products more frequently

Our Strengths:
Forecasting and inventory analysis
Competitor's Strengths/Weaknesses:
Superior partner electronic data interchange (EDI) capability
Outstanding Validation Questions:
Does this map to executive goals?
Do the lower level decision makers understand and agree with this?

Reviewing Existing Information

Now repeat your introduction of the discovery process to each of the customer team members, and reiterate the sources of information to which you already have access. Don't limit yourself to the information they have personally provided to you. If you have performed additional research on their financial reports or through relevant industry analysts, the thoroughness of your approach will impress the customer.

Next, ask your customers what additional sources of information you should be looking at. Here is a sample list of documents to ask for:

> Detailed business or technical specifications not included in the RFP;

> Design specifications for whatever this project is replacing;

> Version and identification information for any relevant hardware or software platforms with which you will be dealing;

> Training materials for the existing system;

> Screenshots (in a software environment) of the current version.

This additional information often exists, but the customer may not think it is relevant to your process. Therefore, if you do get the additional material and your competitor doesn't, you will have the advantage.

Step 4: Interview Key Customers
Your next step is to spend some time with your customers. Your goal during the interviews is to build and refine the list of decision criteria you will address in subsequent demonstrations and proposals. The different members of the team have most likely been party to some of the analysis that led their organization to consider an outside product or service. Try to use the interviews as a way to understand the real, often unspoken, needs behind the objectives of the project. Frequently, a customer will have goals that are not included in the documented requirements they have provided to you. There are many reasons for this omission. The customer might have thought it would be too hard or too expensive to achieve those goals, or the person who owned the decision process may not have felt another group's goals were worthy of consideration due to political alignment. A classic example in the IT world is the break between the business and IT groups. Frequently, those teams will not be aligned, so the project owner or sponsor won't show you a consolidated view of the internal issues. By interviewing the team members, you can ferret out some of those unspoken issues and work them into your value proposition. Consider the following case study, which highlights this classic division between the IT and business groups.

CASE STUDY: DON'T IGNORE EITHER GROUP

We had been working with the IT group at an Internet retailer for 4 months before we got to the point of doing a "bake off," or trial. As part of the trial, we were on site and had extensive opportunities to work with the different business groups. The IT team had told us that they were making the decision and were responsible for representing the proposal we put together to the executives. We subsequently spent a huge amount of time working with the IT team to get to know their needs.

Several weeks into the process, several individuals from the business side approached us and said they felt that IT had "run away" with the project. Not surprisingly, the real decision criteria were still in the hands of the business buyers. This was definitely disappointing because we had been spending time exclusively with the IT team, and they didn't understand the marketing group's needs well enough to make a real decision. It turns out our competitor's sales team personally knew a few people in the business group and had been working with them from the beginning, in violation of the agreed-upon process. We did eventually get the business, but at a massive cost in resources and executive involvement. Our big mistake was not doing a better job of insisting on interviews with the business stakeholders up front. As it turned out, this would have saved us a lot of time and brought the deal in a quarter earlier.

The case highlights the importance of not taking a single group's input at face value. Unless you know who can write the check and what his or her decision criteria are, you must cross-check the facts you have.

The perfect pitch you developed earlier is very useful at this stage. Slides 1 through 3 can be used during any customer interview. Slides 4 through 6 should be shared with customers as you gain confidence that the solution actually matches their needs. In some cases, you will want to make a point of jointly developing those solution slides so the customer feels as if they have contributed to the process. Always position the slides as a work in process and actively encourage your interviewees to correct any mistakes you have made.

Hint: Learning to Conduct Interviews

Although conducting interviews is not exactly an art, some best practices can be employed. We describe some of the basics in this book, but you should try to attend any internal or external training that covers this topic in more detail. If your company doesn't have the resources to implement a training program, work with a senior individual contributor to role-play customer interviews.

We can recommend that you not feel as if you have to give out information during an interview. If you are new to your company, or if you don't understand the customer's need, tell the person you are interviewing that you do not yet have enough information to tell them specifically how your system will address their area of responsibility. You will lose a valuable opportunity to plant your message, but at least you won't dig yourself a hole for later.

Step 5: Observe Current Processes—Get to Know the End User

Spending time with the people your solution is meant to benefit is another great way to gain credibility and build your industry expertise. Generally, this step can be handled concurrently with step 4. Even if there is a representative on the team from the user group, it will help you immensely to maintain direct contact with those users. Ask them what they do and don't like about how they are doing their jobs today. Ask how you can make their job better. Ninety percent of the time, they won't understand your solution well enough to give you a relevant example, but those details will give you a better sense of the situation you are attempting to improve.

You will also begin to build a library of "from the trenches" anecdotes. These tidbits are great for establishing your credibility with the current customer as well as with future customers. You will also start to understand the corporate language and buzz words. Building that into your future presentations will improve your ability to connect with the customer.

> *Hint: Laying Land Mines for the Competition*
>
> *If you know your competition well, then you should use this to your advantage. In discussions with the customer, try to turn a competitor's strength into a "me too" issue for you. The following is an example of this principle:*
>
> > *"These days most databases will have sufficient performance for your needs. Where you will see a real cost improvement is in decreased administration effort with the use of modern tools."*
>
> *In the example above, the salesperson set the expectation that the competitor's strength (high-performance databases) is a commodity and that the real differentiation is in the use of administrative tools. These land mines should all reflect the strategy laid out in your perfect pitch. If you have never tried this before, it may seem like you are delivering the same message many times—and that's accurate. The goal is to begin to have the team repeat those very messages.*

Step 6: Synthesize Information

It is now time to process all the information you have acquired and update your perfect pitch. Much of this should be work you can share with your account executive. Ideally, you should budget at least 2 days between receipt of the final significant source of information and your expected replay of your observations to the customer. Frequently, you may need to conduct additional research internally to make the best possible use of that information. If you have less than 2 days, it is unlikely that you will have time to complete that research.

The process you should follow for this step has two parts. First, work to develop a summary (see step 7) you can present to the customer. Your perfect pitch may already meet this need. Next, review the information you had expected to get during this process. Often, you will not have gotten enough solid data to answer all of your outstanding questions. As long as you have enough information to proceed to the next step in the sales process, you shouldn't worry about missing some of the information for now.

The one exception is that you must be able to identify a solid area of differentiation for your solution. If you cannot do this, then you need to rework your strategy to accommodate additional research, introduce a new solution component, or find a way to change the customer's expectations. The next case study highlights how you can use the discovery phase to "change the rules" on your competitor.

CASE STUDY: CHANGING THE RULES BY CHANGING THE BATTLEFIELD

Companies Business Objects (now acquired by SAP) and Cognos (acquired by IBM) were direct competitors in the business intelligence marketplace. Cognos had a very strong value proposition targeted at financial users and their complex reporting requirements. During the investigation phase, Business Objects would work to expand the deal so that their strengths of end user reporting and executive dashboards were viewed as critical. This flanking strategy proved very effective as the operational executives, such as the CO and VP of sales, plus the corporate end user populations, were more politically powerful than the CFO and his user community—effectively labeling the finance requirements as being very specialized.

Step 7: Prepare and Present Summary
Now you will prepare to revalidate the knowledge of your customer's business processes that you have accumulated thus far. Try to schedule time with the major buying influencers in reverse order of influence. Start with the gatekeepers or recommenders and conclude with the executives. Your goals in this step are the same as they have been for the entire needs analysis process: building your reputation, enhancing your credibility, and validating your value proposition. Often, this may seem like a superfluous step, given that you will shortly be putting together a more formal response, but it is important. A quick phone conversation using the following script should be able to get you that meeting:

"Jane, I was wondering if we could get 20 minutes to review the data we've collected. Your team has had some interesting things to say that I think you should know about."

During this summary, you have an opportunity to make sure the messages you have been getting from the different parties are consistent. Moreover, if the messages are not consistent, then you will have an opportunity to find out why and get the "real story." This will conclude your work on developing the problem and vision that you will begin delivering.

This summary is also a great opportunity to enhance your professional or technical credibility. You should work to make sure you have new information to share with the team. If you can improve their analysis of the situation, then you have done them a great service.

Finally, this is your last chance to "change the game" before heading to a more formal RFP process. If you believe other factors should be included in the proposal, get them on the table and under consideration. This step is particularly critical if you are facing a strong competitor. Here, you can work to flank your strength or add additional components to the solution that dilute your competitor's core abilities.

You can also think of this step as a very early *trial close*. Although you are still a long way from seeing a check or purchase order, it is worth going through the exercise. If an executive commits to you by saying you have the right problem in mind, you can expect him or her also to tell you if that problem changes, as might happen if a competitor successfully flanks your strategy.

Wrap-Up

If you have been successful, then at this point you should have a great deal of detail describing your customer's business. You should also have sufficient information about their needs for your forthcoming proposal to generate a pitch that will really wow them. You have gathered all available data, assimilated it, and replayed your perfect pitch to the customer; you are now ready to take the next step to your formal response.

From the customer's standpoint, they have experienced an effective and educational inquiry process by a trusted vendor. They have met highly qualified personnel who have shown an understanding of the business challenges they face. They have seen their challenges presented in an executive summary presentation and have validated that you are on the right track to developing a final proposal. Their expectations should be high that you will deliver a proposal that meets their needs.

Customizing the Discovery Process

Now that you are comfortable with the general process, take the time to customize it to meet the needs of your business. Are there other buying influencers or user communities you should be tapping to make sure you have all the information? Do you frequently deal with subsidiaries that require approval from headquarters?

Start by diagramming the life cycle of your product or solution for the customer. Try to identify all the people or functions that are stakeholders in the solution you deliver. In this case, a stakeholder is anyone who benefits from, suffers because of, or is responsible for an aspect of the solution. Focus on developing a process that gathers all of the technical and operational information necessary to develop a winning pitch. Spend a few minutes drawing out your discovery process before continuing.

Let's run through an example with a fictional SE, Jennifer. Jennifer sells products for a networking company that specializes in equipment to connect different corporate sites with each other and the Internet. As part of the sales process, Jennifer's sales team has access to the network architecture group of their customer, a large telecommunications provider. Jennifer prepares a needs analysis plan that includes interviews with the key members of the customer's network architecture group. The telesales group is the major customer to the networking group because the telesales group has the largest business application running on the international wide-area network (WAN). Each of these groups can give Jennifer some very specific data on their tolerance for downtime, current and projected bandwidth needs, and the per-minute estimated costs for network unavailability. Jennifer will also need to review the tables included in this chapter to make sure she captures all relevant data. Her company should have detailed technical specifications that will help ensure that she gathers the necessary system information.

Getting the Economics Right

The best way to customize discovery is to focus on the economic benefits the customer desires and then determine what information you will need to develop a proposal to answer those needs. This is what Jennifer does in the example above. The expenditure of any reasonably sized sum of money by your prospect is usually accompanied by a justification or return-on-investment (ROI) document that an executive has to approve. Many organizations are reticent about sharing any cost-saving or incremental revenue-generation numbers with vendors. However, some organizations will share this data or even look to you to help them justify the expenditure on your product.

Traditionally, this is the job of the account executive, although in recent times it is increasingly falling into the realm of the technical-sales organization. To gather this data, ask quantitative questions. Here are some examples:

- How many hours per month of employee time will this save you?
- Do you have a cost per hour for that saved time?
- Are you going to bill your customers for this new service?
- How many additional calls or procedures will you be able to run each day?
- How much time do you spend doing this each day?
- How many people perform this job function?
- Will efficiency improvements drive more revenues or lower costs?

Questions like this will yield a numerical answer that can be translated back into dollars. One word of caution: carefully consider any questions that directly or indirectly could lead to staff reductions. This may be a significant economic element for the executives but will raise a red flag among the rank-and-file employees with whom you will be dealing if they don't have a specific mandate to reduce labor costs.

Adapt Your Questions to Your Audience
Much has been written about successful interviewing styles and how to ask the right questions. This section highlights some common issues and personality types you will encounter when selling technology products. In most cases, your customer interviews will fall into three categories.

The first type of customer views the time spent with you as time wasted. Frequently, this type of individual is an executive, a salesperson, or someone who does not see the project as their responsibility. The second type of customer will inundate you with useless information; this person may be a hardcore techie or may not understand the information well enough to sort out the relevant details. The third type of customer understands the purpose of the interview and is familiar with the business problem. These customers are the most likely to give you feedback that you can use directly.

With the first type, try to ask open-ended questions to draw them out: "Why is the current system not sufficient?" "Tell me about any problems that aren't laid out in the RFP?" "Do you feel the RFP accurately describes what's really going on?" With customers like these, be ready to interject anecdotes describing past customer successes in order to build your credibility and their willingness to listen: "Your competitor had that exact problem. By installing our hardware, they lowered their cost of service by 10%. As you can imagine, they were handing out promotions like candy after that." It may be difficult to come up with a story that compelling, but there is certainly a reason your product is selling, so make sure your customer knows it.

If you are warned that a particular person falls into this category, or if you discover this in the first few minutes of the interview, change the style of the interview. Acknowledge that the individual is in a hurry and that you realize he or she is doing you a favor. Limit your questions to the bare minimum possible, and don't ask questions this person would expect you to know the answers to.

With the second type of customer, try the opposite tactic. Ask a question that is very specific (requiring a factual answer rather than an opinion) and directly related to the problem you are trying to solve: "Gerard, those numbers sound different from what I've heard in the past. Can you tell me how those relate to the goals set for your division?" In some cases, the person you are interviewing will simply not be close enough to the heart of the problem you are trying to solve to give you information you can use. Or, if you are selling a new product, he may not understand enough about the class of product to envision how it would improve his work situation. If the individual refers you to other material, make a note of appropriate reference data and proceed. Try to ask him about his opinions of the situation or to make a comparison with historical data.

When working with the third type of customer, you should focus on getting information that the other sales team doesn't have. Usually, customers of this type are so well prepared because they have been an integral part of the evaluation process. As a result, their inclinations and data are frequently part of the formal communications that have been distributed to all of the vendors. Ask the customer specific questions about what metrics they are interested in and how your solution can support delivery of those business results. You can also use these informed customers to give you feedback on the ideas you will later be presenting to the customer executives.

Hint: Inconsistencies Signal Political Problems

Generally, you will find that for every member of a project team, there is a different viewpoint to be reconciled. So, look for big inconsistencies that have to do with concrete facts or data, things like available budget and funding sources, delivery timelines, or project payback expectations. These can point to poor alignment within a company. If you find such inconsistencies, then you should expect that the sales cycle will be longer than normal. Until a project champion or executive has established specific goals, it will be very difficult for your customer to make forward progress. In these situations, your best-case scenario is selling to a high-level executive and then having to explain what happened to all of the team members after the check clears.

Summary

The discovery process represents a huge opportunity to add value as a sales consultant by bridging the product/market gap. Discovery is important to your company because it is where you customize your generic product to meet a customer's needs. It is important to customers because the output is a solution designed to meet their unique needs. And discovery is critical to your sales team because it is when you develop your perfect pitch or unique value proposition.

Mastering this stage in the sales cycle requires a deep understanding of your products, your competitor's offerings, and the business of your customer. If you can develop these areas of expertise and integrate them with the process we have described, you can nail the discovery phase. If you have accurately developed your perfect pitch, you will also be a step ahead of the competition for the next steps in the sales process.

Skill Building

New SE	Begin by working with a more experienced SE as he or she completes needs analysis sessions. Discovery is a complex enough topic that doing the job well is a suitable goal for a new SE. If your sales force doesn't have a documented process, try to document what you observe others doing. This will help you learn the process and will represent a valuable contribution to the rest of the team.
Experienced SE	As you master the basics of discovery, place more emphasis on the business justification for your solution. Begin to think of yourself as a systems integrator. Look at your solution as an integrator would; are there areas where you could better serve the customer by including external products that compete with yours? Performing this analysis will help you articulate the benefits of your solution and enhance your credibility.
SE Manager	Customize the task list in the worksheet to meet the needs of your sales force. Set up training to role-play progressing through the discovery process. Follow up by helping your direct-report personnel use your worksheet to plan out their strategies in specific accounts. Your goal is to deliver consistently high-quality results, which can be very difficult unless you institute a formal process such as that described in this chapter.

Chapter Goals

Understand strategies for building relationships with technical decision makers.

Know how to find and develop a coach.

Consider what credibility means in your business, and identify ways you can enhance your credibility.

Successful Customer Engagement

The easiest kind of relationship is with ten thousand people, the hardest is with one.

Joan Baez

Think back to when you were new to sales, whether that was yesterday or 20 years ago. When you attended a customer meeting, you would probably go expecting to hear what that customer wanted and have a discussion about how you might be able to solve that problem. As your sales career advanced, you learned that it was not enough to offer the right solution. In this chapter, we discuss the *metarules* of strategic customer engagement. The manipulation of politics and relationship building may seem cynical, even Machiavellian, but it is par for the course in today's world of high-value sales.

Do not assume that the business decision makers are the only ones with whom you need to develop relationships. Although conventional account strategy dictates selling high, you will need to cover key members of the IT team to prevent your competitors from

61

flanking you. Some of the concepts in this chapter touch on overall account strategy. You should be using the same guiding principles to approach the technical organization that the account exec uses with the business decision maker.

First Contact

You helped qualify the lead, responded to the request for proposal (RFP), and made the short list. Congratulations—now the real work begins. Relationships are everything in the sales cycle, and it is now up to your sales team to build the relationship with the prospective customer. As you prepare for your first contact with the customer, take some time to consider the following:

- How do relationships develop?
- What do you need to get out of this relationship?
- What do your customers want out of this relationship?

Your goals in every customer interaction during the sales cycle are two-fold. First, you need to gather the information necessary to satisfy the customer's demand for information while delivering a strong value proposition. Second, you are trying to uncover the unspoken decision criteria. Later in this chapter, we present a case study describing how the stated process often differs from the true process. Remember that in most cases a single individual does not make the ultimate purchasing decision. This is especially true for the technical decision makers on whom you will be focusing.

CASE STUDY: THE PAYOFF OF A GREAT RELATIONSHIP

Dave was part of a sales team working on a deal against two major competitors. The customer had supplied each vendor with the necessary technical evaluation criteria for the sales teams to put together presentations and proposals. Dave's team did so, after engaging in several rounds of discovery and discussion with the customer. After all of the presentations had been made and the vendor proposals were received, Dave's sales team was saddened to learn that they had lost the deal based on the technical criteria. Shortly after, however, the sales team learned that their high-touch customer engagement approach had paid off. The customer's evaluation team decided to change the evaluation criteria to include "Vendor Responsiveness." Dave's team's score was high enough to overcome the deficiencies in their product, and they won the deal. This case is an excellent example of how relationship building can be more important than feature and function differences.

Remember What They Want from You

Let's start at the beginning, with what the customer wants. If you are lucky, the customer wants your assistance proceeding through the sales/purchasing process as quickly as possible. If you are not so fortunate, they want you to come in because they don't know what they are doing and hope to gain some insight by interviewing enough vendors. Although this chapter will generally assume that your customers are not just "tire kickers," you should continue to keep your qualification criteria in mind as you gather more information.

Hint: Make Your Own Luck

If you think the prospect you are dealing with is not serious about buying, try to drive quickly to establish a coach. Find someone with a professional reputation to uphold and the relationship to help you validate whether you should pursue working with the prospect or not.

Think back to your last purchase from a salesperson. If the salesperson was lucky (as defined above), you probably had a certain list of questions you wanted to get answered as quickly as possible. The sales representative you dealt with probably had a lot of information you did not have that may have helped you make a well-informed purchase. In most cases, you did not go into the transaction hoping to make a new friend. When you deal with your customers, they will probably have a similar expectation. Some may even view interacting with salespeople as an unfortunate side effect of buying something—ever bought a used car? As such, you should expect that your early encounters will be businesslike and not overly familiar. This should not be a great revelation for most readers. Interestingly, conduct in initial meetings is actually a greater concern for more experienced salespeople. The more experience you have in dealing with people, and with selling in particular, the greater the possibility that you will begin selling hard too early in an encounter. Keep the charm in check until you know your customers better, and you will avoid the risk of appearing manipulative.

Hint: Divining Personal Agendas

When working with your customers, try to put yourself in their position. Can you see how your solution will benefit them personally? Don't be shy about asking them what their "win" is if the project goes through. If they do not have a win, you cannot assume they will support your solution.

Dissecting Project Dynamics

When you meet with the customer, keep in mind that their organization is just as fragmented and confused as any with which you have dealt. If you are dealing with a group of people, it can be very easy to think that they all have similar motivations and goals. This is never the case. Each will have goals that may only be achieved at the expense of the others'. The IT group may want to get a business group to fund a new project, whereas the business group may expect the project to be funded as part of a previous budgetary exercise. Your access to this information can actually be a good measure of the success of your sales campaign. The more likely you are to win the deal, the more likely it is that the different players inside an organization will try to use you, your company, or your solution to their benefit. Not all organizations are this cutthroat, but if you are dealing with executives, you should be prepared for this type of behavior. Although this may sound manipulative, executives are paid to make the maximum impact with available resources.

It is important that you work with your sales representative to identify the relationships among different groups. Obviously, you want to try to make as many of the customer's people as happy as possible. Unfortunately, it is not always possible to make everyone happy because of resource constraints or conflicting political aspirations.

Back the Strongest Faction

If you are dealing with multiple factions that have mutually exclusive designs on your solution, then you have a decision to make. Once again, make it with your sales representative. Dealing with political infighting is incredibly tricky. The best guidance is that you should try to support whichever group has the greatest influence on the overall decision. This seems obvious, but many sales efforts have failed because the sales team did not understand this principle. The classic example is a sales team that engages with the IT department when the business buyer has purchase authority. An example is given in the following case study.

CASE STUDY: MANAGING DIRECTOR, 1; ARCHITECTURE STANDARDS BOARD, 0

> One of our most painful losses was in a sales effort targeted at a major Australian telecommunications provider. After flying to Sydney on 2 days' notice, we ran an intensive sales campaign over the course of a month. We established relationships

and developed coaches within the system integrator running the evaluation, as well as with key employees at the customer. We spent weeks working with their architecture standards board to help them see that we had a superior solution. At the end of the evaluation, we won, only to find that everything we had been told had been wrong. Our coaches had thought they were responsible for making the decision, and we had won based on their requirements and goals. Unfortunately, their decision was overturned by a managing director of the company to whom we had had no access.

If the sales team in the case study had had a coach within the IT organization, the team might have known that such a power play was under way. Unfortunately, the team did not have the time or access to block their competitor's flanking move.

Identify the People You Need to Know

Imagine yourself meeting the project team. You are in a room filled with 20 people. Each may represent a different group with a different point of view. There is no way you can make a connection with everyone, so how do you decide?

Use Your Intuition

In a free-form group situation, focus on two characteristics of the participants: titles and styles. In general, you should try to connect with the most senior people possible on the theory that they have the greatest decision-making authority. Also look for the people who naturally seem to drive the discussion. These people will usually either have some decision-making authority or represent the interests of those who have the authority but lack the subject matter expertise. A third group does exist: natural boors, people who speak to hear themselves talk. Individuals who match this type are pretty easy to pick out.

But Don't Forget to Use Your Brain

As your sales team gains understanding of the political situation in the account, you should plan your customer engagement process in accordance with the customer's decision process. If the customer is weighting 80% of the decision based on the input of one group and 20% on the input of another, try to allocate your time intelligently across the two groups. You certainly should focus on the more influential group, but not to the extent that you lose the 20% of the decision the other group commands. If you know which specific individuals are making the decision, be sure to ask them about how they plan to make the decision. Managers will usually have trusted lieutenants who may be responsible for different parts of the decision. If this is the case, the managers will usually be happy to have you engage the lieutenant to ensure they have sufficient information to make their recommendation.

Covering the Whole Team, Including the Minor Players

While you are plotting and planning and developing a strategy to connect with the key decision makers, it can be very easy to ignore or insult other team members. You can avoid this by actively engaging the minor players on the team during group meetings, working lunches, and so forth. Usually, the more junior staffers are there because they are either responsible for advising the decision maker on some aspect of the project, or they will be expected to deliver the results you are promising. As such, they need to feel good about your sales team and your product, even if they don't have a significant say in the purchase decision. Giveaways such as T-shirts and coffee mugs are other cheap methods to reinforce the team, even if you don't have the time to spend with each person individually.

Managing the secondary players can pose some challenges. Frequently, they will have concerns that are important in their area of responsibility but not in the context of the decision being made. If the staffer is vocal and his management is not strong enough to keep the team on track, then it is up to you to make sure you satisfy him or her without derailing the larger team or taking up too much of your own time, which is better spent with the key team members. A good way to deal with these situations is by asking to follow up with the staffer "off-line" to address his or her concern. This gives you the option to defer an unpleasant or merely unimportant conversation until later. You can then resolve the obligation in a number of ways, as described in the objection-handling chapter (Chapter 15). Unless you feel further conversation will aid your cause in some way, the simplest approach may be simply to bury the target in marketing and technical material.

Coaches

If you have been in sales for long enough, you know that the most critical person on the team is your coach. Some sales methodologies refer to this individual as a mentor. A *coach* is a person who works for your customer and is willing to give you information beyond that to which your competitors have access. The coach is the person who lets slip information about where your competitors are weak or what pricing the customer is most likely to find acceptable. You should have a coach who is part of the inner circle of decision makers, but anyone with access to important information can potentially be a coach. You should also realize that the coach is usually violating the spirit of the purchase process, in which most companies insist on providing a level playing field for all vendors.

Your sales team should establish a coach within each center of decision-making authority at the customer. Typically, there will be at least three levels of coach: executive, line management, and IT. Your sales executive will generally work to make sure each camp is covered by an equivalently senior person from your company.

The salesperson-coach relationship usually comes about in two phases:

1. You develop a good working relationship with the individual in question.

2. Once you have established the relationship, the future coach determines that he or she will personally benefit from your solution's being chosen.

Take note of the existence and order of these two stages. Only after both have occurred can you attempt to cultivate the individual as a coach. If the potential benefit to the individual is significant, he or she may initiate the coaching relationship. In a technical-sales situation, it usually takes longer for customer team members to evaluate your solution to find how it benefits them, but if you have the right features in your product, the coaching relationship can be very strong. This is especially likely if certain philosophical or standards-oriented differences exist between your company and your competition. A famous example is that of Microsoft and the rest of the software industry. If your products are based on Microsoft technology, a significant percentage of technical architects are fundamentally going to love you or hate you, no matter what else you do from a sales perspective. By finding points of mutual benefit, you can then convince your coach to help you in other areas as well.

Hint: Do You Have the Time to Develop a Coach?

If you are effectively utilizing the coaching concept, you should actually be reducing the amount of time you spend on the account. Your coach should be helping you avoid busywork and deliver more targeted messages. If this is not happening, you don't really have a coach.

Where to Find Coaches

How do you find a coach? Begin by trying to apply the criteria defined above. Make a list of the people you have built a good relationship with during your initial interaction. Next, check off the names of the people who might stand to benefit from the success of your solution. The challenge here is in knowing enough about the team members to have a sense of their personal interests at this point. In some engagements, personal biases come through very clearly; in others, you will have to work to get that information.

What If There Are No Obvious Options?

Go back to your list of friendly contacts, and start buying lunches. If you haven't yet built that level of rapport with any individuals, start asking for one-on-one or two-on-one meetings. You can do this under the premise of doing more research about the customer's needs. If you really have no insight into the organization, therefore no idea who would make a good coach, you should consider approaching groups of two or three people at a time. Having one-on-one interviews with an entire project team would be very time-consuming, and in some cases awkward.

How to Get to Potential Coaches

Be Appropriately Friendly

As the technical side to the sales equation, your best bet is just to be yourself. Technical people often get a bad vibe from someone who comes off too strongly or even simply has a lot of natural charisma. Your organization may have access to information or perquisites the potential coach may value. Try to find out about the potential coach's personal and professional interests. Good possibilities for technical coaches might include free conference passes or inclusion in technical discussions with leaders within your engineering organization.

What If I'm Not a People Person?

Better change your ways—this is sales after all. If you are uncomfortable with the level of personal interaction we recommend, work with your manager to help you develop that side of your personality. Most companies with experienced sales management will not hire someone who doesn't have a certain minimum level of interpersonal skills. One SE was resolutely against professional sports before becoming a salesperson. He found sports to be an excellent icebreaker in discussions with clients. He took up a study of the rules of major sports and now uses sport-related chitchat to find common interests with customers.

Developing the Coach

Once you have established your relationship and identified your potential coach, try to convince that person of the benefit you have to offer. The best way to do this is to be very open. Explain that, based on your analysis, your solution should provide a certain benefit. Engage the coach to see if he or she agrees, then find out if he or she thinks this is a benefit that your competitors do not offer. If your value proposition truly is unique and your potential coach has any personal interest in the value, you should start to see some support. If your product's benefit will result in a raise or bonus for the individual, it is very likely he or she will coach you.

You have now begun the relationship. Your coach's value will depend on the relative value of your solution and the ethical/political bent of your contact. If your coach sees a potential promotion as a result of helping you, it is more likely that he or she will be willing to tell you how you are faring against the competition and other important information.

The Unconscious Coach

Another type of coach you can cultivate is one who doesn't realize the value of the information he or she is sharing with you. This is actually less coaching than just vigorous information gathering. Technical staff members often fall into this category. They have a tendency to let slip details about project budgets or competitive solutions in the midst of seemingly innocuous conversations. The downside of using this type of coach is that you truly are being manipulative. Consider whether this is in line with your personal values before using this approach.

> *Hint: Can You Have More Than One Coach?*
>
> *The best type of coach is the actual decision maker, so it would be difficult to have more than one of those. You can establish different coaches within different parts of your customer's organization. Frequently, you may have one or more technical coaches in addition to your primary business coach.*

Maintaining the Relationship

Follow Up with Natural Frequency

Once you have built your relationship with the coach, you should keep up your communications with him or her. If you let a relationship go cold, you may miss out on important information, and you may find it difficult to reestablish the original rapport. If you only call when you need something from the coach, your approach will become transparent very quickly. If possible, you should try to meet your coach physically for lunch or dinner at least every 6 months, even if there is no activity on the account.

What Can You Ask Them to Do for You?

What type of assistance is it reasonable to ask a coach for? Use your instincts as a guide, but realize that, as a technical person, you may be inclined to underutilize that relationship. If you are asking your coach to do something he or she is uncomfortable with, you will usually discover this very quickly. You can then adjust your approach accordingly.

Here are some common ways a coach might help you out:

- Providing competitive materials;
- Giving you early or exclusive access to inside information;
- Providing you with technical documentation that had not been officially provided;
- Giving you a sense of what really needs to be done in the account;
- Assisting in escalating issues;
- Giving you an idea of how your sales team is doing in the evaluation.

In summary, the coach is your way to find out important insider details that will give you a competitive advantage in the account. Most coaches will do this because they believe your winning the deal will result in some personal benefit for them. If you build coaching relationships and then make them successful when your project is implemented, you can expect the coach to be available to help you out with future sales or career situations.

Credibility

Maintaining Credibility

As a technical salesperson, your position and value in the account is completely predicated on your credibility. Credibility will usually mean a combination of the following traits:

- Professionalism;
- Industry and domain expertise;

▶ Deep product expertise;

▶ Perceived value added in other ways.

Most of what you do is provide information to your customers. If you give your customer misinformation, then what value do you provide?

Losing Credibility

You do not always have to be perfect. Unless you have a very simple product, you will probably occasionally make mistakes or need to involve product specialists. The major negative behaviors are lying or making up answers to customer questions. If you make a statement and later find out that you were wrong, you should definitely consider telling your customer. If they find out independently, you will certainly lose credibility.

Trying to Regain Credibility

Think about the proverbial "sleazy" salesperson. Such people give the profession a bad name because they are willing to say anything to close a deal. Would you trust someone who, either knowingly or through ignorance, gave you incorrect information related to a major purchase? If a house inspector failed to find or mention the termites in the home you were considering bidding on, what would it take to get you to use that inspector again? Your best option is to apologize (if possible) and move forward. If you feel damaged credibility is impacting your effectiveness, you should consider bringing in other salespeople. If you find out that your customer is going around you to speak directly with other people in your company, this is a good warning sign that you need to improve your knowledge and your relationship with that customer.

Know What You Don't Know

Reflecting back on the unsuccessful trip to Australia in the opening case study, you must focus on finding out what you don't know. A good approach is to ask the decision makers you have access to who the final decision maker is. If it is them, then you are in good shape. If they tell you it is someone else, you need to get close to that person. If they indicate it is a certain committee, find out who is on the committee. If they hedge or are evasive, this may mean that there is no process (and perhaps no budget) or that they are not connected with the process. Find out where the buck stops and work backwards to make sure you have relationships with all the key influencers of the final decision makers.

Summary

In sales, the customer is king, and each customer expects to be treated like one. Finding out which of these "kings" holds the real key to the treasure vault can be a challenge. Institute a process by which you can find out which customers will be key to your success. While engaging with the customer, focus specifically on the development of one or more coaches within the account. These coaches will help provide information, clear roadblocks, and let you know your competitors' tactics. Armed with a good engagement plan and a good coach, the account will be yours to lose.

By considering how your customers see and value you, you can learn how to develop and maintain your credibility. Credibility and reliability are everything in sales, and by consciously developing these traits, you will improve your relationships with your customers and make their purchasing from you in the future more likely.

Skill Building

New SE	Work with your manager to understand how to identify the key roles within an account. Think of diplomatic ways to avoid spending time with the less important players who may not be critical to the purchase process.
Experienced SE	Make sure you know how your proposal will advance the interests of each key individual with whom you are dealing. Self-interest will guide more decisions than feature and function comparisons. Build your credibility. Become a professional whom customers like to buy from and would recommend to their friends. Use this credibility to build relationships with coaches in new and existing accounts. Building this network will help you in current and future sales positions.
SE Manager	Make sure your salespeople have a good understanding of the purchase process and the key customer roles in that process. Define the characteristics and "care abouts" for each role. This information will help your salespeople minimize their engagement with those who will not be making the decisions.

Chapter Goals

Develop a structure for the perfect pitch.

Understand the major components of a presentation, including verbal and nonverbal delivery skills.

Learn how to handle special situations.

Learn how to channel nervous energy.

The Perfect Pitch

I'm just preparing my impromptu remarks.
Sir Winston Churchill

The adrenaline flows. You are up in front of an audience ranging in size from 1 to 1,000. Your mission, should you choose to accept it, is to persuade this audience that your solution meets and beats their technical requirements, that it fixes their business problems, and that they would be foolish to buy from the competition. The actual presentation, or perfect pitch, is the culmination of many hours of hard work and preparation.

Public speaking is a difficult and mostly unpopular task—it is, however, an intrinsic part of being an SE. Although public speaking is routinely ranked among the greatest of all fears that people hold, applying some structure and basic principles can help you to prepare and practice for the perfect pitch.

Numerous studies during the last 50 years have attempted to determine what makes the perfect pitch. Every study reveals a slightly different answer, but they consistently indicate that although important, content accounts for less than 20% of the perfect pitch, with nonverbal communication playing the largest role in a presentation. In this chapter, we will help you learn how to structure a perfect pitch and how to do the best job possible of using both verbal and nonverbal delivery skills. So, unless you count yourself in the "I can sell refrigerators to an Eskimo" category, the first step in organizing content is structuring the message.

Developing a Focused Message

Many methods are available for structuring presentation content, and our methodology uses a generalized system based on synthesizing the best of various models. If you have an upcoming presentation, grab a stack of 3 × 5 cards or large Post-it notes and begin drafting your presentation now.

As you begin to develop your presentation, you should start by answering these questions:

- What is the customer's issue?
- What is your purpose?
- What needs to be presented?
- How much time do you have to present?
- How much do you know about the topic?
- How much does your audience know about the topic?
- Which ideas will need support, and where can you find it?

Then specify your objectives:

- What do you want to accomplish?
- What points do you want to make to your audience?
- On what points do you want to persuade your audience to take action?
- What decisions do you want to influence your audience to make?

Start with the Structure

Take three cards, and write one phrase on each as follows: "goal," "objectives," and "closing." Take a few minutes to write down your goal for the presentation, the client's stated objectives, and the closing points or major takeaways you hope to leave with your client. The closing message should achieve your goal by addressing the objectives of the client in a compelling and differentiated fashion. For this step, focus on the high-level value proposition rather than the specific response to each objective. See the example below:

- *Goal:* Show you why ordering our product is the best solution for your needs.

- *Objective 1:* Explain how our product fulfills your requirements for a configuration tool.

- *Objective 2:* Explain how our product fulfills your requirements for a quotation tool.

- *Close:* Our product is the only solution on the market that is proven to work in your industry. Your system integrator has a group that is fully trained on our product and ready to implement it. Our products often cost more for the licenses but generally result in a lower total cost because we have more functionality out of the box.

You have just created a story, one that should be pretty easy to tell. Of course, you haven't actually proven that your product can do any of the wonderful things you claim (we cover that next). It is important to remember that the purchase decision will be made based on this high-level story: "Can this product fulfill my needs." Rarely are decisions made purely on a feature and function comparison. In a feature and function presentation, you can still use this structure; you will just take it down a level and make the presentation more detailed.

Do a Data Dump to Identify Solution and Proof Points
Now, for each objective, create one or more cards or notes to respond to each of the objectives as solutions. Generally, these solutions will be supported by proof points: a combination of demonstrations and customer references. Generate as many ideas as possible. Do not write complete sentences, be concise, and use trigger words or phrases to capture ideas. Include relevant facts and figures, stories, and dates, and don't edit any ideas on the fly. This is the part of the presentation where you, as the subject matter expert, are expected to provide the most value. When creating proof points, it is easy to rely on a product demonstration, but customer anecdotes and "hard facts" regarding live systems often represent a more compelling way to summarize the benefit you bring, with a supporting demonstration performed as necessary.

Organize the Ideas

Move the cards or Post-it notes around to form natural groupings based on a common theme or concept. Title each grouping so that it becomes a *key point*. Prioritize your top three or four key points in order of importance. The ideas within each grouping are known as *subpoints*, which should also be prioritized in order of importance. In a standard corporate-marketing-style presentation, these subpoints become bullets. For the more advanced practitioner, they become condensed, one- or two-word, textual reminders framed by a key image or diagram.

Focus the Message

The fear that the audience will not understand what he is trying to present leads the inexperienced presenter to keep talking, adding more and more points, until the presentation becomes one convoluted series of randomly linked points and opinions. Decide which of your key points you can eliminate or present some other way—to leave yourself with one, or at most two, key messages to deliver. Then, decide how much of your allotted time you wish to allocate to each point, and allow for a buffer of introductions, conclusions, and questions. As a plan B, you should be able to present the one major key message in half the time you have allocated for the presentation. You can do so by going through your presentation and hitting all of the points except for the proof points, for these just give a brief, verbal description for any demonstration or customer reference that is appropriate.

Transfer to PowerPoint

Now (and only now) assuming you use a program such as PowerPoint, transfer your outline from the cards to the computer. Imagine what will be on each of the slides, and mentally confirm that this will meet the objectives for the presentation that the customer has articulated. At this point, you effectively have a storyboard or screenplay and should now fill out and complete the content. Remember the mantra that "less is more," and concentrate on keeping your message concise, relevant, and to the point. You should also consider utilizing other forms of delivery, such as whiteboarding or prepared posters and handouts.

Hint: Bullets Can Be Lethal

The bullet feature of PowerPoint is one of the most overused and clichéd forms of delivering powerful points. While bullets have their place in educational material (such as this book) or as a simple way of presenting a list, they should not be used as a standard mechanism for delivering technical-sales information. Should you have a slide full of bullets, try this technique. Cut and paste the bullet text into the notes, place an image (not clip art) that encapsulates the basic message onto the slide, and then populate the remainder of the slide with one- or two-word segments that summarize your points. You will have a cleaner, easier-to-read slide deck and an audience that pays attention to you instead of aimlessly reading bullet text in PowerPoint.

Nonverbal Delivery Skills

The next time you see a really dynamic public speaker, perhaps the CEO of your company, pay attention to what makes him or her seem dynamic to you. Frequently, such speakers don't necessarily have great content, but they do have great nonverbal delivery skills. There are six key components of nonverbal delivery skills: physical appearance, posture, eye contact, gestures, movement, and facial expressions.

1. On the basis that you never get a second chance to make a first impression, start with your *physical appearance*. Dress appropriately for your listeners, the company, the location, and the purpose of your presentation. Eliminate any distractions, such as extreme fashions, inappropriate hairstyles, big jewelry, and anything that glitters or reflects light. Select clothing that is comfortable for you. Remember that high-contrast colors convey authority, whereas lower-contrast colors are perceived as friendly.

   Hint: Advance Your Presentation Skills to Boost Your Career

   Many technical salespeople are extremely uncomfortable in front of large audiences, so being known as the "big-presentation sales engineer" can be a major career booster and lead to many speaking opportunities.

2. After an initial appraisal of your appearance, *posture* is the next area of nonverbal judgment. People not only listen to you, they watch you. Slouching tells them you are not particularly interested in them, whereas displaying good posture tells your audience you are confident and prepared. This is all before you have even spoken a single word! Use the neutral position when standing—place your feet about hip distance apart and relax your knees, with weight evenly balanced and arms and hands relaxed at your side. When sitting, have your hands in view and open on the table, and sit straight up. In both cases, keep your upper body erect but not rigid. In short, remember everything your mother told you when you were a teenager. A good, erect posture also helps your voice resonate better by decompressing the diaphragm.

Hint: Breaking Bad Habits

The best way to break a habit is with immediate feedback from a set of friends or cowork-
ers. Each person gives a 5-minute impromptu presentation about any subject with which
he or she is comfortable. During the talk, the audience should watch and listen for annoy-
ing habits. After the talk, agree on the top two or three habits and write each of them in
large letters on a poster board. During your next presentation, the audience should wave
the poster boards in the air whenever you repeat a bad habit.

3.   Another key component of nonverbal communication is *eye contact*.
      Attempt to have a series of random one-on-one conversations with
      the audience, including the people seated at the sides or in the back.
      Unless you are unable to see certain audience members, try to main-
      tain about 5 seconds of eye contact with each listener. Avoid eye
      darting, scanning the audience, or continually looking down at your
      feet or even your notes. How many times have you seen a Most
      Wanted picture and thought that the individual had shifty eyes?
      Conversely, do not become too intimate or fixed on an audience
      member by using excessive eye contact. Be aware of cultural norms
      for acceptable spacing and distances when interacting with others.
      An American's personal space is typically 18 to 24 inches; in some
      European cultures, that space is smaller, and in Asian countries, it can
      be somewhat larger.

4.   Combine your movements with *gestures*, as you would in a natural
      conversation. Use a variety of gestures with one hand and both
      hands. Avoid using too many symmetrical gestures in which both
      hands make a similar motion. Extend your arms outward from the
      shoulders with elbows away from the sides. Use gestures to show
      your energy and enthusiasm without resorting to showmanship.
      Beware of making strong gestures when you have a pointer, a pen, or
      some other instrument in your hand.

CASE STUDY: THE SPIRAL STAIRCASE

   Having been educated in a private British school, I had a good grasp of the verbal
   skills required for speaking and an overly formal, but successful, way of
   structuring a presentation. However, my nonverbal communication skills,
   especially gesturing and movement, left a lot to be desired. In fact, after my first
   presentation in the United States, my manager told me I was the first person he
   had ever met who could describe a spiral staircase without using his hands. To
   help cure this awkward habit, he gave me a list of a dozen topics to speak about.
   They included how to throw a ball, how to shape pottery, and the art of karate

self-defense. Anything that would make me move my body and my hands was fair game for a presentation. It took me 2 months to kick the habit of not gesturing, and the spiral staircase example stays with me to this day.

5.   *Movement* can be made purposeful by integrating it with both eye contact and gestures. Standing in the same place, for example, behind a podium, restricts your energy and makes it harder to give a high-energy presentation if that is your goal. Every motion should have a purpose, so look at one person, and then move naturally toward him. Do not pace back and forth; get to where you want to go, and then stay there before you move elsewhere. At all times, keep your body open to the audience. The old presenter's rule of never show your back to the audience is a good one with the exception of whiteboard use.

6.   *Facial expressions* put the final touches on nonverbal content and communications and can be especially important if your image is being projected on a big screen for a large audience. Unless you are delivering grave and somber news, smiling is a powerful cue that transmits happiness, warmth, and friendliness. No facial expression often equates to a monotone voice. So, let your facial expressions be natural (practice in front of a mirror), and make sure your face is visible—large eyeglasses or over-the-face hair detracts from expressions. Combining facial expressions with gestures and changes in vocal pitch is guaranteed to grab people's attention.

Verbal Delivery Skills

Verbal communication is more than words. Practice saying, "This new product is going to be very popular," with as many variations and emotions as you can. Use anger, irony, surprise, and grief, and vary the emphasis on individual words. To quote the great bard, "all the world's a stage," and you are getting ready for opening night. Five significant qualities are important to achieve outstanding verbal delivery of the perfect pitch:

1.   *Pace:* Pace is the measure of how long a sound lasts. Talking too quickly causes words and syllables to be cut short, leaving your audience breathless and struggling to follow you. Speaking too slowly can

sap the energy out of a presentation and make it seem boring. Varying the pace helps to maintain the audience's interest. The optimum pace varies regionally within the United States and internationally. The same presentation given in southern states may take 10% longer than one given in New York.

Hint: Help Yourself to Help Yourself

One common bad habit of technical presenters is speaking too quickly, especially when wrapped up in the adrenaline rush of a presentation. Help yourself by providing a visual cue to slow down during your perfect pitch. Some examples include writing "slow down" on your business card and taping it on the keyboard of your laptop or handwriting "pause" at several places in your written speech or demo script. In one extreme case, a sales engineer placed a small red dot at the end of every third slide to remind herself to stop, slow down, and take a deep breath.

2. *Pitch:* Pitch determines how high or low a note (syllable) is. Higher-pitched tones generate enthusiasm and excitement; lower-pitched tones convey authority and conviction. Other than taking voice lessons, there is little you can do to modify your pitch, but erect posture for clarity and simple pitch variation will take you a long way.

3. *Tone:* Vocal tone conveys emotions—both implicit and explicit. A voice that conveys fear or nervousness can disturb the audience, whereas a voice that conveys confidence or laughter can relax the audience and make people smile.

4. *Volume:* Volume is the measure of how loud or quiet your words are. Even with a microphone, you must ensure that you can be heard. The ultimate goal is to be heard without shouting. If you have a naturally quiet voice and your audience continually has to pay very close attention to hear you, or if the gain on the microphone is turned up too high, causing static, then more brain-processing time is spent gathering the words, and less is spent understanding them. Practice gradually lowering your voice to draw your speakers in, and then raise it to make a major point. Strangely enough, of all professions, most kindergarten teachers have this skill mastered.

5. *Articulation:* The final overriding point for vocal improvement is articulating all words clearly and not running words together. Breathe to keep yourself relaxed and to maintain strength and power in your voice. Eliminate filler words such as "umm," "and," "so," and "okay";

replace them with pauses. Slowing yourself down mentally just 5% can help you do this. Pauses give you time to breathe and think, can create impact, and can even give your audience time to think about what you have just said. Think about how a comedian will momentarily pause before the punch line to "set up" the audience.

Hint: Accentuate the Accent

Many sales engineers are blessed with an accent—either a regional dialect or a "foreign" accent about which they may be self-conscious. Since the audience will obviously notice the accent, our advice is to deal with it up front and introduce yourself, making some joke or comment about your manner of speech. It is important that the humor be directed toward you and not the audience (the New Yorker poking fun at a group of Southerners by saying he will talk slowly for them doesn't go down too well!). In the case of a foreign accent (either by birth or education), make the best of it. I saw a French sales engineer, from a French company, working in the United States remark that he was from HQ, and they were guaranteed to get the latest technical data and some great wine at dinner. A Russian security engineer brought up his heritage and noted his relatives were KGB trained.

If you are presenting in a situation using a weaker second language, get the audience on your side early by asking them to translate a word for you (i.e., how do you say "projector" in German?). This technique is particularly effective for Europeans and Asians when presenting to an audience of Americans, who are generally embarrassed by their lack of foreign-language skills.

Strategize the Start

Almost every presentation course you will ever attend recommends that you start with an "energizer"—a story, fact, or statistic that will make your audience sit up and take notice. Use the mnemonic in Table 7.1 to remember the major categories of energizers. Examples in a technical-sales environment would include a brief video reference, a story about how a similar company saved money, or making a bold, but true, statement about your solution leading the customer to think, "Wow, I didn't know that!"

Hint: Using Numbers to Prove Your Point

One extremely powerful way to start to a presentation is to lead off with a set of three to six numbers on a whiteboard and ask the audience to guess what they mean. Then, use the numbers to tell a story that proves your point. For example:

50   *50,000 euros a month in compliance fines;*

300   *300,000 euros budgeted for hardware to fix the problem;*

6   *Number of months it will take you to install hardware;*

Table 7.1
MasterPieces for Creating Interest
(Courtesy of Deborah Masters of MasterSpeak)

Technique	Purpose
Memorable visuals	To support and strengthen your message
Analogies	To simplify a complex concept
Stories	To illustrate a point from personal experience
Ticklers	To release tension and build rapport
Examples	To make your point stand out and come to life
References and quotes	To enhance credibility

75   *75,000 euros—the cost of our software;*

2   *Number of weeks we need to get it working.*

Interested?

Special Situations

Very Large Audiences

When presenting to a large audience—in the hundreds or upwards—you are often placed on stage, behind a lectern, with bright lights shining down on you. You are usually on closed-circuit projection and are unable to see the audience because of the lights. Even for the most composed and experienced speaker, a situation like this can be terrifying if he or she has never experienced it before. Many of the nonverbal rules go out the window: if you cannot see the audience, you cannot establish eye contact or get a read on how you are doing. So, use the camera to your advantage. Look into the camera to establish eye contact with everyone, and then look slightly away as if you are focusing on someone 5 yards to the right, then 5 yards to the left, and so on. Continue with your gestures, smiling, tonal variation, and all other techniques detailed in this chapter. If asked to use a lectern, also ask for a wireless microphone so that you can move away from it. Use the lectern as a note stand: refer to your notes or perfect pitch outline, and then move away. You will discover that motion will help calm your nerves and relax you.

CASE STUDY: LOCATION, LOCATION, LOCATION

Early in my career, I had to give a 10-minute presentation at a sales kickoff meeting in front of 500 salespeople. The material was very simple, and I had previously given many presentations to large audiences. Due to a variety of logistical issues, I didn't visit the auditorium where we would be speaking in advance to familiarize myself with the approach to the stage or my exit. When the time came to step up onto the stage, I was excited and ready to perform. I climbed the short set of stairs, walked to the podium, turned to face the audience, and was struck dumb by the bright lights and size of the crowd. The auditorium was set up for a later dance production, and the professional light equipment was enough to send me into shock for a gut-churning moment. Luckily, I recovered quickly, and fortunately it was an internal presentation, but the experience highlighted the necessity of investigating the presentation area before showtime.

Presenting Via Teleconference

Teleconferences also present a difficult environment in which to make the perfect pitch. Visually, both you and your audience appear static and stilted unless you have super-high-speed bandwidth. Eye contact is extremely difficult, and gestures become jerky and look uncoordinated. In cases such as this, the voice and variation of tone, pitch, and volume are key to maintaining the audience's attention. For the special situation regarding webcasts, refer to Chapter 10.

Around the Conference Room Table

Conference table meetings can also be challenging, although all of the standard presentation techniques apply except for movement. Energy decreases when you are seated, so your delivery skills need to compensate for this. To gain power or control, stand up; it naturally causes people to focus on you. Move to a whiteboard, flipchart, or laptop to facilitate movement opportunities. If standing up is not feasible, turn your torso when you are connecting with an audience member, not just your head. Arrange seating with a purpose in mind. Make sure you can see and directly address all of the decision makers. Note that when dealing with Asian cultures, different rules for seating arrangements apply, so consult with a local expert.

Hint: Keep It Neat and Tidy

To add one extra professional touch to your perfect pitch at the conference room table, ensure that all power cords and projector cables are out of sight or neatly wrapped up with Velcro ties. As well as providing a safer working environment, your first impression will be very professional.

Feature and Function Presentations

As mentioned previously, these techniques are equally applicable for feature and function presentations. We have made presentations in which we were expected to demonstrate compliance with 200 technical requirements. Even in these dry presentations, you should use the structure above because it will help you focus on the key business benefits you provide, beyond the explicit presentation requirements. One modification that we have used with some success is providing handouts that include the following: an index of the required features and screenshots or product diagrams corresponding to the desired features. This is generally a good idea if you can provide supporting pages that represent 50% or more of the features you are demonstrating. One concern is that your competitors may gain access to the document and be able to better position themselves around the benefits you describe. If it truly is a complex presentation, the upside of having your customer be able to remember what you showed and how you were compliant with their request may outweigh the potential downside. Consult with your manager or sales rep when considering this type of approach.

Using Humor

Used effectively, humor can defuse some tough situations and be the perfect icebreaker. On other occasions, humor can leave both the speaker and the audience feeling very embarrassed. Our advice is to go with whatever seems natural for you, but if in doubt, leave it out. Certainly reject anything with a religious, political, sexual, or cultural theme—you must avoid offending anyone in the audience under all circumstances. Remember that you are being paid to educate and persuade your audience, not to have them rolling in the aisles with laughter. Our personal favorite subjects are either sports or something self-directed ("a funny thing happened to me on the way to the auditorium") so that the audience can chuckle with you. If all else fails, you can resort to the old standby of "on this day in history" when asked to give a last-minute presentation and you have just a few minutes to conduct some Internet research. In a sales situation, starting with a joke is a risky proposition.

Using Nervous Energy to Your Advantage

The main enemy of a presenter is tension, which ruins posture, voice, and spontaneity. The voice becomes higher as the throat tenses. Shoulders tighten and the legs shake and cause unsteadiness. The presentation can become "canned" as the speaker locks in on his or her notes as a crutch and starts to read directly from them in a monotone voice.

The first rule of nerves is to welcome them and not to fight them. Actors and politicians recognize the value of nerves: they can add to the value of a performance because of the impact of the adrenaline coursing through the system, which is a leftover from the "fight-or-flight" reflexes of our ancestral cavemen. If nerves win, then you go into flight mode by withdrawing from the audience; if you welcome the nerves and the adrenaline, then you are in fight mode, ready to stand your ground and make the perfect pitch. You do not need to get rid of tension and anxiety; you need instead to channel them into concentration and expressiveness. Some techniques that have proved effective are listed here:

- Mentally visualize yourself giving the presentation beforehand, including the audience and the room.

- Relax your body. Sit or lie down and focus on tightening and then relaxing each major muscle group, starting from the feet and moving upward.

- Drink water. Avoid alcohol for obvious reasons and soda or coffee because of their caffeine content. The adrenaline is stimulant enough. Try to keep two bottles of water near you.

- Understand that your anxiety is more noticeable to you than the audience.

- Visit the bathroom, wash your face and hands, and check your appearance. Don't you look great?

Even the best presenters make mistakes. The important thing is to continue on after the mistake. As you continue your presentation, your audience will continue to listen, and you will seem more personable to them. Don't point out any minor typographical errors or glitches unless they are so obvious or funny that your audience reacts to them.

Hint: Cool Down That Nervous Energy

If your pulse is racing, your voice is trembling, and the words keep spilling out more and more quickly, stop for a water break. Often the few seconds it takes to locate your water and take a sip will be enough to calm your nerves and let your brain catch up to your mouth.

Everybody gets nerves before the perfect pitch—if you don't, then you should be questioning your mental mind-set for the day. Read any interview with an actor, politician, sports figure, or newscaster, and see how they answer questions about nerves and stress. Of all the techniques, we strongly recommend visualization as a method to relax. By convincing your psyche that you have already given this speech a half-dozen times, you can bring your stress levels down considerably as your body starts to feel familiar with the situation and locale.

Finish Strongly

Even if you do not feel that you have given the perfect pitch, you are likely to be far more critical of yourself than the audience. The important aspect of the conclusion is to finish with strength and conviction. Should you need to have a question-and-answer section of the presentation, don't make that the final piece of your pitch so that you finish with a weak, "Well, I guess that's all the questions. Thanks for coming." Take the opportunity to very briefly summarize your presentation, reiterate the "so what," smile, and then conclude with a call to action for the audience. Remember the analogy that in most professional sports tournaments, if you win your very last game, you are the champion.

Summary

The perfect pitch involves far more than merely putting words together in a persuasive fashion. More than 75% of your audience's impression and interaction will be through nonverbal means. Strong posture, eye contact, gestures, and movement, coupled with a confident manner and some smiles, are a solid foundation for any speech.

As with almost every task in the sales engineer's life, preparation is the key to success, and strong nonverbal and verbal delivery skills can make even the most mundane topic seem interesting and topical. Don't take your presentation skills for granted; work with small groups or in front of a video camera to emphasize your strengths and improve your weaknesses.

Remember that nerves are a positive—welcome them and use them to your advantage. Relax and visualize your perfect pitch in front of the audience. Above all, smile and look like you are having fun. After all, you are the technical person in the team!

Skill Building

New SE	1. Listen to your own voice. Be aware of your accent, pace, volume, and tone.
	2. Present to a peer group. Have them pick your top three annoying habits. Eliminate these habits through repetition and feedback.
	3. Videotape yourself at every opportunity.
	4. Practice facial expressions and mannerisms in front of a mirror.
	5. Smile, particularly when picking up the phone or before a difficult conversation.
	6. Experiment with a number of asymmetric hand gestures.
	7. Make a point of always rehearsing your presentations aloud.
	8. Accept nervous energy and redirect it.
Experienced SE	1. Accept speaking engagements outside of work (church, school, local government).
	2. Develop a complete repertoire of presentation energizers.
	3. Experiment with the concept of using numbers to make a point.
	4. Seek out opportunities to speak to very large audiences.
	5. Mentor a new SE and guide him or her through points 1 to 8 above.
SE Manager	1. Require that your SEs rehearse every presentation with you, by phone if necesary, until you are comfortable that they are rehearsing on their own.
	2. Encourage your team to take advantage of presentation skills training classes at work or at local colleges. (Refer to http://www.masteringtechnicalsales.com/services).

Chapter Goals

Appreciate why the "dash to demo" occurs.

Learn the planning and logistics of demonstrations.

Learn how to entertain the audience.

Discuss the segmenting of an audience.

The Dash to Demo

In selling, as in medicine, prescription before diagnosis is malpractice.

Jim Cathcart, Relationship Selling

The eager rush to demonstrate your product, which we will refer to in this chapter as the "dash to demo," often sounds the death knell for any sales opportunity, whether you are selling a $99 piece of software or a $3 million piece of medical equipment. In essence, it is the abandonment of any disciplined sales strategy in the haste to show the prospect the product. Inexperienced salespeople, or even experienced ones in a hurry to close the deal, become fixated on the belief that a world-class demo of the product is the key to progressing rapidly through the sales cycle. In fact, in the overwhelming majority of cases, the exact opposite is true.

Before discussing the demo itself or the preparation required beforehand, step back and apply some logic to the situation. In the life cycle of any product or service, the period during which it is deemed "hot" is very short. Using Geoffrey Moore's "crossing the chasm" analogy (Figure 8.1), this is usually either as you are accelerating to jump the chasm or just after you have safely landed. At this point, the market believes you are "hot," the world is beating down your doors, the sales force is overly confident, and orders are taken by someone standing next to the fax machine or by the webmaster.

Your product or service is now viewed as so unique that it virtually sells itself. A generic demo (known in the trade as "show up and throw up") is usually all that is required. The prospect sits back, realizing that the product will save time, money, and be very, very cool. You leave the office with the ink still drying on the purchase order. This sounds like a dream come true, but history is littered with just such examples. A few that come to mind include Digital Equipment in the mid-1980s selling VAX/VMS machines, Oracle in 1988 and 1989 with its database, Sybase in 1992 and 1993 with its database, and Sun Microsystems at several points in its product life cycle. During the dot-com era of 1999 to 2001, companies like JDS Uniphase, Ciena, and Nortel with optical networking gear and Siebel Systems with their sales-force automation software were all the dominant 800-pound gorillas in their product areas. The closest current approximation to this phenomenon is Google.

Most of us, however, are not fortunate enough to experience this type of phenomenon even once in our careers. So, unless your product is in that "hot" mode right now, immediately put aside all thoughts of rushing into a demonstration without fully understanding the situation beforehand.

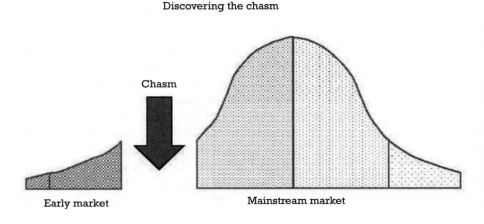

Figure 8.1 The technology adoption bell curve. (Reproduced with permission by the Chasm Group, LLC.)

Why Does the Dash to Demo Occur?

The salesperson's best friend in the dash to demo is often the prospect himself. To overcome objections early in the sales cycle, the phrase "you will see that in the demo" is used. This is a truly awful phrase for a rep to use and a downright criminal one for anyone in the sales-engineering organization to utter. You are simply setting higher and higher expectations for the eventual unveiling of the product. The higher the bar is raised, the greater the pressure disproportionately placed on you, your organization, your time, and your product. The salesperson can almost stop selling because such an intense focus is now placed on a single event.

The "day of the demo" is now poised above you like the sword of Damocles and effectively creates a make-or-break situation for the entire deal instead of just being a step along the way to closure. The demonstration should be a proof statement to gain more credibility ("See, it does what I said it would do"), but when the sale is entirely predicated on it, then the team needs to very carefully reevaluate the opportunity.

We stated earlier that the prospect is often an unwitting accomplice of the dash: "Just come in and show it to us. You don't have to change a thing." Should your sales team buy into this invitation, your chances of success drop dramatically. During this discussion, we have constantly referred to "the product." The product's definition is *precisely* what needs to be determined before proceeding any further.

"The Product" Becomes "The Solution"

By following the discovery process outlined in earlier chapters, you should be in a position to define the products or services you are selling as the solution to your client's problems. You are aware of the "pain points" the prospect is experiencing, the business and technical challenges it faces, and the impact of your proposed solution. A good discovery process, aided by quality interactions with the prospect, allows you to define the product as it best fits your solution. The dash to demo precludes any of this from happening. How can you effectively sell if you don't know why the prospect is buying?

We are also assuming that you have been fully briefed by the account manager, informed of any hot buttons and areas to avoid, and know how to express your benefits and features in terms of a solution-oriented, return-on-investment (ROI)–driven sale. In spite of all the best sales processes in the world (as an aside, we wonder why no sales organization implements a customer buying process), you will still be driven by the desire to dash to demo.

Risk Mitigation

The primary role of the demonstration during the sales process is risk mitigation. If selling is defined as carrying the prospect from their current state toward their desired state, the demo is the reinforcement and support of the sales bridge that will carry them there. It is not the bridge itself! The demo supports your message and your capabilities, serving to convince the prospect that you are the low-risk solution to their business problem. The demo should be wrapped with conviction, references, and user stories that all serve as proof points for your solution—it should not be held up as the keystone of your sales cycle.

Failing to Plan Is Planning to Fail

With a dash to demo, one fundamental problem is that everyone in the audience will have different expectations, and the sales team is not likely to anticipate them all. This is a recipe for disaster. There is so much more downside than upside in this unprepared approach that the odds are stacked very much against you. An unscientific survey of over 300 sales opportunities conducted by one of us in 2006 and 2007 revealed a win rate of 10% with a standard demonstration versus 45% for a customized one. Bear in mind the following:

> ‣ Not everyone in the room knows that this is a generic or "rushed" demo. Even if this is carefully explained to the audience, someone with influence will likely be disappointed.

> ‣ An important technical issue will be missed. As you are setting up, some IT analyst will ask, "This does run under native LINUX doesn't it?" or "Is there a Japanese character version?"

> ‣ An important business issue will be overlooked. Either just before or just after the technical issue, a business manager will mention that his or her business processes are in diametric opposition to your proposal.

> ‣ You or the sales rep will say something that may sound stupid to the audience. This could happen anytime, but because you have performed

almost no discovery beforehand, the chances of doing this are significantly higher.

▸ The sales pitch may completely miss the mark because you have misunderstood the prospect's business problems. The prospect becomes offended because they feel you have not researched their issues, and the sales team is summarily dismissed.

The odds of any or all of the above happening are greatly increased if a third party is involved. This may be an independent consultant or a huge systems integrator (SI) trying to keep you at arm's length by protecting what he regards as his turf. Most companies will disapprove of an end run around their SI. One successful approach is to document all interactions and discussions with the SI (in the sales force automation system we hope your company has). Then, use this as the agenda for the demonstration to reconfirm what has been agreed on and what the individual expectations are. Sending such a document to the SI as an inclusive sales measure a few days in advance of the meeting can be very beneficial.

CASE STUDY: LEMMINGS

One dreary Monday afternoon, a very senior vice president from a large information services company called one of our account executives and announced, "Our foreign securities division needs your product. Be there at nine on Wednesday morning to give them a demonstration." We had never dealt with this company, although its parent had been a successful user of our software for years. Our contacts within the company were unable to give us any specific data about this division, and our requests for at least a few hours of telephone discovery were indignantly refused.

Cooler heads prevailed, and we attempted to call off the session. However, this was the salesperson's first big opportunity, it was a marquee account, and we had a new VP of sales. Over the objections of the technical team, we sprinted down the path of the dash to demo and were instructed to perform the demo. This was totally contrary to our well-established sales process and caused severe conflict within the sales team. The sales engineer on the account, being a true professional, decided to make the best of it and spent hours preparing with only limited information.

Needless to say, within 5 minutes of starting the meeting, our plans fell into disarray. The senior vice president took offense that we hadn't prepared adequately and didn't understand their business. Ten minutes later, he decided our product was not a good fit for his division and asked us to leave, berating the account executive for wasting his time. Ironically, with a few tweaks, we would have been an outstanding fit for his requirements. The vice president then called almost every executive in our organization to complain and bad-mouthed our company to every single one of his own peers. A multi-million-dollar pipeline dried up for the next 12 months until we could repair the damage this one individual had wreaked, with our spineless collusion, on our product and organization.

We will now shift our focus and emphasis toward the preparation and eventual execution of the demonstration. Whether you have fallen victim to the dash to demo or have undertaken a slower, leisurely stroll through discovery leading up to the demonstration, at some point you will actually need to start planning your approach.

Logistical Implications

Obviously, it pays to plan the demonstration out carefully, with a laser-sharp focus on how the product will solve the prospect's business problems economically and expeditiously. This means that every action during the demonstration has either to lead back to one of these solutions or to reinforce a competitive advantage.

In terms of logistics, you should always double-check some of the basic facts surrounding the event:

- Number of people attending;
- Names, titles, and phone numbers of attendees;
- Third parties who will be in attendance;
- Part-time attendees, particularly any key decision makers or executives;
- Amount of time allotted;
- Projection and sound facilities needed;
- Network access or strength of wireless signal;
- Availability of an electrical power supply;
- Handling of breakfast and lunch breaks;
- Requirements regarding signing of a nondisclosure agreement;
- Availability of an electronic map of the location, with driving instructions.

When presenting to a very large group, it is often worth visiting the facilities beforehand, which can be arranged by the internal coach, to personally check on all of these requirements. This can also present a marvelous opportunity to meet informally with some of the attendees in advance ("I just happened to be in the building").

Hint: Check the Signal Strength

Many organizations now routinely use the Internet as part of their demonstration environment and utilize a wireless Internet access card to obtain service from a national provider such as Verizon or Vodafone. Always look for an opportunity to check the available signal strength and coverage, especially if you are situated in an internal conference room or the basement of a convention center.

Whether in person or via telephone or the Web, it is vital to determine what the attendees *expect* to see. Great expectations may be fine for Charles Dickens, but it is your role to help set expectations with the potential audience. Based on what you learn, you can either give the audience what they want or set the groundwork beforehand if you cannot immediately meet some aspects of their requirements. In essence, you are able to define the product by matching the prospect's requirements against your capabilities.

CASE STUDY: I HEARD WHAT YOU SAID, BUT I KNOW WHAT YOU MEANT

A software engineer told us, "We sold a utility package that could significantly speed up any packaged application such as Peoplesoft Human Resources or the Oracle eBusiness suite. A brand-new sales rep set up a demonstration of our product and provided me with his somewhat brief discovery notes. From the notes and a subsequent conversation with him, it was obvious we were dealing with an Oracle packaged application. I arrived at the customer site, set up the equipment, and used the next 10 to 15 minutes to conduct my own discovery with the audience members as they arrived, as the rep had refused to let me have access to them beforehand. To my horror, I discovered that they were indeed running Oracle, but only as a database, and used Peoplesoft as their standard application! We were totally unprepared for this and obviously had the incorrect slide deck, demonstration, and marketing collateral. It was, at the time, the most embarrassing sales call of my short career. I vowed *never* to prepare for a demonstration ever again without explicitly talking to the customer beforehand. Learn from my experience!"

The Agenda

The most important preparatory tool of all is the agenda (see Appendix 8A). Whoever controls the agenda controls the show. The agenda explicitly gets buy-in from the prospect about the length and content of the meeting. It also allows the pace and format of the meeting to be set beforehand. One of the most common mistakes is going into a demonstration session, or in fact into any customer meeting, without an agenda.

An agenda is not something to be typed up quickly on the morning of the meeting or casually added to the front of a PowerPoint presentation. Do not feel rigidly bound by what you traditionally expect to see on an agenda. You can include names and titles of attendees as well as the presenters. If you are bringing in a subject matter expert, include a short biography on this person and include a picture if he or she is remotely dialing in. You can also list the key elements of any session, some discussion points, and even potential problems about which you want to raise the attendees' awareness.

You will note that the sample agenda in Appendix 8A does not place the corporate overview as the lead-off item; nor are any of the demonstration sessions any longer than 45 minutes. We will cover this in more detail in the following chapter.

Preparing the Way

All too often, the demonstration consists of one sales engineer sitting at the keyboard of a laptop projecting onto a screen in a slightly darkened conference room. Before even dealing with the content of the demonstration, let us examine the logistics.

> ▸ Can everybody see and read the screen? Sit at the back of the room, and try to read your most complex screen or chart. Bear in mind that not everyone has good vision. You may need to increase the font size (most applications are in 8 or 10 points) up to 12 points and modify some colors to make the screen legible. Red, purple, and green are notoriously poor colors for display purposes and text. Somewhere between 5% to 8% of your audience will have a color blindness issue.

> ▸ Always make sure that you maintain eye contact with the sales representative. This means the rep usually has to sit on the opposite side of

the table or directly across from the podium. The sales team will only be able to communicate with each other nonverbally, so the visual aspect is crucial. Should trouble develop, or if the rep needs to tell you to speed up or slow down, some small gesture is all that is required.

‣ Have an emergency phrase or gesture prepared. In the event of a potential catastrophic meltdown of equipment, your nerves, or the presentation, this signal notifies the rep that it is time for her to step in and take charge.

‣ Never, ever be alone in the room. In a team-selling situation, it is very tempting for the rep to quietly leave the room to make a few calls or to handle Blackberry e-mail. This is a guaranteed way of ensuring that equipment will malfunction while he or she is away. An agenda can help in dealing with logistics if presenters are coming and going during the course of the day. It is the function of the account executive to ensure attendance in the room. A presenter *always* needs assistance in the event of equipment failure or even in handling the audience.

‣ Have a backup prepared. For example, if you are using a PowerPoint presentation, make sure a copy is available on a USB memory stick or stored on a colleague's machine.

‣ Always bring a spare power cord, extension strip, Ethernet cable, and so forth.

‣ Print out, in color, copies of key slides or screens. Make sure they have the company name or logo on them. Label them "Proprietary and Confidential" if necessary.

‣ Clear the way. Should you need to get up out of your seat and approach the screen, make sure all leads and power cords are tucked safely away. When presenting from a conference room table, ensure that all cables are rolled up with ties rather than having connectors snaking across the table.

‣ Turn off, or place in vibrate mode, all cell phones and pagers. I once worked with a sales engineer who reminded everyone before each meeting by saying, "Set phasers to stun."

‣ Approach your meeting sponsor, if appropriate, and ask him to announce beforehand that laptop lids should be closed to prevent surreptitious e-mail reading by the audience.

The Audience

Nothing is guaranteed to put the audience to sleep more than a 6-hour monotone delivery showing every feature and function. In fact, the very act of creating the agenda should bring this home to you. Just as variety is the spice of life, it is also the spice of a good demonstration. We are not suggesting a Las Vegas–style multimedia presentation, but sometimes you need to give the eyes and ears a rest.

CASE STUDY: A MULTIMEDIA SUCCE$$

One of the most successful sales engineers I ever had the pleasure to work with was a gentleman named Gary Sing. He was so successful that his peers used to call him "Gary $ing." Gary firmly believed that a demonstration was as much about presentation as content, so he used to choreograph almost every step in the demonstration. *Choreograph* is the appropriate word, because Gary used to set up and script role-plays for everyone on the team. Not only did this keep everybody involved, but it also made the demonstration more fun.

When demonstrating call-center software, Gary would play the role of the customer-service agent, the sales rep would often be a really irate customer, I would be the call-center manager, and one of the other sales engineers would be a repairman dispatched to fix the problem. Gary gave everybody his lines and some props (for example, hats) and made us all practice. On one occasion, he even used Lego bricks to make a point. Needless to say, his approach proved so successful that other sales engineers started to imitate his methodology. An additional hidden benefit was that it forced the sales representative to be present throughout the demo preparation (often late into the night) instead of turning up on the day of a corporate presentation.

We received almost uniformly positive reactions from customers. In a market crowded with similar products, they always remembered the demonstration and the way it was performed. That was often the only edge needed to make the short list in a selection. I personally believe that this approach resonates so well because real life is all about interactions as opposed to one-way dialogs.

Customer participation is often another way to differentiate a company. I can still recall a half-dozen demonstrations when I was made part of the show. On one occasion, I had to provide a blood sample to a medical-device maker. Building audience participation into your demonstrations helps engage customers on a subconscious level. They will be more attentive and likely to voice opinions because they are interacting within a familiar function. Use the entertainment factor to highlight the crucial parts of your demonstration, particularly if you can help internalize a financial saving or ROI calculation for an executive.

Segment the Audience

Presenting a demonstration to an audience that includes business and technology people is very difficult because each group looks for different things. Executives require information at a higher level than systems analysts. It is an incredibly complex and difficult task to craft a demonstration that will appeal to these varying constituencies. Questions that can only be answered by using technical talk will go over the heads of business people and most executives. A question about business processes or economics is immaterial to technicians. It is not your fault that the question is asked, but because the answer is not relevant to certain members of the audience, they become disinterested, and you lose their attention.

Hint: Capture the Questions

Unless you are being deluged with questions, have colleagues write them on a poster board. This shows that you are not avoiding the issue and intend to answer them later. Crossing off these questions as they are covered later in the session makes for a powerful indicator of progress and resolution. For a segmented audience, you can even label them "business" and "technical."

The solution is to always divide and conquer. Offer to provide a separate session for the technical staff that will dig deep into the product or service and explore every possible issue that may be raised. In return for committing to this, ask for permission to defer any questions judged as being too technical to this session. This is also a good tactic for not answering a technical question you're not prepared for or for buying time for a feature that is not quite ready to be demonstrated.

Similarly, break out an hour for a high-level executive overview. Typically, this overview may include only two or three slides but will involve whiteboarding and drawing many diagrams to engage attendees in conversation. Dealing with executives is an art form in itself (see Chapter 16), but simplicity and directness are key. Remember that you can often *tell* an executive how something works instead of *showing* them.

Dealing with Technical and Business Audiences

When forced to deal with a mixed audience of executives, technical people, and business people, decide who comprises the most important segment, and structure the agenda to be sure to address their concerns. In most cases, this will be the executive or business groups because they are frequently the most difficult to reach (in terms of availability) and also the least patient. Technical staff members are usually willing to wait for the subject matter that interests them. Often, business-oriented decision makers lose interest and begin having themselves paged to escape; executives may simply get up and leave. Your prospects understand this pecking order too, so do not be unduly concerned about putting this group before another.

Should the technical team be the most important group to reach in a mixed group, then state this during the agenda review. Put the bulk of the available time into the line items for the technicians. Introduce your agenda by saying, "Our understanding is that we are here today to make sure our solution has a fit with your technical vision." If this is incorrect and isn't the purpose of the meeting, the business side will quickly make that known. At this point, the average sales team thinks fast on its feet and either adjusts on the fly or postpones. The professional sales team will already be prepared for this eventuality and have a response prepared.

If you primarily need to reach the business group, comment on that during your introduction: "We understand that we have been given a green light by the technical team, and we are here to validate our understanding of your business requirements." Then, throughout the presentation, whenever a technical person asks a question that deviates from the goal, you can promise to follow up with them via e-mail. This avoids diluting your message and also provides a good reason to contact that person in a less formal setting.

Checkpoint Charlie

There is an old maxim for public speaking: "Tell them what you are going to tell them, then tell them, and then tell them what you told them." This tongue twister should serve as a reminder to keep checking throughout the demonstration that you are still on target. It can be very annoying for one person to continually ask, "How are we doing?" so the sales team needs to divide this task up beforehand. The purpose of the agenda is to set the stage for what the audience is going to hear. Any salesperson worth his salt can summarize the events of a meeting. All that remains is the telling and making sure the points are being communicated effectively. One technique used very effectively is to summarize at the end of each agenda item (assuming that they are spaced 30 to 60 minutes apart) and gain agreement on the summary before proceeding.

Hint: Branding Is Key

Just as your product or company may be branded, so should the demonstration. Decide beforehand on just a few key phrases to use repetitively throughout the day: "cost-effective," "number one," "industry leading," "safe," "domain experts," "huge installed base," and so forth. Award yourself bonus points if at least one member of the audience repeats a sound bite during the day.

Summary

Preparation is the key, so always make sure you have contacted as many members of the audience beforehand as possible, and target your demonstration toward their stated requirements. Never perform a blind demo unless you are desperate. Prepare the product, prepare your team, prepare the environment, prepare an agenda, and prepare to differentiate yourself. Connect your product or service to the customer's business requirements (repeat as needed), and, above all, loosen up and enjoy the day.

Skill Building

New SE	1. Be prepared. Start with an agenda.
	2. Allow an experienced SE to conduct your first discovery session.
	3. Keep the demonstration short and simple.
	4. Focus on 2 to 3 key benefits.
	5. Pay attention to the meeting environment.
Experienced SE	1. Employ multimedia within the demonstration.
	2. Seek out an opportunity to have the audience "test-drive" your product.
	3. Create scenario-based or role-play-style demonstrations if appropriate.
	4. Pay attention to the smallest of details.
	5. Learn to handle mixed audiences.

Appendix 8A: Sample Agenda

Agenda
Tuesday, May 29
Vendor Presentation for New System

Attendees		
Acme.net	Phillip Thrasher, regional sales director Amy Tanner, account executive Martin Lawson, systems engineer Valerie Trulove, senior systems engineer Michael Loo, product manager	
Integrator	Romy Paschal, principal	
Outline		
Morning Session		
8:30–9:00 a.m.	Breakfast and introductions	
9:00–9:15 a.m.	Agenda review	Amy Tanner

9:15–9:30 a.m.	Goals of meeting:
	    Gain agreement on technical architecture
	    Presentation of reference sites
	    Validation of economic assumptions
	    Development go-forward plan
		Amy Tanner

9:30–9:50 a.m.	Quick, scenario-based demonstration	Martin Lawson

9:50–10:45 a.m.	Technical architecture
	    Hardware requirements
	    Linux version support
	    Scalability
		Valerie Trulove

10:45–11:05 a.m.	Break	

11:05–11:35 a.m.	Product demonstration I
	Basic principles
	    Customer analysis
	    Service metrics
		Martin Lawson

11:35 a.m.–12:00 p.m.	Corporate overview	Phillip Thrasher
12:00–1:00 p.m.	Lunch	

Afternoon Session			
1:00–1:45 p.m.	Product demonstration II Handling your business Increasing productivity Decreasing costs Improving customer satisfaction		Martin Lawson
1:45–3:00 p.m.	Split session		
	Room A:	Product futures and technology	Michael Loo
	Room B:	Economic justification	Phillip Thrasher
3:00 p.m.	Wrap-up		All
	Outstanding questions Achievement of goals Next steps		

Meeting Goals

1	Gaining agreement on technical architecture
2	Presentation of reference sites
3	Validation of economic assumptions
4	Development of go-forward plan

Michael Loo is the product line manager for Acme.net's eBusiness Systems. Mike has been with the company for over 4 years and designed his first e-system in 1995. His responsibilities include setting product direction and investigating technologies for inclusion into our product lines. He has been published in *CIO Magazine*, *Infoworld*, and the *Journal of eCommerce* and is regularly quoted by industry and financial analysts.

9

Snap Demos

Much wisdom often goes with brevity of speech.

Sophocles

Impromptu, or "snap," demonstrations are increasingly common. You may run into a client in an airport or have an ad hoc meeting with a prospect at a hotel bar at a trade show, or a senior executive might join a meeting and ask for the abbreviated version of your two-hour presentation. Regardless of the setting, a snap demo can be a great way to learn more about a client's needs and set the hook for a future sale. Learning how to structure snap demos effectively can also help you improve your delivery for longer presentations.

In this chapter, we will address the following topics: scoping, structuring, and execution of the snap demo. We note that certain concepts in this chapter are relevant for short, scripted demonstrations of the type that frequently take place on a trade show floor, but such demos usually provide the opportunity to script and rehearse the material. Such luxuries are not typically present in the "snap demo" we are discussing.

> Example: One of us went to visit an existing client interested in extending their use of his products. After hours of flights and driving to reach the meeting, the sales team learned that the technical decision maker might not be able to attend the meeting. After an hour, the decision maker showed up and said, "I had an emergency come up, but you have 5 minutes to tell me why we should use your product for our new project." The author brought up a single screen and employed the Snap Demo Structure below (using the information gathered in the first hour of the meeting). The decision maker became friendlier, delegated the handling of the emergency, and joined for the rest of the meeting. While this was one of many steps, the process did result in a large sale, and the local sales team was very impressed with the author's ability to condense two hours of planned material into 5 minutes.

Scoping the Snap Demo

When you begin to deliver an ad hoc demo, you should start by mentally cataloging what you know about your prospect and then ask the following questions of the attendees to make sure you confirm certain crucial information at a minimum:

- What is their role in the organization (end user, administrative, managerial, technical)?
- Are they using (or familiar with) another comparable product (competitive, in-house, or other)?
- Do they have any familiarity with your product or your company?
- What do they believe they need?

When a prospect asks you to show a particular product, it can be tempting just to jump in and run through the demonstration specific to that product line, which you may have memorized. Before doing so, you should run through the minimal needs analysis described above and mentally plan how to respond to the prospect's needs and establish appropriate next steps.

Structuring the Snap Demo

Once you have the information described in the scoping section, you should organize your presentation around those key data points. The sample snap demo structure below provides an illustrative agenda for a snap demo.

Hint: Use External Touch Points to Shortcut Long Topics

In a quick demo presentation, when possible, try to address questions that are not key selling points verbally, frequently including specific feature and function discussions. In particular, it can be helpful to contrast your product features with those of a competitive product where you compare favorably or at least offer an equivalent solution. For example, if you have a vertically focused order-management system, you could refer to features that your product has in common with Oracle, SAP, or Salesforce.com, then focus on those features that differentiate your product.

Begin by stating what you are going to show, any key features, and associated benefits. Just as in any presentation, you should tell your audience what you are going to show, show it, then tell them what you just showed. While this structure may seem overly redundant, given the brevity of your presentation, the small amount of time will help your audience retain your key messages.

Exhibit 9.1: Sample Snap Demo Structure

1. Perform a mini "needs analysis."

2. State the business problem(s) you intend to address and the products that you will demonstrate.

3. Demonstrate the product (briefly), and deliver key messages.

    ‣ Explain key product features.

    ‣ Highlight benefits and key selling points.

    ‣ Repeat as necessary.

4. Tell your audience what they saw; explain how it addresses their expressed need and describe other tangible business benefits or differentiators; confirm that this was responsive to their needs.

5. Ask about next steps or follow-up.

The next sections will focus on optimizing snap demo delivery.

Hint: Do the Last Thing First

Peter Cohan, author of the book Great Demo![1] and high-impact-demo training consultant, advocates beginning your software demo with your most impactful screen and then backing up to perform the full presentation. By doing so, he believes you will improve your audience's attention during the rest of the demo, and you will make sure that any executive who cannot stay for the whole meeting gets the benefit of seeing your key selling point. In a snap demo situation, this technique will have a similar benefit, especially if you get sidetracked and run out of time. More on this technique can be found at Cohan's Web site: www.secondderivative.com.

Keep the Demo Snappy

In a snap demo, you will not be able to show a prospect a full demonstration of your product; nor will you be able to provide a detailed response to most questions asked. The first issue can be particularly problematic for software or complex hardware, as "seeing the product in action" can take a long time. Instead of performing a full demonstration, bring up a key screen on your computer, or present your prospect with the most interesting aspect of your hardware product. Then, provide a brief narrative of what the product does, highlighting key sales points, user benefits, and strong differentiators.

- *Hardware example:* "This laser is capable of modulating between four states while in use and has an 8-year duty cycle. When compared with existing products that can only achieve two states over a 4-year cycle, our customers can reduce their field inventory by half and save 50% over an 8-year product life when you factor in reduced costs of maintenance and service."

- *Software example:* "This forecasting screen is a lightweight way for account directors and regional and corporate management to easily share quota, order, and quota achievement information. *Briefly highlight key fields and features on the screen.* Relative to legacy products that are hard to maintain, our clients tell us that over 90% of their sales forces keep their accounts current on a weekly basis, enabling regional managers to manage resources and giving executive management the ability to manage inventory and financial expectations."

---

1. Peter Cohan, *Great Demo!* (Bloomington, IN: iUniverse Publishing, 2005).

In response to any questions that may arise, focus on verbalizing an answer without demoing the product. Highlight features on a screen or demonstration unit using gestures, but avoid "jumping in" unless showing the requested feature is significantly impactful. Unlike in a formal presentation, you shouldn't feel compelled to provide proof on the spot that your product does everything that you say it does. If you are able to address in the snap demo all of the key topics your prospect requested, then offer to go back and provide an in-depth demonstration if they have additional time. You definitely don't want to spend 3 minutes of a 5-minute demo responding to a question with a lengthy response or a detailed demonstration of a small feature.

Wrapping the Snap Demo (Tell Them What They Saw)

After the demonstration is complete, reiterate what attendees saw and how that maps to their needs. Confirm that the prospect can see how the demonstration addressed the points requested. This is a good time to perform further qualification to expand your understanding of the prospect's needs and the fit of your product.

Snap Demos for Executive Audiences

When doing a snap demo for a business executive, you must be even more mindful of the previously mentioned differences between a full demonstration and a snap demo. In addition, it can actually be helpful to skip doing a demo at all; simply bring up the key screen that supports your sales message and talk about what your product does. Supply customer anecdotes, and talk through use cases without actually doing the demo. Following this path reduces the chance that the executive's attention span will be exhausted before you hit your close.

> *Hint: Use a Metaphor or an Example to Connect with an Executive*
>
> *A metaphor can be a great way to quickly explain the benefit of your product in a memorable fashion. The sales management of Siebel Systems, a former maker of customer-relationship management software acquired by Oracle, used to say their use of their sales-forecasting system let them "see around corners" to know when a change in the business environment was going to take place and react before their competitors. This simple positioning helped establish a fairly basic product as providing a nearly supernatural benefit for their customers.*

Closing the Demo and Establishing Next Steps

If an account director or sales executive is present, he or she should step in at this point and try to schedule additional follow-up. If you are presenting solo, and you feel the prospect is qualified, you should proactively offer to set up a follow-up call, meeting, or webcast to be able to provide a complete demonstration and more fully respond to outstanding questions. If the prospect declines, ask for his or her contact information in order to send additional information by mail or e-mail.

> *Hint: Prescripting Snap Demos*
>
> *While you frequently won't have the ability to script a full snap demo, you can do some homework. A good practice is to try to become facile at delivering the introduction and closing portions of a typical demonstration script, cutting out the 90% in the middle that addresses the step-by-step walk through of the product. It can also be helpful to maintain a library of supporting customer case studies attesting to how your customers have been successful with a given product. A customer anecdote can often quickly and impactfully illustrate the benefit of a product.*

Snap Demo Considerations

The typical gotchas in delivering a snap demo include (1) misassessing a customer's needs and showing them an "inappropriate" product, and (2) using time inefficiently. The key to avoiding the first issue is gaining experience with your products and their qualification criteria. Reiterating what you are going to show the prospect in step 2 of the sample demo structure above should help mitigate this issue as well. Time management is a big challenge in any demonstration. When there is a question, err on the side of showing less, not more, deferring an in-depth demonstration until you have provided a cursory review of all items on the agenda or for a follow-up.

Summary

Snap demos provide a good way for prospects to qualify your product and for you to qualify whether a prospect warrants a full meeting or demonstration. Short presentations can be more complex because you may have no advance notice of the agenda and because many products can be challenging to demo in a few minutes. Learning to quickly perform a needs analysis, show a product, and drive home key benefits is critical for snap demos and a useful exercise for full-length presentations.

Skill Building

New SE	1. Develop familiarity with product features and key marketing messages by presenting at trade show booths.
	2. Memorize the "elevator pitch" for your key products, and think about how you can emphasize key messages in a very short presentation.
Experienced SE	1. Practice giving short, "narrative-heavy, product-light" demonstrations when presenting to business executives.
	2. Work on effectively qualifying prospects and achieving follow-up actions without the benefit of a sales rep's presence.

Chapter Goals

Discuss the pros and cons of using webcast technology.

Build a checklist before each webcast.

Learn how to gain the audience's attention and establish credibility in the first 3 minutes.

Learn Web presentation techniques and how to avoid bad habits.

Remote Demonstrations and Webcasts

Talk low, talk slow, and don't say too much.
John Wayne

The advent of high-speed Internet connections, notably for the home-office worker, has dramatically changed the landscape of traditional product presentations and demonstrations. An increasing percentage of sales calls are now conducted remotely, through the Web, instead of in a classic face-to-face meeting.

The Basic Premise

The rationale behind the use of the webcast is twofold. First, it offers a significant saving in travel costs, both in terms of time and money. Second, it allows the sales team to reach an audience located in disparate locations (and increasingly in different time zones and countries) with a single session. Corporate best practices, especially for a low-cost or a low-margin solution set, may dictate that

113

webcasts be the primary form of customer interaction. However, for the enterprisewide, relationship-oriented sales force, a remote demonstration is just another tool in the sales-engineering arsenal. Just like any other tool you may have in your garage at home, when used correctly it can be a major productivity aid. Yet, you need to be aware of the "when all you have is a hammer, everything looks like a nail" syndrome when proposing a webcast.

Advantages and Disadvantages of the Remote Demonstration

As previously stated, the main advantage of webcasts is that they reduce the cost per sales call and provide the logistical benefit of being able to reach more people in a single session. In addition, webcasts can be set up on short notice, although preparation time should still be scheduled for a demonstration or customized presentation. Most webcast software offers the option of recording the session so that it can be replayed at a later date, used for training, or even posted on the corporate Web site. Webcast technology is best used for short presentations with a single key message or for the purposes of an upgrade or "what's new"–style demonstration for an interim (not major) release of your solution. Webcasts are also very effective for covering a few outstanding points or issues after a longer face-to-face demonstration or presentation. They can further be useful in building consensus among different functional groups by "getting everyone on the same page" regarding user requirements.

Case Study: Touching All the Bases

As part of a sizeable transaction with a very large international manufacturing company headquartered in the eastern United States, we had developed a sample executive dashboard for their operations managers. Although we had the approval of senior IT management and the budget from the business units, we were asked to "validate" the design with operational teams based in multiple locations. Physically visiting each of them, even with the cooperation of our international offices, would have been a drawn-out process and could potentially have pushed the sale out of the quarter simply due to timing. We also knew from prior experience that getting the operations units at this customer to agree on any common guidelines or a common look and feel was an exercise in futility. Since the actual demonstration was 15 to 20 minutes long, this was a perfect opportunity to use a webcast. We set up two webcast sessions to account for time zone variances and business pressures, arranged for a sales person or sales engineer to be physically present in the customer's main U.S. and European offices to chaperone the audience, and carefully rehearsed the presentation. The technology and our product behaved flawlessly, and 90% of the stakeholders viewed and validated the solution. Having them all online significantly cut down their differences of opinion, and we rapidly gained consensus for deployment. More importantly, the transaction closed within the current fiscal quarter and was large enough to make a sizeable upside difference to our financial results.

The primary disadvantage may be so obvious that it is barely worth mentioning, but *you are not in the same room as your customer.* You have no mechanism to "read the room" and lose the benefit of most of the nonverbal techniques covered in Chapter 7. As discussed in that chapter, 93% of your message is conveyed through nonverbal communication[1], and of that 93%, 55% is facial and body language. Therefore, in a webcast, you are presenting with 45% effectiveness at best, assuming you fully utilize words, content, and vocal tones. Our advice is that, although you should approach each opportunity for customer interaction with unbridled optimism, you should assume that you are competing against e-mail, Blackberries, side conversations with the mute button on, and even feet up on the desk behind closed doors. A comprehensive list of the positive and negative uses of remote demonstrations is detailed in Table 10.1.

This means your message needs to be highly tuned to the media in play and totally focused. There is no opportunity to restart or hit the reset button halfway through as you can with a live, face-to-face session. The webcast is not a tool to use if your presentation skills are below par. Indeed, even good presentation skills do not always translate well to the remote-demonstration environment because of the constrained nature of that medium.

The webcast also restricts the length of the presentation, which may actually be a blessing in disguise. Most effective webcasts run between 45 and 75 minutes, which is enough time to cover a topic without the audience growing bored simply because they have looked at a screen for too long. For a purely business-oriented audience, 30 minutes is often the maximum attention span you should expect.

---

1. Albert Mehrabian, *Silent Messages: Implicit Communication of Emotion and Attitudes*, 2nd ed. (Belmont, CA: Wadsworth, 1981); www.kaaj.com/psych.

Table 10.1
Positive and Negative Uses of Remote Demonstrations

Positive Uses and Attributes	Negative Uses and Attributes
They provide an outstanding tool for lead generation.	Complex presentations don't work well.
They can easily be recorded and replayed.	They are limited to 75 minutes maximum.
They work well for "what's new" and "upgrade" messages.	You have no control over the audience.
They can be used to cover outstanding points after a face-to-face sales call.	They are unsuitable for complicated architecture situations or detailed Q&A sessions.
They can be multilocational and multinational.	Third-party technology may crash or require distracting and lengthy setup.
They can be set up and rescheduled at short notice.	There is no effective way to whiteboard.

Best Practices in Preparing for a Webcast

You should approach a remote demonstration just like a standard sales call—because it is just that. Several days before the webcast, time permitting, you need to have researched the company and the audience and to have agreed with the sales representative and any other presenters what the core of the message should be. For a lead-generation event or a seminar, you are most likely presenting standard material provided by the marketing department, designed to reach a fairly broad audience. For a webcast with a single customer, your message needs to be laser focused to the expected audience and the specific business and technical problem to be solved.

In keeping with standard practice, you should also build an agenda, even if you don't display it during the webcast. This prevents any misunderstandings and will help to keep you on time. As a matter of best practice, you should allow 5 to 10 minutes at the start for introductions, setup confirmation, and latecomers. Remember that attending a webcast does not generate the same sense of urgency that a regular meeting might on the part of your customer. You should also decide whether to take questions throughout the session—which we strongly encourage—or to defer them to a Q&A near the end.

Ask for the name of a technical contact at your customer, and send them the webcast link at least 24 hours beforehand. Even if you have presented a half-dozen times to the same customer at this same location, you should still do this in case of firewall changes or software updates. Also request that this same contact sign on to the webcast software at least 15 to 20 minutes beforehand to insure that everything is working at their end. Most customers are perfectly reasonable about this and will agree to help you out to ensure everything goes smoothly.

It is also good practice to e-mail a copy of a few of the key screens or presentation slides to the attendees beforehand, particularly if there is a slide or even a business point you need to refer back to constantly. We recently watched a vendor webcast presentation where the lead sales engineer had distributed a two-pager that summarized her entire presentation and contained a key screen shot as a form of "proof statement." The audience found this technique very appealing and effective in helping them understand the content. This can also help in situations where one of the participants cannot access the technology due to travel or technical logistical difficulties.

Several hours before the presentation, you should recheck the technology, making sure that Internet connection, firewalls, and routers are all stable and functional. Prepare for the webcast as you would for a standard call. In the case of a demo, make sure that everything works and is loaded and cached for optimal performance; for a presentation, ensure that you have the correct slide deck. Should you be using prerelease software or have doubts about the stability of your demonstration, take screen shots as a backup. A webcast is best conducted from a quiet conference room, as opposed to a cubicle in some busy office. Where possible, have as many participants from your team in the same location so that you can have some "back-channel" communication. Should you have participants from other offices, such as product-marketing or technical-support personnel, set up an Instant Messenger (IM) session with them shortly before you start in order to allow for some on-the-fly coaching if necessary. Needless to say, the IM session should not be on your live webcast machine. Another best practice is to have a second machine or laptop in the room to serve as an audience monitor, enabling you see what the audience is seeing in case of transmission delays. Use this machine for the back-channel IM sessions. The final touch is to use a headset instead of a speakerphone to gain the best possible sound quality.

Hint: Clean Up Your Desktop Beforehand

Make sure that your desktop is clear of distracting icons, that all IM and news programs are turned off, and that your recent files lists have been scrubbed to avoid the embarrassment of 100 people seeing that the last image you viewed was surfing_dog.jpg or reading that IM from a colleague asking, "How's the job hunt going?"

Note that an updated and comprehensive, time-driven webcast checklist is available on the www.masteringtechnicalsales.com Web site.

The First 3 Minutes are Critical

In the absence of face-to-face contact, successful remote demonstrations follow the "Rule of 3s."

> *30 seconds:* First impressions are formed about how you present.

> *3 minutes:* Decisions are made about whether you are credible.

> *30 minutes:* This is how long you have to deliver a key point.

The main presenter (i.e., you, as the sales engineer) should *not* start the webcast off with pleasantries, introductions, and the obligatory "can everyone hear me/see the screen?" That task should be left to the account manager or another sales engineer acting as the host. Checking on the volume level is an easy task; checking on the screen resolution and image quality can be a little trickier. When the target audience is in a single location, place a small icon at both the top left and the bottom right of your introductory start-up slide and have the main contact at the customer site confirm that he or she can see both icons, which serves to confirm the screen resolution. For the occasions when you have multiple viewing locations or for a lead-generation-type webcast, introduce the use of the built-in polling and feedback mechanisms in the software (refer to the next section for further detail on including interactivity in the session) and request that the attendees signal yes or no through a poll as a way of familiarizing them with these capabilities.

The host should now briefly go through the agenda, then introduce you as the main speaker. We suggest that you provide the host, even if it is the rep you work with every day, with a very brief, written biography so that your introduction is carefully scripted. During the biography, you should move onto the introductory slide or screen of your presentation. This slide should contain your name, title, any relevant professional qualifications, and a photograph of yourself. Relevant professional qualifications would include CISSP certification for security professionals, PMP certification for project managers, or a CPA/PhD for domain experts. The photograph is an interesting idea first developed by real estate professionals in the United States as the visual helps to personalize you and "put a face to the voice." Under some circumstances, you may be introduced by your coach at the customer site or by a third-party partner. On these occasions you should supply a lengthier biography and a scripted introduction, leaving nothing to chance.

You may also need to hand over, or share, control of the webcast at some point. Be conscious of the "Rule of 3's" relating to the next presenter, and practice the handover beforehand (both verbally and with the technology) or decide whether the account executive should step in as the host to effect the transition.

Once you get into the meat of your presentation, consider starting with a visually impactful slide to immediately grab the attention of the audience. All too often, a webcast spends 30 to 40 minutes leading up to the grand finale. Starting off with the one slide, screen, or report that really highlights your solution will make the attendees want to spend the remaining time learning how you did that. Refer back to Chapter 9 for more details about the snap demonstration technique for compelling presentations.

Effectively Constructing and Delivering PowerPoint for a Webcast

Most standard PowerPoint decks need to be substantially reworked for Web-based viewing as animation, slide builds, and other advanced graphics do not always translate perfectly to the remote medium and frequently display incorrectly. Should you need to use a complex slide with builds, test it very carefully beforehand. Be aware that in certain parts of Europe, such slide builds are viewed with disdain as "American marketing." As in most situations, a picture is worth a thousand words, so employing a graphic and speaking to it is usually preferable to burying the audience with bulleted text. At the best of times, bullets within a sales presentation (as opposed to an educational or informative presentation) are boring and can lead the presenter to read from the slide. In a webcast situation, you want the audience to pay attention to you (again, imagine you are competing for their attention in reading their e-mail) and listen to your voice instead of focusing all their attention on reading text from the screen. When you must use bulleted text, aim for a maximum of five bullets of five words or fewer. For executives, cut this down to three bullets of five words or fewer (see Chapter 16). This also provides the side benefit of making the font larger and easier to read.

Familiarize yourself with the tools available to you within the webcasting software. Most tools allow you to use a highlighter to call out sections of the slide and a pen to annotate a slide on the fly or even, if you have the talent, draw a picture. In order to keep the audience's attention, you need to engage them constantly and attempt to keep the sessions interactive. You can accomplish this either by verbally asking open-ended questions, which can be risky, or by using a set-up slide to ask a closed question. These questions can be either yes/no or red/green, or you can ask the audience to select a number from 1 to 5 denoting a specific answer or range.

Should you find yourself needing to present an unusually long or complicated demonstration, consider breaking it up into smaller sections. Switch from the demonstration across to PowerPoint several times to introduce and subsequently summarize the key components of your presentation. We have witnessed several creative modifications to the standard webcast. We referred to the first in the previous case study—just because you cannot be physically present does not necessarily mean that the account manager or another colleague cannot be onsite. A second option is to "coach your coach" and allow him to participate in, even drive, part of your presentation. A third alternative, more applicable to the mass market, is to offer a prize or a raffle for attendees.

CASE STUDY: MAKING SURE YOU ARE STILL OUT THERE

Deloitte Consulting, the consulting arm of Deloitte, runs a series of informative webcasts called "Dbriefs"[2] on a variety of topics of interest to both their customers and general business audiences. A benefit of attending some of the sessions is that you may earn continuing professional education credits. However, in order to earn these credits, you need to respond to a number of questions asked and polled during each session. These not only keep the sessions interactive and meaningful but also yield a wealth of consumer data and a wonderful set of leads for Deloitte.

Some Really Bad Habits to Avoid

In effect, all you have is your voice, the mouse, and a screen display to attract your audience's undivided attention. It is important that you utilize all three of these attributes to gain maximum impact. Any bad habits you have in the vocal department will be magnified in the webcast arena; plus, you have the opportunity to exhibit many new bad habits. It is essential that you speak clearly, a little slower than normal, and at a comfortable volume

---

2. Deloitte Touche Tomatsu Corporation, www.deloitte.com/dtt.

for the attendees. If you are nervous or have a tendency to use filler words, we suggest that you write out your opening remarks for the first 3 minutes so you don't have to concentrate on the words and their sequencing.

The concept of appropriate speed applies to your use of the technology during the remote session. Two common faults of novice presenters are "screen kung-fu," where you jump from screen to screen to screen with little explanation, and the "zippy mouse" syndrome, which involves using the mouse to rapidly and repeatedly move the cursor across the screen, leaving your audience dazed and confused. Should you need the mouse cursor to point out some detail on the screen, use a larger cursor to start with and utilize the webcasting software's built-in highlight/pen tools. Another bad habit to avoid is location transference. This involves the presenter's physically pointing to his own screen with a finger and saying, "If you look right here."

Engaging the Audience

Another common bad habit is the use of the weak interactive question, "Does anyone out there have any questions so far?" This is almost always guaranteed to elicit a deafening silence from the crowd. It is far better to use the polling mechanism or to directly ask a question to one of the attendees in the form, "Steven, now can you see how … ?" If it is not a lead-generation webcast, try to make sure that you "call out" each of the participants during the discussion. This will help encourage the audience to pay attention, and it is about as close as you can get to making it feel as if you are in the same room.

Another strong technique is to refer back to your agenda and ask for confirmation that you have addressed each point in turn: "Steven, did that meet the requirement you mentioned in your e-mail?" This can be a little riskier than when you are presenting in person, as you do not have the opportunity to whiteboard a response, and it may be tricky to extend your demo ad hoc. However, it is always better to know that something did or didn't work so that you can propose appropriate follow-up.

Prime Time for Webcasts

The best time for a webcast varies according to its purpose. For a seminar or mass-market lead-generation webcast, most events are held during lunchtime when more people are available. When presenting to a single client, the hour before or after lunch usually works out best and provides the fewest opportunities for absenteeism. When planning a webcast for a multiple time zone or international audience, the start time needs to be arranged within the business day to encourage as many people as possible to attend.

As a general heuristic, the optimum days for webcasts are Tuesdays, Wednesdays, and Thursdays, avoiding the first and last days of the week, which are typically already full of meetings. Webcasts arranged for early Monday or late Friday have a higher probability of being canceled or suffering from poor attendance. Also bear in mind that Fridays are a day off in Israel and most Muslim countries, and the Southern Hemisphere will be operating on summer time during the Northern Hemisphere's winter.

Table 10.2 shows the time zone chart for coordinating an international webcast. The top row represents the standard time zone offset based on the Eastern United States.

The Wrap-Up

Finish with a summary of the material you have covered, targeted toward the key messages and business problems you established before the presentation. Do not end with a Q&A session as you have no control over the questions, and it will lead to a weak conclusion. Plan for a short wrap-up

Table 10.2
Time Zone Offset Chart for Webcasts

−5	−3	−1	0	+2	+5	+6	+16
Hawaii	Western USA	Central USA	Eastern USA	Brazil (Rio)	UK	Europe	Eastern Australia (Sydney)
6 a.m.	8 a.m.	10 a.m.	11 a.m.	1 p.m.	4 p.m.	5 p.m.	1 a.m. (next day)
7 a.m.	9 a.m.	11 a.m.	12 p.m.	2 p.m.	5 p.m.	6 p.m.	2 a.m. (next day)
8 a.m.	10 a.m.	12 p.m.	1 p.m.	3 p.m.	6 p.m.	7 p.m.	3 a.m. (next day)
9 a.m.	11 a.m.	1 p.m.	2 p.m.	4 p.m.	7 p.m.	8 p.m.	4 a.m. (next day)
11 a.m.	1 p.m.	3 p.m.	4 p.m.	6 p.m.	9 p.m.	10 p.m.	6 a.m. (next day)

Note: When you near daylight savings time adjustments, times can vary significantly even within individual countries.

after the last question has been asked and answered. It is usually a good idea to leave the key slide, screen, diagram, or report you started with up on the screen while wrapping up and even during the prior Q&A session. Thank the attendees and (optionally) follow up with a transcript of the Q&A if you answered any relevant or objection-busting questions. The account manager or webcast host should again confirm with the key attendees that the objectives of the webcast were met, as well as next steps.

Summary

Although we prefer face-to-face sales calls, the financial dictates of modern business necessitate the use of modern technology. Treat a remote demonstration as seriously as a physical sales call, performing all the required research and preparation. Then, tune your message to the bare minimum number of key points, and focus upon the visuals and maintaining audience interaction. Some of the most commanding in-person presenters become very ordinary over a webcast when they refuse to adapt their styles. Your goal should be to become a demo master no matter what the delivery mechanism is!

Skill Building

New SE	1. Practice your first 3 minutes of the webcast.
	2. Take every opportunity to use interactive questions.
	3. Customize the webcast checklist for your own personal situation.
Experienced SE	1. Aim for bullet-free PowerPoint slides.
	2. Experiment with visual aids and graphics. Practice describing everyday objects (a house, your car, a great meal) using only the resources available across the Web.
	3. Have the courage to start with the grand finale.

Chapter Goals

Understand trial negotiation and overall success strategy.

Be able to plan and execute a trial.

Learn how to avoid a trial through use of references and other proof points.

Evaluation Strategies

If you can't make it good, at least make it look good.

Bill Gates, founder of Microsoft

One of the few things worse than a request for proposal (RFP) or a multiday demo is the dreaded evaluation trial, now more commonly known as the proof of concept (POC). This is often a trial in every sense of the word—draining resources from the sales organization with little effect.

Developing the Strategy

Conducting an Evaluation: How Did We Get Here?

This is a simple question lacking a simple answer. These exercises have many names: prototype, conference room pilot, evaluation, or trial. Customers usually ask for an evaluation for one of two reasons. First, they are unable to determine whether a claim you made during the sales process is true. This may be related to the esoteric relationships between components of the customer's legacy environment, or it could be because you are pitching a brand-new, unproven product. Second, the customer "just wants to play around with the system." This often signals that the customer doesn't really *know* what they want. They probably believe that they will know it when they see it, but that puts you in a tough spot. How do you know what to show them if they just want to play with the product? Whatever the reason for a trial, it is critical that you know what the customer's goals are. Without clearly understood success criteria, an evaluation can truly become a trial.

Negotiating Engagement in a Trial

When a customer asks for a pilot, evaluation, or trial, you should consider this a negotiating point. Just as with a full project, you will be expending valuable resources in return for some consideration from the customer. The customer's initial stance may be that the "consideration" is continued progress in the bid process. If the total time expended on the trial is one week of labor or less, this may be acceptable. If more effort is required, you should prepare a statement of work for the estimated resources required to complete the trial.

Next, work with your sales rep to present the statement of work to the customer. The customer will respond in one of three ways. "Tire kickers" will quickly back away from the idea of the evaluation. Serious prospects will realize that they are asking you to incur significant cost, and they will attempt to build your evaluation costs into their project budget. High-value prospects may be offended that you are asking them to pay for such services. Dealing with this last group can be a bit tricky. If you think a customer may fall into that category, ask your sales management about how to proceed.

> *Hint: Beware of Corporate Architecture or Best Practices Teams*
>
> *Many of the larger multinational corporations, notably in the financial-services arena, now employ a specialized team whose sole function is to evaluate vendor products in a laboratory or test environment. Such evaluations often lead to your solution's being approved for inclusion on a preferred suppliers list—with no guarantee of an eventual sale. This may well be an acceptable way of doing business for your company, but you need to be aware of the costs.*

You should already see the benefit of this approach because you are either identifying unqualified prospects or arranging to get paid for services rendered. Either outcome is a huge win over simply going in and doing the work gratis. To sweeten the pot for the customer, you should consider giving them some credit for evaluation-related services toward the final contract. While you are working with the customer and your sales management to determine time frames and available resources, you must simultaneously consider your ability to win the evaluation.

How Do You Define Success?

Your ability to negotiate success criteria is probably the most critical step in the evaluation process. If you cannot find an intersection between what your customer needs to be convinced of and the value you are able to demonstrate, then you may as well quit now. Ironically, you may be able to improve your chance of winning by negotiating a smaller pilot. If you are facing a competitor with greater resources or a more feature-rich product, you will benefit if that competitor is not able to bring those resources to bear.

How to Win: Determining the Success Criteria

Begin by asking the customer why they want to engage in a trial. Then, try to answer the following questions:

1. *Do we need to prove specific points or give the customer a general level of comfort?* Be wary of situations where you need to provide a customer with an undefined comfort level. This will frequently result in the customer's wanting to play with your solution to "get a feel" for it.

2. *Has the customer provided objective success criteria?* Could a third party with limited knowledge of your solution judge whether your pilot is capable of meeting the success criteria? If not, you are in danger of having political alignment or other unknown factors impact the evaluation. Although political issues are always going to be a reality, you need to try to identify and nullify those issues that you cannot control.

3. *Are biased consultants or advisors involved?* Many times customers will hire consultants to help them evaluate products. Try to determine if the consultant has her own agenda, especially if she may have a commercial interest in the implementation of the product.

CASE STUDY: ARE THE DECISION MAKERS READY FOR A TRIAL?

Be wary of customers who rely heavily on consultants for the initial screening and evaluation of products. The consultants may not be educating the decision makers as you educate the consultants. An anecdote illustrates the danger:

> I gave a demo to a Hollywood studio on a solution where the consultant involved did a very poor job of preparing the customer for what they were about to see. The demo was intended to be a 2-hour educational session on the features of our phone system. Instead, we spent 4 hours, 2 of which were spent explaining the very basic details of telephony fundamentals to a completely unprepared executive, who was very arrogant and disagreeable. Since we were first, the customer essentially cut their teeth on our demo, then went on to have much more pleasant, productive sessions with our competitors. Not surprisingly, we lost the deal.

If the sales team had known that the executive had not been involved in the process up to that point, they undoubtedly would have taken a different approach with the presentation. Some consultants will consciously put you in this position if they hope to see you fail.

4. *Can you make proof points that your competitors cannot? Are they in support of your message or sales strategy?* If you believe you can score well on a pilot but that the scoring doesn't correlate with your value proposition, you have a major problem. Either your competitor has significantly influenced the customer, or your value proposition does not fit with the customer's vision. Your response must be to change your value proposition, change your customer's requirements, or quit the game.

Once you have answered these simple questions, you can begin to develop your strategy. The key is to make sure your sales team knows exactly what to do to win this stage in the sales cycle.

How to Ensure Success: Evaluating the Success Criteria

Once you have an understanding of the success criteria, you need to make sure you can actually prove each of those points. For each of the items, ask the following questions:

1. Are you better than the competitor?

2. Can you prove the point?

3. Can you prove it with the resources and time available?

Once you have answered each of these questions for each item to be proved, you must ask one more question: will you score higher than the competitor? This last question is complex. Be sure to factor in your understanding of the competitor's available resources and political connections. There is nothing more painful than being beaten by a competitor on an item that you consider to be a strong point. Consider the following case study.

Case Study: Losing on Your Strengths

We had a competitive situation where the prospect wanted to engage in an evaluation. The prospect understood the costs involved and only wanted to have a single vendor move to the full-evaluation stage. We had a series of meetings to discuss and negotiate the success criteria. One of the customer's key criteria was the ability to integrate with external systems. Our solution was widely regarded as superior, so we felt very confident that we would be selected. We knew we were better, it had been proven publicly by prior projects, and we had the resources necessary to prove it for the customer. Unfortunately, our competitor had a forthcoming release with new features that we did not know about. Based on these new—and admittedly exciting—features, the customer decided to go with the competitor. We also found out that the competitor's sales rep had been a college friend of the decision maker. These two factors turned a deal that should have been a slam dunk for us into a painful loss.

The case study illustrates that it can be difficult to answer the questions about whether you will score higher than your competitor, but it is important for the team as a whole to answer this question. Once the team has decided, you will have the commitment of the group for the stressful period that lies ahead.

Intellectually Closing the Deal

Once you have identified the success criteria, you or your salesperson should then get the customer to commit to their willingness to "do the deal" if you successfully complete the trial. Present your estimated costs in terms of manpower, time, and equipment, and make sure the customer realizes that their company will be making similar investments.

One good practice is to bring in a sales manager at this point to help you confirm the customer's readiness to proceed. If you don't complete this step, you run the risk of winning the evaluation and then having the customer not go forward. This is most frequently the case when the evaluation is run by the IT staff, who may not have the authority to move the project forward. If you cannot get this commitment, don't agree to the trial.

Working Backward from the Definition of Success

Now that your team is convinced, try to envision what it would take to get a perfect score. Put together a presentation meant to show the end result you intend to achieve. Have your sales rep validate your result with the prospect, asking directly if you will get the business if you can deliver the solution described. If your prospect wavers, something is wrong, and your sales team must ferret this out if they are to have any chance of success.

If the prospect agrees, use this to begin a dialog between your executive management and that of the customer. Use the shared definition of success to build that executive relationship. Ideally, your executives can get the prospect's executives to commit to going forward once the solution is delivered. The key is identifying the people who will stand up and say that you have won when you have reached the negotiated goal. Once you have achieved that level of alignment and understanding of the customer's business problem, begin working backward to determine the tactical steps needed to achieve that result.

Running a Trial

If you are put in charge of a trial, be sure you are ready for the responsibility. Evaluations are costly, high risk, and high visibility. If your trial melts down because you did a poor job, it can taint you for the rest of your career with the company. Ideally, you will have prior experience in project management and a deep understanding of your solution. Without these two strengths, you will have a difficult time succeeding. If you feel weak in either area, consider asking your manager to bring in a more experienced person from whom you could learn the appropriate skills. Table 11.1 shows the high-level account management steps for a trial.

Trial Phases

The trial steps should then be grouped into phases that can be used to build a project plan. The phases of a trial are shown in Table 11.2, and details are discussed in the following subsections.

Phase 1: Document Success Criteria

This phase has already been described. Work with the customer to establish what the expected deliverable is for each item. Ideally, you can prototype the system with the customer and then work backward to identify any necessary engineering tasks.

Table 11.1
High-Level Account Manager Trial Steps

1. Ask the customer why they want a trial and begin to define success criteria.
2. Try to find ways to limit the scope of the trial by using references, published documentation, and so forth. If necessary skill sets are in short supply, confirm a tentative schedule with key team members.
3. Determine whether you have the solution and the resources necessary to win. If you think you do, continue. If not, you must either change the requirements or refuse to compete.
4. Confirm new success criteria with the customer after you are comfortable that you can win.
5. Work with the salesperson to write a "win agreement" for the customer.
6. Build a storyboard for presenting winning results to the customer.
7. Work to get customer executives to sign off on the win agreement and storyboard.
8. Build the project plan necessary to deliver the winning results.
9. Do the real work of the trial.
10. Present results and move to next phase in the sales cycle.

Table 11.2
Phases of a Trial

1. Document definition of success criteria
2. Mini-discovery
3. Development
4. Test
5. Deployment (if necessary)
6. Demonstration and validation
7. Presentation of results

Table 11.3 shows an example of a success criteria form. This form will serve as the central point of discussion for not only your negotiations with the customer but also for any necessary engineering work. If you are not the expert on the details of your solution, you should consider getting an expert involved to generate these documents. Frequently, trivial changes in the wording can result in drastically different outputs from your engineering team.

Table 11.3
Sample Success Criteria Form

ID	ACT-1 (Use an intuitive numbering scheme if none is provided by the customer.)
Description	Prove ability to reach through to legacy account information.
Success criteria	System should be able to access, present, and update legacy account information.
Related documentation	Identify any schematics, screen shots, or other related diagrams. Obtain description of legacy account system APIs.
Business impact	Describe quantifiable business impact if possible. Reach-through saves the cost of developing batch interfaces. Additionally, reach-through provides better quality of service to customers.
Detailed description	The system shoud be able to access and display legacy checking and credit card account data when accessing the system's built-in account information. The system should display a new grid on the "Account" screen with the legacy data. The grid should have the following fields (as defined in the API documentation): Type Account ID Account Name Account Balance When an item in the grid is double-clicked, a new form should be brought forth with details about the account information. This form is detailed in ACT-2.
Sign off on requirements	_____
Sign off on completion	_____

Phase 2: Mini Discovery

Once you have documented the success criteria, ask to have access to the people responsible for using the functionality. Spend the time reviewing your documented success criteria to ensure that your goals accurately reflect their business needs. Pay particular attention to whether there are other quantifiable business benefits.

Conclude this phase by having the customer sign off on the requirements. Once again, this is to get their commitment that your document describes the result they need to keep the purchase process moving.

Phase 3: Development

The development phase is when the real work starts. Your company will have its own style of working, but the following suggestions are valuable for any company. First, pad the schedule by no less than 30% because the unexpected *will* happen. If necessary, negotiate your way out of some of the requirements.

Second, compartmentalize the key development phases. Most developers are used to having the flexibility to spend extra time on particularly sticky problems. By "time-boxing" key deliverables, you can help ensure that a single setback does not affect multiple downstream deliverables. This is not intuitive for traditional developers, who will frequently claim that a given deliverable can be completed "in a few more hours." Be firm when this happens; tell the person the requirement will be addressed once all of the other requirements are taken care of first.

Hint: Prepare for the Worst

Before you even get onsite for the trial, notify your corporate support department that you will be conducting a trial and provide them with as much technical information about the prospect's environment as possible. Ideally, ask for a dedicated support engineer to call and a backup for that individual.

Phase 4: Test

Budget time as necessary for testing. If your deliverable is simply a demonstration, you may need to do very little testing. If usage testing is required, then you should allocate significant time for testing. Real use always unearths unforeseen problems. You are almost always better off being seen as the "stable" solution, even if you miss a few of the success points based on available time.

Phase 5: Deployment

If you will be deploying your system onto customer equipment or sites, book a preliminary deployment when your initial development is complete. Problems will frequently pop up during deployment that you can work on in parallel with development.

Hint: Always Check Out the Network

In our experience, the most common problems with trial setup and logistics have to do with the customer's networks. If your system relies on interconnectivity with any other system, be sure to have your access and passwords nailed down in advance.

Phase 6: Demonstration and Validation

Once you have completed the requirements, present the implementation to the customer. Depending on the nature of the audience, you may wish to use a formal approach as described next for phase 7. In many cases, the validation of the results will be an informal discussion with the customer's technologists. In either case, present the customer with your documents, and ask them to sign off on your success criteria.

Phase 7: Presentation of Results

This "payoff" presentation may be given to a broad group or only to the decision maker. If it is just to the executives, the salesperson will probably deliver the presentation, but you will have to help put together the content. We recommend an agenda that includes the following:

- Overview of requirements;
- Discussion of project approach;
- Project results;
- Unique business benefits.

Clearly, the focus should be on the unique benefits of your solution. Have the stack of signed-off success documents handy as well. It will make for an impressive prop when you are dealing with the executives.

Basic Trial Organization

Depending on how complex your product is, you may be able simply to deliver your product to the customer and cross your fingers. If your product is that simple, you can probably skip this chapter. For the unlucky majority of us, a trial will require anywhere between three people and the entire set of resources available to your company. Listed below are the *roles* involved in the trial process. Multiple individuals may be associated with some of these roles, or single individuals may handle multiple roles. The following case study provides a high-level view of how a challenging evaluation was planned and implemented.

CASE STUDY: PILOT STAFFING AND PLANNING

A software company was engaging in a pilot with a large potential customer. The customer wanted to have a customized version of the software deployed to 20 users who would perform usability testing over the course of 3 days. The pilot was judged as follows:

- 50% ability to meet certain business scenarios;
- 20% user satisfaction as measured by surveys after the pilot;
- 30% scoring performed by the IT department.

The pilot was scheduled to begin in 20 calendar days, and the resulting contract would initially be worth $5 million.

This was an extremely challenging pilot scenario. The requirement to have 20 users live meant that the system had to be well tested and well documented. To meet the requirement for the IT department, the system would be measured on installation, administration, and customization features. We ended up having more than 10 sales engineers associated with the pilot. Five days were needed for up-front installation and development, requiring six technical-sales SEs. Then, the remainder of the pilot required a mixture of training, technical, general sales, and project-management skills to deal with the IT, business, and user communities. We had a total of eight people working simultaneously across the groups. We had a project manager for the entire pilot, as well as sales leads for each decision-making community. The project manager was responsible for general resource allocation across the subprojects. The sales leads were responsible for the customer contact and the validation of the different deliverables. Although this was a very challenging evaluation, we won the decision because we were willing to commit the necessary resources and to use advanced pilot-management techniques.

The Technician

The technicians are responsible for developing the solution. Technical staff associated with a trial must be very smart and sales aware, very flexible, and very technical. It is difficult to find professional-services people with all of these characteristics. Usually, the best technicians will bristle at the fluid nature of a trial, preferring well-documented requirements and processes. Additionally, most technical people are not used to delivering to a 2-day project cycle. Make sure your team understands the necessary turnaround times and is comfortable operating in that environment. Emphasize that the solution just needs to be "good enough" for the trial and that you don't expect it to be reflective of the true quality of their work.

Also, either the technicians must be comfortable dealing with customers, or you must shield them from customer inquiries. The last thing you want to happen during a trial is for your technical staff to give the customer answers to questions that may contradict those you have given during the sales cycle. In such cases, either you, as the senior SE on-site, or the salesperson must "run interference" to allow the technical team to complete their tasks with minimal distraction.

The Salesperson

Someone has to focus on acting as the interface with the customer, as well as making sure that the steps performed in the evaluation are meeting the customer's requirements. This person should also focus on relationship building. In a trial, this person should often be an SE. The account manager is better off spending her time working with the customer executives. The person fulfilling this role must understand the value proposition and the relevant technical details. Having a view into both aspects of the trial will enable this person to make the tough calls when trade-offs are required between features and technical roadblocks.

The Project Manager

Depending on the complexity of the trial, this role may require a full-time person or only a fraction of a person's time. The project manager is responsible for tracking all of the tasks to make sure that the success criteria are met. The project manager must also manage time and technical risks for the project. The risk-management requirement is key. If your team has 3 days to prepare for a trial, the project manager will have to make sure people are on schedule or reduce the scope appropriately. A very common situation is to have a given piece of technical work take longer than is feasible. Left up to the individual engineer, these "slips" in the timeline can extend indefinitely. In a trial, it is often better to give up on a challenging piece of development and admit that it is too difficult to do. Of course, the message to the customer is that it could be done given additional time. The project manager is also responsible for bringing in additional resources and managing logistics.

Training

When your customer wants to use parts of your system, you will have to train them first. This can be a 5-minute or a full-day exercise. In any case, it is certain that you will have less time to train them than would normally be required. Don't underestimate the difficulty of developing and delivering training during a trial. Usually, the training can only be developed after most of the engineering work has been completed for the trial. This will frequently mean that the training materials will be completed in a rush the night before they have to be delivered. Try to budget enough time to complete quality materials and walk through the training at least once.

Documentation

You will want to document the work performed during a trial for three reasons:

1. *Proof points:* You can use the documentation to support your claims in representations to the customer.

2. *Training:* If you have to train your customer on the system, you will need to document any customer work done.

3. *Handoff to postsales:* If you win the deal, you will need to give the postsales team documentation so they will understand the expectations you have set.

Depending on the complexity of the trial, this may be a good role for the project manager to hold as well. Use the documentation to coordinate development across the different roles in the trial. Update the documentation as you change your sales pitch or the solution you are delivering in support of the pitch. Having access to these materials after the trial will make it much easier for your customers to remember exactly what you did during the trial. Sometimes they will even forget minor errors or issues if you have credibly documented the solution.

Equipment
Equipment can be a significant issue during a trial. In many cases, a customer will want to use their equipment instead of, or in conjunction with, any hardware you provide. The point is, after all, to try out your solution in a real-life situation. In particular, you need to be aware of the legal issues if you are asked to interface with any hardware or software that is part of the customer's production environment as presales engineers are not usually bonded in the event of any mishap to the customer's systems.

Software Installation
If you must install software on a customer's equipment, then you must be very familiar with the risks and issues related to such installations. Determine the standard installation time required for your software, then double that and build the larger time into your project plan. If possible, have the software install completed days before any work begins. The difficulty is that you will be unable to anticipate all of the problems related to software installation. Even software programs from large, well-established corporations occasionally run into significant issues during installation. Frequently, customers will have old machines, dated operating systems, or other odd situations. All of these factors make software installation a significant risk factor for an evaluation. If trouble does arise, make sure that your help desk or support line knows you are calling from a customer site with a significant deal on the line.

Hint: Be Prepared

At least a week beforehand, provide the prospect with a checklist of minimum require-ments for your product. Include everything you can possibly think of, including operating system, memory, network speeds, languages, security access, and power supplies. Leave nothing to chance, and ask for the completed checklist to be returned to you several days before the trial commences.

Bring Your Own Hardware

Another option is to provide your own hardware with any necessary soft-ware or other systems preinstalled. This is an excellent approach if you can afford it and if your customer will accept it. One way to make this option more acceptable is to offer to provide your customer with a "fixed bid" for installation of your services. In this manner, you can eliminate their risk and limit the need to include that in the evaluation.

Networking and Access

There is nothing more frustrating than working on a trial and finding out, after hours, that you don't have access to another machine on the network or, even worse, that you have rebooted a machine and can't log in because you don't have access.

You can mitigate this by providing the customer with a very specific list of required access points and passwords. If they have systems that are too sensitive for you to access, suggest that the customer either provide a test system or establish a "dummy system." A dummy system can be set up for most software applications that can trap appropriate calls and provide a rea-sonable baseline for evaluation.

Anticipate and Outdeliver Your Competitor

By now, you should be in good shape. You have put together a plan to meet the customer requirements and tried to anticipate competitive responses. Now you need to add something to the trial process that will catch your competitor unaware.

You should have some differentiator that the customer didn't ask for but that supports their decision criteria. If you do, be sure to include it. Even better, use your keenly honed understanding of the customer's business to offer them something based on your normal solution but that is also new, perhaps even unique. The reason for doing this is that we must assume that the competitor is as smart as we are. If this is true, they will anticipate our likeliest flanking moves based on their understanding of our company's products and value proposition. So, by proposing something new and unique, you will be able to eliminate any possibility of a response. Even better, this strategy can even destabilize the competitor's core value proposition. Consider the following case study.

CASE STUDY: EFFECTIVE USE OF THE "HEAD FAKE"

We had reached the final stages of the sales cycle to a large media company. The customer had asked the two finalists to develop a prototype representative of five user scenarios. We were to present the scenarios to the 50 key stakeholders in the division. We were ahead in the account based on what we were hearing from the customer, but the SI who was running the evaluation favored our competitor. Because of this, we knew that any work we did would be shared with the competitor. The format for the presentations was a daylong session from our competitor, followed by another day devoted to presenting our results. We had done a good job of arranging to make sure we went second so that we could respond to whatever our competitor did. Unfortunately, they claimed that one of their sales team had a last-minute conflict, so they would have to go second. We were incensed because we knew that they would have full access to our presentation and pitch. So, in response, we expanded the deliverable to include some new options for the customer. These were very flashy features that were "really nice to haves," not "need to haves." We didn't mention these to anyone until the day of the presentation. Not only did we show the new stuff, but we handed out a 12-page, full-color guide. We knew that this would cause the opposing sales team to respond and that—given that they had one night to put together their presentation—the effort would distract them from their core material. What we heard from their presentation confirmed this; even though they had more time to prepare, they did a poor job of conveying the critical material because they tried to change at the last minute to respond to our expanded pitch.

❖ ❖ ❖ ❖

Avoiding a Trial

By now you should have a feel for the time, expense, effort, and implicit risk of doing a trial. Because of the high cost, you should only engage in a trial when you know you can win and when a win will result in a sale. If you are not sure of either of those points, you should seriously consider trying to avoid the trial.

Does the Customer Do Trials?

Ask your customer if they have done product evaluations before. If they have not, be prepared to help them establish a clear decision process. You will also have to be very sure they have access to appropriate technical staff to make the trial happen, unless you are providing all of the hardware. You might also ask if their salespeople perform trials with their own products. You may find them more sympathetic to your requests if you can establish common ground around trial requirements.

Are They Paying for the Pilot?

Your sales representative may be uncomfortable with this, but you should get your customer to pay for any trial that takes more than a day or two of your time. The only exceptions to this are if evaluations are especially common in your industry or the customer is a major partner or a strategic account.

You can offer to have the costs of the trial applied toward a future order. This is another good qualifying technique. If your customer wants a trial but balks at the expense, then they are likely not seriously looking to buy. In addition, if your customer is paying for the time and expenses incurred, you can field a stronger team for the trial. You will usually not receive any personal compensation for hours you bill as part of a trial, so try to arrange an internal "exchange" to use that revenue to pay for additional support from your professional-services organization.

CASE STUDY: QUALIFYING OUT OF A PILOT

> One of us was working with a local sales team on a deal that the team had been pursuing for three-quarters of a year. It was with a respected manufacturer who had a solid need for our product but a haphazardly defined project with no clear budget. During our visit to the customer's site, we had a series of great meetings that left the customer very excited about our products. Our sales team felt great about the opportunity and was looking forward to moving toward finalizing the sale.
>
> While discussing the next steps, the IT manager mentioned that the company would be interested in doing a pilot. We told the manager we would be happy to move on to the pilot once we had received an assurance from the executive with signature authority that the company was ready and willing to go forward with the deal once the pilot had been successfully completed. We also told the IT manager that we had a policy of charging for any services required during the pilot, but those fees would be credited toward the final contract.
>
> As we found out during the next few weeks, we had been chasing a nonexistent project. The IT manager had no authority to approve any level of expenditure; nor

did he have the backing of any executive. A deal never did emerge from the company, and we were pleased that we were able to qualify ourselves out of a time-wasting sales effort.

Using References

Once you have determined the success criteria for the trial, you should try to eliminate certain tasks by using references or published reference material. Your customer should understand that the trial is being performed at significant expense to both organizations. If you can prove one of the key points in another way, both of you will benefit.

The best way to meet the requirement without performing the task is to reference another customer who has implemented a similar solution. This approach is also in your customer's best interest because they will learn more of what is really involved than if they just perform the test in a sterile lab environment. Unfortunately, many customers believe that they have unique requirements that reduce the worth of references.

Hint: Avoid Unattended Trials

Unless your company has a specific strategy related to unattended trials (perhaps aimed at midmarket customers), you should refuse to accept this as a requirement. If you don't have a salesperson present when the customer is evaluating your system, you place your sales effort at a huge risk. If you see this requirement frequently, work with your marketing and engineering teams to develop an appropriate response.

Summary

Trials are difficult to control and time-consuming. Unfortunately, customers sometimes insist on them. When they do, make sure they are aware of the costs of doing the trial. An evaluation must be positioned as a material step toward a significant partnership. Use this discussion to further qualify your customer. Simultaneously, work to establish a set of clear-cut success criteria that are in line with the value your solution can deliver.

Once you have negotiated the commercial terms and the business value of the pilot, engage with gusto. Use the special short-term project-management techniques described within this chapter to complete the trial. Create a compelling way to present the positive results of the trial, and use that to move to a close for the overall project.

Skill Building

New SE	If you are put on a trial, focus on the following: Be sure you understand the customer's need and your value proposition. Try to think of other aspects of your product that could be included to strengthen your value proposition. Work hard! This is a significant investment on the part of your company—you certainly don't want to be the one to let the team down.
Experienced SE	You should be involved in developing the value proposition and the overall strategy. You can add value by overseeing the work of less experienced team members and by developing relationships with the customer. If you are called upon to act as an individual contributor, do so with gusto, and set a good example for the others.
SE Manager	Aggressively interview the team, including the sales manager, to make sure their strategy is sound. Act as a devil's advocate to try to anticipate your competitor's strategy in the trial. Help make sure the team has all resources necessary to win the trial.

Contract Negotiation and Pricing

Nuddink, I know nuddink.
Sergeant Schultz, Hogan's Heroes

This chapter deals with the SE's involvement in the endgame of a sales transaction—contract negotiation and pricing. This is one of the shorter chapters of the book because the key to success, unless you are an extremely experienced SE, is not to get involved.

As we have now stated many times, one of the primary advantages of being an SE is that the prospect will often inadvertently give you information they would never dream of giving to the salesperson. The downside, however, is that the experienced prospect will view you in a similar manner. You might tell a purchasing agent or midlevel manager some factual snippet that the salesperson never would. Frequently, this *reverse leak* entails pricing information or contract items.

Let us be perfectly clear on this point. The best defense is zero tolerance—plead total ignorance about the subject, no matter how or when it arises. Contract negotiation, including pricing, terms, conditions, and any legal requirements, is best handled exclusively by the salesperson.

Rarely, however, does such a black-and-white delineation of responsibilities exist within a sales team. An inexperienced SE may be tempted to enter a discussion prompted by an apparently off-the-cuff remark. Just as you should share any useful information gathered in a conversation with your sales team, assume the prospect's organization is equally efficient in gathering information.

CASE STUDY: How $500,000 DISAPPEARED IN 5 MINUTES

> It was the last day of the quarter, and an $8.5 million proposal was sitting on the CFO's desk, ready for signature. The board of this telecommunications company had approved the expenditure, and all that remained was the formal signing of the paperwork. All legal terms and conditions, discounts, and pricing schedules had been agreed on. As a favor to the prospect, a junior SE had been dispatched on-site to install software so that development could start the following week.
>
> During lunch in the company cafeteria, the lead purchasing manager joined the technicians at their table. After some small talk, the conversation turned toward business. "I guess this deal means a lot to you?" the purchasing manager casually said to the SE. "Yes, it does," replied the helpful young SE. "This deal will put us a half-million dollars over quota for this quarter."
>
> The conversation moved onto sports and last night's Yankees game. Two hours later, after much yelling and acrimony, the contract was signed for $8 million, because that was "all we needed to make the number." One casual remark, seemingly not even connected to the contract, had cost us $500,000.

An Introductory Approach

For the inexperienced SE, the one and only rule is obviously that silence is golden. Simply cut off any conversation by declaring that you know nothing about the subject. As the case study shows, even discussing a tangential subject can lead to disaster. Rather than forcing new hires to pretend ignorance and lie to prospects, it is easier just to skip the pricing and contracts section in their training altogether. There is more than enough to learn at this stage without bothering about something that can only cause you harm.

Creative Ways to Say Nothing

At times, you will be forced into a corner and will need to say something about pricing and contracts. Should a legal question arise, simply state, "Company policy doesn't allow anyone outside of our legal group to get involved in legal issues. I am sure you can respect that." An inexperienced SE can disclaim knowledge and merely say, "I'm just on the technical side and don't know anything about pricing. They never tell us anything about it anyway." You can even make a joke about it and defuse the situation: "Well, we have to let the salespeople do something, don't we?"

Understanding the Quote

It is your responsibility to double-check configuration data, capacity information, and any other technical aspects of the proposal for completeness and accuracy. This absolutely includes product availability and delivery. Improperly configured quotes embarrass everyone involved. Aside from ensuring that the quote is technically correct in terms of technology details, you should also review all the nonproduct items. For most quotes, that specifically includes training, technical support, and professional services/consulting, as selling a product without the necessary training and implementation services is a recipe for disaster and will lead to shelfware (where the product sits on the shelf and is never deployed). Should a mission-critical system be sold with only 12 hours per day, 5 days per week support, or a complex solution without the requisite training, you should question those omissions. Depending upon your relationship with the salesperson, you may directly engage with them or go through your manager, but you owe it to both your eventual customer and to your professionalism at least to request a review of the nonproduct line items.

> *Hint: Covering the Legalities*
>
> *During the course of a complex sale, the technical configuration and proposal may go through multiple revisions. Ensure that the legal (negotiating) team is aware of any cost/benefit trade-offs so that they are not negotiated out of (or into) the final contract.*

An Advanced Tactic

Once you are comfortable with the products and services you are selling, it may be time to learn about the pricing structures and contractual requirements that surround the sale. You should pay special attention to issues around revenue recognition. There are strict guidelines regarding a contract's wording, as well as delivery of product and conditional items included in a contract (such as the right to return the product), which may impact whether a signed contract can be booked in a given month or quarter. This need is more for career development, should you ever wish to move into a direct sales position, than it is to gain a tactical sales advantage.

However, the knowledge can be used to the benefit of the sales team. At an account strategy session shortly before the initial proposal is made to the prospect, agree on a few sound bites with the salesperson. These are phrases you can drop into a conversation when dealing with purchasing agents or management. Examples include the following:

1. Your competitor got a 15% discount.

2. You should ask about concurrent user pricing.

3. Our CFO loves it when clients pay in cash.

Fewer than 1 in 20 salespeople will even be willing to allow the SE to participate in this area of sales strategy. Our advice is to learn pricing if it can help your career; otherwise, give the subject a wide berth.

The true role of the senior SE during a large, complex sale is to know more about the interactions between their solution and complementary partner products than anyone else on the sales team. Understanding how these pieces dovetail and their interdependencies can help build the value behind the salesperson's proposal. By establishing this value-added aspect (for example, how your solution may solve three other problems), the salesperson can maintain margins when being beaten down on price. Such information effectively gives your team another advantage at the negotiating table.

Summary

In most sales situations, ignorance is bliss. Unless you are a very experienced SE who does understand pricing, discount structures, and all of the legal terms and conditions, you should simply stay out of the way.

Skill Building

New SE	1. Say nothing. 2. Be in a position where you can honestly disclaim knowledge about pricing. 3. See rule 1!
Experienced SE	1. Learn basic pricing structures. 2. Be familiar with relative pricing—which modules or services cost more than others. 3. Double-check configuration and capacity data in the proposal. 4. Use agreed-on creative sound bites to help pricing negotiations. 5. Identify the value-added aspects of a solution when partner products are involved.

Chapter Goals

Understand appropriate
account engagement
after the sale closes.

Be able to construct an
effective transition plan.

Build a plan to maximize
potential opportunities
presented by ongoing
account management.

Understand what special
circumstances can
happen in the postsales
transition and how to
respond.

Sanity after the Sale

Success breeds complacency, complacency
breeds failure. Only the paranoid survive.

Andrew Grove

This chapter will begin with a basic how-to
guide with step-by-step suggestions for a
successful handoff from pre- to postsales. We
then present you with several justifications for
these postsales activities based on their potential
to improve your future sales and career. Even
more importantly, we will suggest options that
let you gain the benefits of these interactions
without drastically impacting your ability to
bring in new business. Finally, we close the
chapter by addressing special situations that can
arise in a postsales context.

Postsales support is a tricky subject for any
SE. Because we are all creatures motivated by
our compensation plans, our thoughts after the
sale usually relate to running to the bank to
cash the check. The classic presales organization abhors postsales work because it detracts
from generating more revenue. If you are

covering major accounts, such that you only have a total territory of three to five accounts, postsales support is almost unavoidable. More important than technical support is the ongoing account and relationship management. Although this is generally viewed as the sales rep's responsibility, there are advantages to your being involved.

Developing the Transition Plan

Congratulations, you have made the sale! Now it is the second week of the new quarter, and you have reacquainted yourself with your family and begun to think about work again. You are getting copied on long e-mail threads going back and forth between your professional-services group and the customer project manager. What do you do? Build a transition plan. This plan is a handoff document for the team that actually makes your solution work. Table 13A.1 in the appendix at the end of this chapter provides a sample "Sales-to-Professional-Services Transition Plan." Your plan should document any information you captured during the sales cycle that could benefit the implementation team. In general, this should take the form of a two- to five-page summary that frequently references other documentation. By communicating appropriate information, this document will help limit your interaction with the implementation team, while making them more effective.

Hint: Keep Your Work

In 2008, $1 would buy over 1 GB of storage for a desktop computer, which means that there is effectively no cost to—and absolutely every reason to—keep every bit of work you produce, during or after the sale.

It is also good practice to burn several CDs that contain the request for information (RFI), request for proposal (RFP), and discovery documents, plus any other notes pertinent to the account. Copies of demonstration scripts and modifications should also be added to the CD. This CD can then be provided to the professional-services group or systems integrator responsible for installation or implementation. This approach can also help lower your administrative work later. Instead of getting calls whenever someone needs access to a document or wants to see a demonstration, you can provide them with the CD and let them serve themselves. Make sure you are aware of (and compliant with) any document-retention policies as well.

Ongoing Engagement Plan

Now establish your plan to maintain your relationship with the customer. Even if you chose to avoid the deployment phase, you must maintain the relationship. In this section, we highlight key milestones in an implementation. Table 13A.2 in the appendix at the end of this chapter provides a sample "Ongoing-Account Engagement Plan." Use this sample plan as a template to document the steps critical to your customer's life cycle. By mapping out the high-level project plan, you can establish a schedule of project or customer interactions, balancing time investments with relationship maintenance. Combine these summaries for all of your customers and post them on a wall next to your desk; they are a great way to help you track ongoing activities.

Customer Meetings: Project Kickoff

You should work with the professional-services organization to make sure you are part of the project kickoff meeting. This is when you should review the transition document with the customer and the implementers. You should also be prepared to give a presentation on why your solution was chosen. Frequently, the implementation team will not have been part of the formal evaluation process. If you give them a presentation on your proposed solution and highlight the critical components, from a business perspective, you are helping to make sure that the implementation will actually resemble the product for which the executives think they are paying.

During Deployment

During deployment, you want to remain apprised of the current situation and determine whether the project is hitting or missing critical milestones. The worksheet shown in Table 13.1 should help you keep track of this information. You also want to be made aware of any changes in the project scope or deliverables. Form a relationship with the project manager and ask him to critique your engagement plan. Also find out how you can help the project team to be successful. Frequently, you may be able to help escalate issues to customer executives when the project team hits roadblocks.

After Rollout

You should try to meet with your key contacts at least once every 6 months. Your challenge is to spend the minimum amount of time possible in gaining the information you need and maintaining the relationship. A starting agenda for such a meeting might look like the one shown in Table 13.2.

Table 13.1

Deployment Planning Worksheet

1. Schedule a transition workshop at which you meet with the implementation team to transfer all of your knowledge, documents, etc.
2. Have them present their project plan, project charter, list of deliverables, and key milestones to you.
3. Make sure you are on the distribution lists for major project milestones.
4. Attend the project kickoff meeting with the customer.
5. Attend any celebrations related to the rollout. If the customer doesn't have one planned, see if your company can sponsor one. The goodwill will go a long way.

Table 13.2

Postrollout Planning Customer Session Agenda

1. Review project status.
2. Discuss new products that may be relevant.
3. Discuss other new requirements or systems that may be in place.
4. Ask if everyone is happy with the solution.
5. Review current reference to determine ability and willingness to be referenced in the future.
6. Review current customer staff and organizational chart.
7. Review your technical profile documentation.

Your goals for these meetings are simple: identify add-on opportunities, detect competitive attempts at entry, and maintain an accurate view of the customer and the relationships you made. If you have free time, you can spend it with the customer. This is a great way not only to further the relationship but to deepen your understanding of the customer's use of your solution. Such meetings also help the customer feel "in touch" with your company.

Hint: Never Eat Alone

My first sales manager used to tell me that anytime we ate alone, we were wasting a sales opportunity. Even if your day is busy, use an early breakfast or a lunch to catch up with existing customers. They will appreciate the free food, and you will keep the relationship current.

Leveraging the Rest of the Sales Team

Luckily, you are not alone in maintaining these relationships. The sales representative should be involved, but others should also be engaged. Consider how each of the following groups can advance your relationship with the customer.

The Inside Sales Team

You can transfer most relationship activities that you do not want to be involved in to your inside sales team. Be cautious of delegating too much for the reasons listed earlier. Frequently, an inside sales group will be compensated for add-on sales to existing customers. These groups can be invaluable in their ability to make the customer feel appreciated through low-cost contact via phone, e-mail, or Internet-based presentations.

Executives

You can engage your executives with your existing customers. Your customers will usually appreciate the opportunity to hear from an industry expert and regard the attention as an investment in the relationship. Most executives are interested in engaging with customers to keep in touch with the market. So, if you become aware that an executive or marketing staffer is going to visit your area, see if you can get him or her to spend an afternoon with the appropriate personnel of the customer. This is also a good opportunity for you to raise your level of visibility back at headquarters.

Having a Fallback Strategy

Our recommendations reflect an all-inclusive strategy where you have an infinite amount of time to devote to nonrevenue-generating customers. Most of us do not live in that world and will have to pursue a subset of the options presented. *At a minimum,* plan on reviewing your account profile document with your customer every 6 months or so. That will at least keep you up to speed on the critical information you need. The key is to have a strategy that will at least let you keep in touch with your key contacts while consuming appropriate amounts of your time.

Personal Benefits of Postsales Support

So far, this postsales activity may seem like a lot of work with little reward, but many benefits actually accrue to you and your company. We will discuss why it is in both of your best interests below.

Hint: The Downside of Postsales Support

Watch out: some companies require ongoing support on the part of their salespeople but do not pay for it. Over time, such policies will end up forcing salespeople to leave as they are forced to spend more and more time in nonrevenue-generating activities.

Personal References

One of the most immediate benefits you will receive is having this customer act as a reference for you in future sales engagements. Depending on the maturity of your company and its products, you may have few existing references. If this is the case, your ability to cultivate them will represent an important coup internally. If your company does have a number of existing references, then this reference will personally benefit you because your existing customers will be more likely to accept calls from your future customers. This can be done even if the implementation is not yet complete. You can have customers tell prospects why they chose your solution. Strictly from a time-benefit standpoint, you may have to do less selling in the future because of the credibility your existing customer base will give you with new prospects. If you can confidently tell prospects that another customer across town is doing the same thing that the prospect wishes to do, then you will have to do less busywork to convince your prospect. From this argument alone, you may be able to justify the level of postsales engagement we recommend. The following case study illustrates this principle.

CASE STUDY: WHAT GOES AROUND COMES AROUND

When running the pharmaceutical sales-engineering team at Oracle, I noted that one SE spent twice as much time engaged in postsales activities than anyone else. Initially, I attributed this to the fact that Mark dealt with two of our major accounts, Merck and Johnson & Johnson, who were more demanding than some of our other customers. I felt that Mark was such a nice guy that he was unable to say no to our customers and that they were taking advantage of him. Because this behavior was not impacting revenue and Mark was able to handle his workload, I let it pass, although we talked about it frequently. Then, we hit a tough quarter, and two large opportunities we were depending on were floundering due a lack of technology references. I went to Mark and asked him to give me a list of Oracle DBAs who would help us out. Though I was expecting one or two names, he gave me six—and a big "I told you so" smile. We closed both deals and made our quota, Mark made his point about postsales, and I learned a valuable lesson.

Maintain Relationships for Add-On Sales

A long-term benefit of engagement with the customer is the relationships you build within your sales territory. As you get to know more of the executives and staff, you will become a known quantity if you move on from your existing company. Most good salespeople can justify their employment based as much on their Rolodexes as their ability to sell. To quote an anonymous VP of sales interviewed by *Field Force Automation*, "We hire experienced people and expect them to bring talent, ability and territory equity to the party. We pay for performance and the good ones make it. We offer a competitive pay package and provide two weeks company/product training before we parachute you into your new territory."

Hint: Using Newsletters to Stay "Top-of-Mind" with a Minimal Time Commitment

Newsletters are a time-tested way to add value and stay in touch with your customers. With e-mail, there is now effectively no cost to putting them together. Consider putting out a quarterly newsletter highlighting the top trends in the industry and within your company. New product announcements, white papers, partnerships, or major new customer wins are all great topics for a newsletter. Try to include technical tips or success stories from other customers. You can also distribute your newsletter internally to other sales and marketing staffers. It can be a great way to highlight your expertise, and you will help them by providing information they can pass on to their customers.

Keep Your Reservoir of Customer Stories Full

Postsales engagement also helps you build your base of anecdotes. These can be critical to establishing your future credibility with prospects. If you can drop occasional references to highly relevant implementation details, the prospect is much more likely to see you as an authority on the subject at hand. You can also speak more directly to the business benefits your past customers have achieved if you have kept in touch with them throughout the implementation.

Potential for Customer Satisfaction Objectives

More and more companies are compensating their sales forces based in part on the satisfaction of their customers. If this is the case, you should expect to have more involvement than is described here. One common approach is to provide a portion of an MBO (bonus as part of a *management-by-objective* program) related to a customer-satisfaction survey. If you are a sales manager, you may wish to consider implementing such a program. It does take time away from new sales activity, but it will encourage the many benefits described in this chapter, especially add-on sales, customer references, and bringing your company closer to the current business needs of its customers.

Good Way to Build Skills

If you are interested in "crossing over to the dark side," then this is a good way to test the waters. Your sales rep will probably be happy to have you shoulder some of the account-management burden for low-revenue existing accounts. You don't want to go too far down the food chain in the territory though. If accounts are divided into A, B, and C accounts, you want to work with the B, not the C, accounts. Otherwise, you learn the trade but get no reward. See Chapter 18 for more details.

Benefit to the Customer: Free Consulting

Customers should see these ongoing interactions as a positive opportunity. Brief meetings will keep them up to speed on your company's latest developments. If you are doing your homework, you can also help them by discussing best practices employed by other customers. Point out that they are getting a $300 to $400 an hour value for free. Of course, this may encourage them to ask you to be more involved than you are able. If your customer seems to be heading in this direction, be sure they understand that you specialize in helping them plan for future product use, not doing all of the heavy lifting associated with an ongoing project.

Justifying Engagement with Your Management

Most companies give lip service to ongoing account management, but salespeople cannot spend the time necessary to do the job. It is a good idea to let your manager know how much time you are spending on postsales engagements. She can help you make sure you are balancing your time appropriately. Many sales engineer activity-tracking programs in place within vendors differentiate between pre- and postsales work. These systems let your manager monitor and provide appropriate feedback regarding your level of engagement.

Where to Draw the Line

You should be asking yourself several questions when considering your engagement. Are you being taken advantage of? Is the customer asking you to do things for which they should be paying? Is there a near-term revenue opportunity? Are you able to take advantage of long-term opportunities with a reasonable investment of your time? These may seem like very obvious questions, but they highlight the need for a conscious strategy on your part. The needs of your customer and your company, as well as your own goals, will pull you in a different direction. You should always be able to defend your plan, especially if the plan is to provide *no* support.

Troubleshooting the Handoff

You should be familiar with the following scenarios or special circumstances that can impact the handoff to the implementation team. Each of these will introduce challenges that will change the way you approach your plans for transition and ongoing engagement.

Major Accounts Have Special Requirements

Certain customers will be designated *major accounts*. Usually, these are identified based on one of three criteria:

1. They provide some strategic benefit.

2. They have spent a lot of money with your company.

3. They may spend a lot of money in the future.

Major accounts require different methods in many ways, and if you are responsible for covering them, you should adjust your strategy accordingly. Expect lots of work that is not necessarily tied to a deal. In some cases, customers will only make a purchase once every 2 years. Be sure your compensation plan takes these longer cycles into account. The following case study provides a common example of dealing with a major account.

CASE STUDY: DESIGNING THE APPLICATION ARCHITECTURE AT A MAJOR CELLULAR PROVIDER

We had a very large customer who was a significant telecommunications provider. They had purchased our software about 3 years previously in a contract that represented the largest deal our company had signed at that time. They now wanted us to come in and spend time with them helping to design their next-generation application architecture. On the one hand, we were happy to do so because they were an important customer. On the other hand, they wanted to spend a lot of time with us, and there was no direct revenue opportunity. So, we ended up working with them to define the architecture. This work took a total of 8 working days over four trips. Including travel, this entailed a minimum of 12 days' time. Several months later, we did end up signing a very large deal with them. Because we had our top sales team actively engaging in the account, we were well positioned to win the business. Had we left the account management to our professional-services team, we would likely have had to reengage, rebuild relationships, and develop a new set of coaches on the fly.

The icing on the cake was being able to reference the fact that I had personally taken a lead in the development of the architecture for the customer's new system. This personal referenceability gave me a level of technical credibility I could have earned no other way.

You should also work with marketing to publish brief customer case studies or testimonials for use by the rest of the sales force. Everyone wants to know what the leaders are doing, and it will accrue to your benefit to have your name front and center with the marketing materials. Finally, major accounts are also the most highly sought after references, so maintaining a close relationship with the technical decision maker can be a great help to you as you provide references for future prospects.

Customer Skimps on Training
If your product is complex enough for you to be reading this book, it is almost certain that your customers will need to attend training classes to use those products successfully. You should do whatever you can to convince customer executives to send their people to training. It will increase their probability of success, decrease costs related to professional services, and lower their time to implement by reducing the turnaround time associated with external support. If your customer is reluctant, consider giving them free training if they purchase more expensive maintenance programs. You can pitch this in the interest of partnership, when the reality is that such a move will lower your cost of maintenance and provide your customer with all the benefits defined earlier. Given the importance of training, a good practice is to try to begin scheduling training immediately after you get the contract. An unofficial rule of thumb in enterprise applications is that training may take up to 6% of the overall project budget.

Customer Tries to Do It Themselves
Customers may frequently attempt to lower their costs by installing or customizing your products on their own. If this is your customer's plan, you should still develop your transition plan. Now the customer is the target for the transition meeting. Make sure you give them an honest account of their situation. Unless they have worked with your product before, they are likely to have a difficult road ahead. If you obscure implementation details, it will decrease the customer's ability to plan appropriately. In this scenario, it is even more critical that you explain appropriate support options for them; otherwise, you should expect to be the first-level support person for every issue that arises. Be clear when discussing the pros and cons of any support options they have chosen; it should then be clear to your customer

that they are expected to pay for the support they receive. It should also be clear that you are not an appropriate channel for most inquiries. If your customers are slow to learn this lesson, remind them that you spend a significant time traveling. Provide them with a more responsive resource from your service organization, and they will usually change their method.

Working with System Integrators

If the same system integrator (SI) who was involved in the purchase (if any) is handling the implementation, then delivering your transition plan should be relatively straightforward. If you are dealing with a new SI, then get ready to do another sales job. It is the SI's job to provide expertise not available internally to the customer. Therefore, almost by definition, the SI will be compelled to point out holes in the proposal you have developed. If the customer's check has already cleared, this should not be a big deal. If your deal has not closed yet, however, you should view such SIs as potential competitors.

Developing a joint transition plan with the SI is a good strategy. This will let him or her bill some hours to the customer, as well as show that person's expertise up front. You should always get together with the SI beforehand to iron out any differences. After all, you will likely be working together again in the future on some other opportunity. If your customer confronts you about any differences between your proposals and what the SI has put together, explain that there are multiple ways to solve any problem and that your proposal was based on your company's experience. Go on to explain that the SI is involved in the project because he or she brings expertise relevant to the customer's business problem. Just because the SI's approach differs from yours does not mean that either is wrong. If, however, the SI's approach will result in significant differences from expected costs or business results, you should probably get involved to find out what happened. If it turns out that you inadvertently misrepresented a significant item, you owe it to your customer to be honest about this error.

Summary

Ongoing customer interaction is crucial to the success of the customer, your company, and your career. By identifying the key individuals and milestones in your customer's project, you can benefit while minimizing the effort required on your part. Always remember that the most valuable aspect of your customer relationship is the relationship itself. Even if you have little time to be involved in the ongoing status reports of the project, develop a plan to maintain those relationships. You can keep in touch, spending only hours per quarter, by effectively using newsletters, lunch hours, and periodic communication with your postsales team. Such an investment of time will pay off in future sales opportunities, either with your current company or your next one.

Skill Building

New SE	You have a lot to gain by building your network of contacts and references. This is an area where you should invest a lot of extra time. The relationship equity you build will enhance your position within the firm and is transferable if you choose to go elsewhere.
Experienced SE	You should be working on two things:
	1. *Receiving the same benefits with less effort.* Refine your process so that you can keep the relationships and references without investing a huge amount of time. As your career progresses, your network will expand in a linear fashion. If you don't find a way to keep it up without expending additional effort, you will lose touch with those valuable contacts.
	2. *Finding ways you can leverage this work internally.* By keeping in touch with your customers and their needs, you will gain huge internal credibility with marketing and individual executives. There is no more powerful anchor for an argument than, "I was speaking with *<customer executive>* last week, and she told me it's critical that our company do this." This type of information can make you a real heavyweight and help you get wherever you are hoping to go.
SE Manager	Your job is to help your staff perform effectively all the activities described, but to do so in a reusable context. You want to make sure that if the employee leaves, you and your team will still have access to the reference information, contacts, and so on at that account. Focus on developing transfer and maintenance processes with appropriate documentation. By periodically collecting and reviewing the documentation, you can help make sure your team is doing the right thing, while capturing the information for use by other members of the team.

Appendix 13A: Record-Keeping Forms for Postsales Information

Table 13A.1
Sample Sales-to-Professional-Services Transition Plan

Account Name/Names of Sales Team:
Payback Requirements (identify any specific financial or operational criteria used to jusitfy the project.):
"Sexy" Requirements (list functions that may be deemed to be secondary, but which helped generate excitement among the user community of the IT staff.):
Basic Requirements (usually quite extensive. Reference attached customer documentation but try to write up the major elements of the customer requirements in a seminarrative form.):
Major Customization Shown (list any major modifications represented during the sales cycle. Also identify where they can be accessed, for instance, on a server or through an implementation partner.):
Major Known Milestones (list known business or technical milestones identified during he sales cycle.):
Key Customer Contacts (list name, phone number, and e-mail for the key contacts from the sales cycle.):
Key Account Team Contacts (list everyone who presented to the customer during the sales cycle. Also list titles or areas of responsibility.):
Attach detailed documentation (especially current system configuration).

The following two templates can be joined horizontally in a word-processing document. You can then place two or three customers (arranged vertically) on a single page for easy reference.

Table 13A.2
Sample Ongoing-Account Engagement Plan

Client Executive Contact:
Upcoming Actions (Identify any specific financial or operational criteria ised to justify the project.):
Project Milestones:
Currently Referenceable?
Milestones to Referenceability?
List Historical References and Dates:

Table 13A.3
Sample Site Reference and Review Document

Name of Customer Project Manager:

Name of System Integrator/Consultant Manager (if applicable):

Account Name/Names of Sales Team:

Progress Toward Payback Requirements (review current progress toward payback expected by executive sponsors.)

Current Issues (review outstanding change log.)

Current Implementation State Overview (high-level descrition of what has been done thus far; very useful in communications with marketing or prospects.)

High-Level Plan for Future Implementation (this discussion can be key in terms of identifying add-on sales opportunties and potential competitive threats. Include dates when possible.)

Major Known Milestones (list known business or technical milestones identified during the sales cycle.)

Key Customer Contacts (review previous lists of key contacts to see if there has been any change.)

Executive Interaction Plan (schedule appropriate contacts between executives at customer and your executives.)

Chapter Goals

Learn tips that will help
you succeed in your first
6 months on the job.

Develop a success plan
to make your ramp time
shorter and more effec-
tive, enabling you to sell
sooner and more
successfully.

Use the 30-/90-/180-day
concept to help you
structure your success
plan.

Getting Started

The dictionary is the only place where success comes before work.
Arthur Brisbane, American journalist

As a new SE, you will have been given a
laptop, a cubicle, and some marketing
literature, and you will have been to boot camp–
style corporate training. What next? The first 90
days, as any good manager knows, represent a
critical time. This chapter will help you maximize the opportunities present when you are
newly employed and help you hit your sales
quota more quickly.

The Ramp Process

Ramping refers to the time it takes for a new
employee to acquire the minimum level of skill
in his job to perform effectively. This is an
important metric for companies because it has
a direct impact on the lead time necessary to
experience revenue growth. If, on average, it
takes 2 months to hire an SE and 6 months for

163

him or her to "ramp up," and your average sales cycle is 6 months long, then your company must hire 14 months in advance of new revenue! Obviously, this is a significant concern for growing companies that may be taking out loans or selling equity to finance this investment in future sales. It is an issue for larger companies as well, because that initial ramp time is basically a sunk cost for them, with no prospect of any sales occurring.

Now that you know this, what can you do? Make the most of your up-front education, and try to bring in revenue as quickly as possible. If you can even bring in some small deals a few months before you are expected to be "up to speed," you have an opportunity to really impress sales management. Additionally, because you are usually given quota relief, if you can close any deals during your ramp period, you are much more likely to reach your yearly quota.

Setting Goals with Your Manager

The first thing you should do upon being hired is meet with your manager and discuss what you need to accomplish to be successful. Table 14.1 can serve as a guide for that discussion and subsequent one-on-ones. Your company should have a set of expectations for your abilities at certain key milestones. Be sure you understand what the expectations are.

You should also request that your manager have a one-on-one chat with you every month for your first 6 months. This should be a semiformal review of your progress to date and your plans for the following month. Even if you see your manager every day, it is still important to have periodic, formal progress reviews. Some managers are reluctant to point out weaknesses during the regular course of doing business. Your periodic reviews will help make sure you get appropriate feedback, as well as help you both develop a joint understanding of each other's communication styles.

Find Out What You Need to Know to Succeed

Now that you have defined your goals, the next step is to find out what you need to know to achieve them. Clearly, some of this information will come from your first meetings with your manager, but you should be prepared for an iterative process. Key areas of information will usually include a combination of the following:

- Product knowledge;
- Organizational structure and processes (where to go to get things);

Table 14.1
Sample Planning Process with Your Manager

---

1. How do I define success?

   a. Quota requirements (timing, bonuses, accelerators);

   b. "Club" trips or other perquisites;

   c. Job grades and requirements for advancement.

2. What do I need to be successful?

   a. Product expertise;

   b. Presentation and professional skills;

   c. General technical skills;

   d. Key support groups and individuals at corporate;

   e. Company's sales process and knowledge of how I fit in;

   f. Informal processes (how things really work around here);

   g. Knowledge about how to make my manager successful.

3. How do I get the information I need to be successful?

   a. Recommended product training;

   b. Recommended professional training;

   c. Recommended technical training;

   d. Escalation path or sales issues (technical, product, or process);

   e. Location of documentation;

   f. Access to intranet/knowledge management/marketing encyclopedia.

4. How do I compare to others (benchmarking)?

   a. Who are the internal leaders in my area of focus?

   b. Who are external leaders or sources of validation in my area of focus?

5. What is the training policy?

   a. What are the timing and logistics issues involved in signing up for the internal training classes needed?

   b. What is the corporate reimbursement policy for external training, periodical subscriptions, and membership in industry organizations?

- Corporate overview (basic details about the company);

- Sales process.

Identify the key skills you will be expected to have and when you will be provided with the opportunity to build each skill. If you have any gaps in your background, discuss how you will improve in those areas. Frequently, new SEs will lack either technical experience or sales and presentation experience. If your company's training program assumes you have a certain level of competence in either area, make sure you are on track to meeting or exceeding the requirement. If you attend a training session unprepared, you will waste your time and the opportunity to learn the more advanced material.

Boot Camp

Within most companies, a sales training group will host a boot camp session to get you up to speed on the products you will be selling. Unfortunately, many SE organizations focus 90% on product training and 10% on the other skills. Before going to any training session, put together a list of objectives for the training. Begin by building your own list of "need-to-know" information, and check the items off as you feel your introductory training covers them. Review the list with your manager or other senior SEs. When your training is beginning to come to a close, spend a few minutes with the training staff to ask how you can get up to speed on some of the other areas you need. Do not be surprised if they are dismissive of your request. In the eyes of the trainers, they have just told you everything you need to know. Frequently drawn from headquarters staff, the trainers may not fully understand your needs. Be friendly and persistent, and they will usually give you some good pointers. If the trainers are not helpful, work with your manager as well to figure out how to improve your skills in those areas.

Why Use Benchmarking?

Benchmarking is an important component of your success plan. Why do you care how you compare to others in your group? *You* may not, but management does. If your goal is to continue to hit quota and remain in your current position, then this may not be important to you. If you are hoping to be promoted, want to overachieve on your quota, have high standards for personal excellence, or need to avoid layoffs, then this type of friendly internal competition may be crucial to you.

Another good reason to try to benchmark yourself internally is to establish an idea of how you might compare to the competition. Sales is a competitive profession, and by striving to be the best within your organization, you will increase the probability of your comparing favorably with the sales teams against which you will be competing.

Benchmarking Yourself

Benchmarking is one of the most difficult components of the plan you are building. You need to find a way to evaluate your skills relative to others'. Typically, this is best done in sales by finding out who is highly regarded in a certain area of expertise and then trying to work closely with him or her. By watching someone else do a presentation and interact with a crowd, you can gain valuable insights into the holes in your own knowledge. If your company has structured training programs, then you can complete the tests, which can help you gauge your level of expertise. Material may also be available to your professional-services group that could help you chart your progress.

When working with your customers, ask them to contrast your style with your competitors' sales teams. This type of discussion is really only possible if you have a good relationship with the customer in question. Often, the best time to ask is after you have already won the deal. If you have lost the deal, the customer may worry about offending you. Ask the customer what they like about how you have interacted with them compared to the other sales teams. Frequently, the customer will focus on things such as how responsive or friendly you are, but they may tell you about specific points where the competitors did a better job than your team. Tell them that honest feedback is important for you to continue to improve your skills and provide them with superior service.

Hint: Consider Focusing on New Products

A great way for you to differentiate is to specialize in a new product. First, you should, of course, make sure that there is enough business to warrant focusing on the new line. Many existing SEs will not want to focus on new products because doing so poorly leverages their existing experience. You have no such equity, so there is no incremental cost for you. What's more, becoming an expert will take less effort because the new product will likely be less complex than products that have been on the market for several years. By focusing on new products, you are more likely to have a chance to interact with their marketing and engineering staffs. These contacts may be able to help you if you later move to focusing on older products as well. Of course, you should not attach yourself to a product that will not allow you to make your quota, so validate this strategy with your manager or mentor.

Develop a 30-/90-/180-Day Plan

The next step is to move beyond focusing on the generic ramp process and to begin focusing on your personal success. We recommend that you define your goals, then break them into components that can be achieved in 30, 90, or 180 days. This approach will enable you to leverage your ramp time best by driving toward concrete milestones.

Begin working with your manager, your sales reps, or other experienced SEs in your office to build your personal definition of success. Your primary target, of course, should be making your quota. By now, you should have a better understanding of what you need to do to make successful deals in order to achieve that quota. Try to identify what those winning characteristics are, and attach goals to them. If your company has a management-by-objective (MBO) variable component to your pay, then you will probably be required to do this. Even if it is not required, goal setting is a critical part of putting together your plan. We firmly believe that if you don't know where you are going, you won't get there. Your definition of success should enable you to meet your corporate goals, as well as any personal objectives. A mission statement in the following form is good way to envision this goal:

> Achieve 120% of first year's quota by utilizing superior sales skills and in-depth product knowledge and by providing superior customer service.

At this point, build specifically on the organization's definition of success. Do not start with a goal of "become branch manager in 9 months." In sales, if you can meet any initial quota, build a good network, and develop beginning product expertise, then you are off to a great start. Let's turn these goals into a couple of possible success plans.

Example Plan 1

> • *Mandatory ramp activities:* Complete demo training, and pass demo certification.

> • *Achieve 120% of quota:* Work with rep to close two deals, achieving quota.

> • *Provide superior customer service:* Build a good relationship with product marketing so they return calls.

> • *Gain in-depth product knowledge:* Become recognized as the regional expert in a new product.

Though reasonable, this plan could be better. The plan's strength is in its specificity regarding the different areas the SE thinks are necessary to meet quota. You should try to make your plan detailed enough that you will know whether you are on track to get there. We also want to introduce a concept of time that we call the *30/90/180 plan*, which simply refers to three different time frames in which you should focus on achieving different sets of goals. By tying specific goals to a time frame, you will find it easier to sequence and prioritize your activities.

A more specific plan might look like the following.

Example Plan 2

- *30 days:* Focus on mastery of corporate information.
  - Memorize the key metrics and measurements of the top 10 customers.
  - Learn and be able to deliver corporate presentation.
  - Know enough to be able to respond to typical request-for-proposal (RFP) questions related to corporate information.
- *90 days:* Focus on beginning to master tactical skills.
  - Complete demo training.
  - Pass demo certification.
- *180 days:* Master intangible aspects of success plan.
  - Begin implementing differentiation plan.
  - Build a good relationship with product marketing so they return calls. Focus on Jane M's group because their products have the greatest revenue potential. Meet marketers during a scheduled training session, and have lunch with at least one of Jane's staff.
  - Become recognized as the regional expert in the new product. Find out who the experts are in other regions, and go see at least two of them in action.
- *Post-180 days:* Focus on long-term tasks.
  - Work with rep to achieve quota by closing two of three deals, focusing on the Acme Corporation business-process reengineering project, the Safeway terminal project, and the San Francisco municipal-improvement project.

The second plan is clearly more action oriented and will be simpler to execute because the initial steps are well thought out. However, if at this point you don't have enough information to develop a plan like the second one, don't worry. The rest of the chapter gives specific recommendations on how you can take your top-level goals for your ramp period (as shown in example plan 1) and turn them into a more detailed action plan (example plan 2).

The 30-/90-/180-Day Structure
As you saw in the preceding example, the 30-/90-/180-day concept provides a simple structure to try to organize your early progress. We recommend that you try to take your overall set of goals and assign them to the

30-/90-/180-day structure. In our example, we broke our goals down based on three categories: corporate information, basic product mastery, and relationships and intangibles. You should also certainly consider dependencies between your goals, as well as opportunities provided by travel, when putting together your personal plan. For example, if you spend your first week at the corporate headquarters, you should begin working on "relationships and intangibles."

Qualities of a Good Plan

A good plan should be clear and actionable. Do not place items on your plan that you don't understand or don't know how to execute. If you like, have a separate section for goals. Have the actions relate to defining success or the implementation of those goals. This segregation will help you make progress on the concrete items while remaining open to ideas about how to accomplish the others.

Your plan should also include dates where appropriate. If you know when you are going to have product or other training, commit (to yourself) that you will set up the lunch meeting with the marketing team. Periodically review the tasks that do not have definite completion dates to see if you can schedule them.

Ready to Go

Spend a few minutes working on your personal plan right now. Be sure to incorporate ideas from your manager, this book, and past experience into your goals. The balance of this chapter consists of tips for achieving the goals you identify. When you complete your goals and your plan, share them with your manager, your sales rep, and your spouse. Philosophies differ about whether it is a good idea or not to commit publicly to certain goals. In this case, you are still learning what's possible and how best to succeed. By being open with those around you, you will get good feedback on how to improve your plan. Sharing your plan with a spouse or significant other is also a good way to communicate how demanding your first 6 months on the job will be. You may want to build rewards into achieving certain goals to make those successes more noteworthy for you and your significant other.

CASE STUDY: SUCCESS SECRETS FROM A SERIALLY SUCCESSFUL SE

We interviewed a former SE (Jason) who has been a sales rep, sales-engineering manager, and senior individual contributor at multiple high-tech companies. He had the following suggestions:

- During your first 6 months, practice what you are learning with small deals or current customers. They will be forgiving, and you may even make some money.

- Ask every successful sales person you meet what the top three reasons are for their winning or losing a deal. You can then parrot these reasons to your customers until you understand enough to develop your own.

- While you are getting up to speed, go sit with a professional-services team while they are at a customer site. You will make some great contacts with both the customers and your service organization, plus you will learn how people really use your products.

- Build your network within the company.

The result? We would not include his tips if he weren't successful, but Jason overachieved his quota during his ramp period at every company he joined. In addition, most of Jason's hires were able to do the same.

Tips on Making the First 6 Months a Success

Find a Mentor

This will probably not be your manager. Find a senior SE who is the go-to person for a product you would like to sell. Shadow that person in meetings; help him or her work on RFPs, whatever else he or she needs. Once you get out of your ramp period, you will probably be expected to be more self-sufficient, so take advantage of this opportunity. It is even better if you can find someone who is located in a different geographical area. You can become the local expert in your area and have access to the mentor's peer group in that other area.

Finding a mentor can be difficult. You can't walk up to someone you have just met and ask them to mentor you for the next year. In addition to being strong in an area where you are weak, a good mentor candidate should have a reason for helping you. This reason will usually be related to their experiencing personal satisfaction from helping out a coworker. In particular, look for people with whom you share common interests or who have held a position similar to yours because they will be more likely to sympathize with the challenges you face and more willing to share their experiences. Most people will be flattered if you ask their advice on how to improve your skills or pursue aspects of your career. Such questions show you hold them in high regard.

Read the Manual—Really!

Reading the manual is especially critical if you are dealing with your company's engineering or marketing teams. They have developed the training materials, marketing materials, and product documentation specifically so they do not have to deal with a bunch of one-off questions. If you go to them with something covered "in the book," you are going to lose credibility and hurt that relationship. On the other hand, if every time you go to them, you expose them to new customer issues they haven't dealt with before, then you are representing an important source of market information. Understanding the contents of the manuals is also essential when dealing with a customer's or prospect's highly technical contacts. They *will* have read the documentation, and you can be sure they will ask you about some obscure setting or flag mentioned in a footnote. It also pays to be up to date on documentation such as new release notes or bug and recall notes.

Watch the Video

Almost every company now keeps a library of video-based training on its intranet. While some of this training is standard corporate fare, you will also find copies of specific presentations by the masters of the trade within your company. You should review these videos, download them if possible, and borrow as much material as possible for your own use. Another growing trend is the use of weekly or monthly training podcasts, so sign up for the service; also go back to review the last 12 to 24 months of material for diamonds in the rough.

Master the Technology

Your first 6 months are the perfect time to ask all of the potentially embarrassing questions about how to plug in, start up, set up, and configure your product. Being able to "fieldstrip" your demo kit and rebuild it from the basic components will serve you well in the future when odd glitches occur at critical times. Spend time building relationships with your customer-support team in case you are ever in a jam at a client site during a trial and need emergency help.

Master the Product

Some SEs focus so much on the sales aspects of their jobs that they neglect to become expert in the products they represent. Take the first 6 months to get a really solid foundation for your future success. You will probably never have a similar opportunity where your expected revenue contribution is low and you are expected to spend a lot of time on product training.

Boot Camp Training Contacts

Contacts from boot camp will be your support in hard times. Build your network and support it. You will find that the time you invest here will reap benefits in relationships, personal satisfaction, and support in your times of need. Focus in particular on identifying those individuals whom you can call on during your sales cycle. Ask your manager if you can expense lunches and dinners with these key contacts. Also, ask your manager for suggestions as to people you should try to get to know.

During boot camp, your top priority should be learning the material. Frequently, social events and other activities are often planned that could dilute your focus on the training sessions. It is easy to view these types of activities as "team building" or networking. In moderation, they can serve as pleasant distractions and also provide networking opportunities. Many SEs will reach and exceed the point of diminishing returns. For example, do you really need to stay out at a bar until 2 a.m.? Although this example may seem humorous, this type of activity will take its toll and possibly decrease the benefit you receive from your training.

Work in the Factory

If you have the option of working at the headquarters for the first few months, instead of at home, take it. At the office, you will have the opportunity to take part in short-term projects that often arise. Product testing and demo development are two examples of special projects that build your skills while exposing you to valuable contacts.

Face Time and Relationships

This aspect of success has been mentioned several times elsewhere, but it is worth calling out once again. Specifically, budget your time to get to know the right people. Invest more in them than they invest in you. If you do this, you will have all the support you need when that big deal is on the line.

Practice, Practice, Practice

As degrading as this sounds, become a "demo jockey" if that is relevant in your sale. Know how to use your product forward and backward. If your product is too large to do this, learn the most common 20% of the product so that you appear to be an expert. You should also practice worst-case scenarios. Know what happens if you are pulled off the standard demo track.

Learn About Key Customers and How They Actually Use Your Product

Until you build your own references, you will have to use those of others. As we discuss in later chapters, customer references are key in any sales process. Early on, customer references can also be key in helping you understand your own value proposition. We have been impressed by how new sales reps can appear to be extremely well versed in their company's products by mastering the use cases for referenceable customers.

Understand the Financials of Your Value Proposition

If you already understand the basics of finance, this can be a great way to quickly understand a new product. Learn how your solution impacts your customer's business from a financial perspective. If you know how to read an annual report, you should be able to see how your solution could affect the customer's income statement. Being able to articulate your solution's benefit at this level will establish your credibility during the sales cycle. Best of all, it won't take more than a few months on the job to get the necessary information. If you don't have an inclination toward finance, read the management discussion and analysis section from the annual reports of your major customers and major prospects. You should be able to identify some of the corporate trends that drive purchasing decisions for your products. In most cases, product return-on-investment (ROI) analysis is a good starting point. Most marketing organizations build them in so that customers can easily understand them, so you should have no difficulty at all.

CASE STUDY: GETTING ATTENTION AS A NEW GUY

One of us used to be an overlay salesperson responsible for traveling throughout the United States to help sales teams on deals. He had recently helped out a new sales team from Detroit on a couple of customer conference calls, and 2 weeks later he received a gift certificate to an on-line bookseller as a "thank you." The author was impressed not only by the thoughtfulness of the SE but also by his savvy strategy at getting the attention of people back at corporate. Consider how you can use this strategy to add value to those on whom you will need to draw later. In addition to gifts, consider sharing your technical or industry expertise in the form of forwarded articles or custom-made customer presentations and deliverables.

Learn the Math; Don't Just Memorize the Answers

Be sure you understand the why of your value proposition. If you have access to the marketing team, try to build your own expertise over lunch or dinner. Time invested here will pay off later on when you are dealing with customer management staff who really want to dig into how your product benefits them. Select a current prospect, and discuss how you could develop a customized return-on-investment analysis for that customer.

Understand Content, but Don't Feel Overwhelmed

If you find yourself bombarded with too many new concepts, make a list and slowly try to understand each. If you have a complex product set, as many as a dozen MBAs may well be working on this material. It is okay if it takes you a few months to get up to speed. By learning in a methodical way and working from a list, you can be sure you will not get caught flat-footed in a customer meeting.

If You Can Use Your Product in Everyday Life, Do So

Even if it is a bit inconvenient, this is the best training possible. This applies primarily to products that could be used by salespeople or professionals in general. You will really know how your solution works. It also doubles as great demo training. If you don't use your product (and you could), be prepared with a story for why you don't. Your prospect will likely be suspicious of the fact that you don't use the product you are trying to sell.

Get Feedback—From Everyone

Getting feedback is a much simpler process than the benchmarking discussed earlier. Whenever someone else has the opportunity to see your work, ask for feedback. Customer feedback is especially valuable. Ask them what they did or didn't like. Ask customers if you have met their needs and if there was a more efficient way you could have done so. By engaging in this type of discussion, the customer may also tell you what information you did not communicate effectively. In addition to receiving a suggestion for your personal growth, you will have found a problem to fix during your next communication with that customer. Don't feel badly if you get "constructive feedback"—people willing to tell you what they believe are your weaknesses do so because they want to help you improve.

Review Your Plan Weekly

Did you forget about your plan already? Did you take the time to begin writing up your goals and the actions to achieve them? If you didn't, stop reading and do so now. Allocate all activities to a specific week. Reviewing your goals weekly will help keep them fresh in your mind. You may decide that some of them have become less relevant. If so, remove them. Then, try to plan for the week ahead. Do you have any downtime? Have you already budgeted a certain amount of time to study the product? If so, identify the highest-priority goals and slot them into those times. You will find that your downtime is more effective if you have already planned how you will fill it.

Summary

There is plenty to accomplish, but by starting with your goals, then developing and refining a plan enabling you to achieve them, you can get there. You will have certain unique opportunities in your "ramp" period, and you should be sure to take advantage of them. Focus on building the skills and internal relationships you will need to be successful in the future. Share your plan with your manager and possible mentors and enlist them to help you deliver on the plan.

Skill Building

New SE	1. Focus on defining what success is.
	2. As a new employee, you are especially likely to get drawn into activities that consume time but don't help you progress toward your goal.
	3. Find a mentor (perhaps your boss), and ask him or her to help you evaluate your plan.
Experienced SE	1. Focus on the relationships.
	2. Look for areas of differentiation that will support your revenue goals.
	3. Skip ahead to "Your Personal Value Proposition: Self-Branding" in Chapter 17, and try to apply that principle during your ramp period at the new company.
	4. Think about how you behaved and were perceived in your previous company. You now have a "clean slate," so build a plan that makes you the success you want to be.
SE Manager	1. Think of ways you can help support your new hires.
	2. Build a sample plan to give them, and think of ways they may wish to personalize it to meet their goals.

Chapter Goals

Discuss how to categorize objections.

Learn the basic techniques of objection handling.

Improve your ability to work with third parties and consultants.

Objection Handling

Problems are only opportunities in work clothes.

Henry J. Kaiser

Entire books have been written about objection handling, which is one of the pure sales areas with which an SE needs to be intimately familiar. Although this chapter is titled "Objection Handling," it could also be named "Managing Questions" as it is very important for the SE to understand that questions are a good thing. They should be viewed as neither adversarial nor confrontational in nature, but as a natural means to progress the opportunity through the sales cycle.

Before You Start

Every sales organization should have a list of the top 10 most common objections they face when selling. Along with the objection should be a standard, corporate-approved reply. Think of this as analogous to a frequently-asked-questions (FAQ) document for the sales force. It must be realistic and cover the hard questions as well as the easy ones. Entering a meeting thinking, "I hope they don't ask me about ...," virtually guarantees that the prospect will raise the objection.

> *Hint: Create a List of Common Objections*
>
> *If you don't have a written list of answers to the most common objections your organization meets, create one now. Collaborate with your peers, managers, marketing, and whomever else you need. Take the initiative, and get it done now.*

Categorizing Objections

Customers raise objections for many reasons. It is important to determine why an objection is being raised and its origin.

A Valid Objection

Contrary to first impressions, this is absolutely the best kind of objection to have raised. It represents a legitimate chance to remove a sales obstacle standing between you and the signing of the contract. The objection may be difficult or easy, but once voiced, it can be dealt with and then effectively eliminated.

For a technical objection in particular, ensure that your answer is clear, concise, and understood by the person who raised the objection. Gain a verbal commitment that you have successfully handled the objection and then proceed. When debriefing after the meeting, should the sales team feel this was a key objection, then follow up with the answer in writing or via e-mail, citing additional sources of information if appropriate.

A Competitive Objection

The internal coach of a competitor usually raises this form of objection. Typically, this individual has three or four questions written on a pad or contained in an e-mail that are designed to point out a perceived flaw. Take the high ground, at least initially, and answer these objections exactly like any other. It is highly probable that you have heard them before, and they are part of the top 10. Because you, as an SE, are most likely answering a technical objection, the onus is on you to gain closure. Ask directly if you answered the objection satisfactorily. If you haven't, press for clarification, and answer as clearly and briefly as possible. Do not volunteer extraneous information that could lead to follow-up questions.

<u>*Hint: Stay on Safe Ground*</u>

Remember that you know more about your products and services than your prospect. Conversely, they know more about their business and environment. Stay within your strengths, and do not wander into, or express an opinion about, their territory. It can seem extremely rude and arrogant if you position yourself as knowing your prospect's business better than they do. The prospect may also take this as a challenge and lead you in a direction you do not wish to go.

When there is no closure on an objection, and no one from the audience has stepped in to assist, then defer the objection to later, writing it down or posting it on a board.

CASE STUDY: SILENCE IS GOLDEN

This incident occurred when I was a rookie SE with less than 3 months of experience under my belt. I have never forgotten it. I was visiting a bank in Newark, New Jersey, with Mike, one of our newest account managers. The purpose of the visit was to conduct a technical question-and-answer session after a prior fact-gathering visit. We were competing head to head with our closest competitor, but I felt that we had the deal. The only major stumbling block was Phil, the MIS director, who obviously wanted to buy our competitor's product.

Even though I was still a trainee, I knew our product really well and was handling everything Phil and his gang could throw at me. The 1-hour session had already taken 90 minutes, and some of Phil's peers and his boss were getting a little impatient. Finally, Phil had me cornered and asked, "Should I run your software under CICS or TSO [two IBM interactive systems]?" I looked him in the eye and replied, "Well, Phil, which way would you like to run it?"

A few seconds of silence stretched into 5 seconds, then 10 seconds. I leaned forward as if to break the silence, and Mike kicked me. Phil looked around the room, back at me, and then down at the ground. By this time, it seemed as if a minute had passed, but it was probably only 15 seconds. The room stayed quiet, and all eyes were on Phil. Finally, he replied, "Well, I guess it doesn't matter."

The meeting ended on that note. Mike went into the vice president's office and got the paperwork signed. I still believe to this day that if Mike had not kicked me, I would have broken the silence, and Phil would have wriggled off the hook. Sometimes silence is better than a thousand words.

The Seymour Objection

A *Seymour* is a highly technical member of the audience whose only interest is to "see more" of the product. These people will often ask the most elaborate and detailed questions—we hope in the cause of intellectual curiosity—but often just to see if anyone knows the answer.

The key to dealing with a Seymour (who is rarely a decision maker) is to answer the question briefly and then offer more detail using documentation or a reference Web site. Above all, when finishing the answer to a Seymour objection, make sure you have eye contact with someone else. Maintaining eye contact will guarantee a follow-up question; breaking eye contact allows another member of the audience to interject with a question or comment.

This technique applies to any person whose floor time you are trying to reduce, but executives and senior managers will typically ask their follow-up anyway, while Seymours are more reticent.

Hint: Is That a Great Question?

Avoid the "That's a great question. I'm so glad you asked it" approach. Unless it really is an insightful question, the response is artificial and can even be deprecating toward the questioner. Also avoid the "A lot of people ask me that" response. As well as indirectly questioning the intelligence of the audience, it also leads to the implicit reaction of "So, why haven't you already dealt with it then?"

The Seymour objection is usually more disruptive than insightful because an unlimited discussion about technical minutiae will lose a high percentage of the audience. When working with a mixed technical/business audience, the Seymour needs to be dealt with politely but firmly so that the session can proceed at your pace.

The Coaching Objection

This is the exact opposite of the competitive objection because it is asked by one of your supporters. It is designed to show your products and services in the best possible light by providing an opportunity to answer the objection in a positive fashion. Treat this objection just like any other, and do not be so eager to answer that you forget to listen and pause. After answering the question, make sure the entire audience fully comprehends the significance of the answer by soliciting verbal feedback.

Although it is important to provide the coach with several objections, do not overuse this opportunity. An even better approach is to ask the coach to suggest several objections that include the prospect's own terminology and acronyms.

If your rapport with the group is strong, you can even pose a coaching objection yourself in the form of a question: "A typical issue with this type of system is the propensity to burst into flame. Can you see why this wouldn't be an issue with what we are proposing?" Such prompting can help you get the audience to the "ah-hah!" point at which they grasp a complex subject after ongoing discussion.

The Hostile Objection

A very small number of vendor-prospect meetings become confrontational and hostile. It is a much rarer occurrence than popular sales folklore suggests. Nevertheless, be prepared to deal with a hostile crowd and to identify their rationale. Three common situations follow:

First, you have a group of people who, through rudeness or lack of interest, play "bait the vendor." They will steadily grow louder, rowdier, and angrier during the session. A technical audience is more likely to dissolve into this behavior than a business audience. At some point, the SE needs to look to the senior member of the sales team and force a go/no-go decision. A group session rarely recovers to get back on track, and stopping the meeting is the best solution.

Second, something said or done may have upset the audience. This can be a problem particularly in dealing with multinational corporations and non-Western cultures. In this situation, face the music, apologize profusely, and continue. Admitting error and continuing, as opposed to becoming defensive, is the recommended course of action.

Finally, and most commonly, the hostility is confined to a single individual. In this case, it is again important to maintain composure and stay calm. For an SE, whose technical prowess is being challenged, this can be difficult to accomplish. However, proceed at a slow and measured pace, lowering your voice slightly. The antagonist then has to concentrate more on the reply instead of formulating the next barb, and the pace will slow. Either the objections will peter out, or the individual will cross the line to such an extent that another audience member will react negatively to the constant questioning. At this point, unless you are accused of being unethical or deceptive, gracefully give the antagonist an exit by offering some form of follow-up and proceed.

When possible, try to personally approach the problematic subject after your meeting is concluded. Ask if his or her questions were answered, and, if appropriate, apologize for anything untoward you may have done during the discussion. Usually, this approach will help the person realize he or she's been acting toward you in a hostile fashion. Frequently, he or she will even share with you the reason he or she was unhappy during the presentation. It is entirely possible that you are recommending a course of action that contradicts a long-standing policy or would cost someone a job. By apologizing, you help cast yourself as an innocent in any ongoing game of office politics.

CASE STUDY: AN EXTREME RESPONSE

As an SE manager at Oracle, life was always entertaining. The salespeople were aggressive, successful, and prone to taking risks. The SEs scrambled to keep up, but together we were a well-oiled machine. Bruce, our district sales manager, had been working on a sizable database opportunity with a chemical company in Pennsylvania. After many months of selling, it had come down to Oracle and IBM as the finalists. The business side wanted Oracle, and the IT department, dependent on their IBM mainframes, wanted their DB2 database.

We were invited to corporate headquarters for the day to conduct a lengthy series of presentations, discussions, and demonstrations. We had followed all of our rules and knew exactly who would be in the audience, their hot buttons, and our weaknesses and strengths. In short, we had done our homework. Our major technical advantage was a feature called *row-level-locking*. It allowed our database to process an incredible number of transactions per second compared to IBM's offering. It was brand-new technology and a major leap forward for Oracle—and it even ran on an IBM mainframe.

Fifteen minutes into the second session of the morning, one of the SEs started to discuss row-level-locking. The IT folks took this as an opportunity to drag us down a rat hole, and, sure enough, down we went. Finally, after the third explanation of how we accomplished this magical piece of technology, one of their senior systems analysts said, "I don't believe you. You're lying."

The room fell silent. Bruce picked up his pen and notepad, put them into his briefcase, and declared, "Okay, that is enough. We didn't come here to be insulted. We are leaving." We complied and trooped out of the conference room and gathered together outside the building. Bruce looked at his watch and said they would be out after us within 10 minutes. After 5 minutes, the senior business sponsor approached us in the parking lot, apologized for the behavior, and invited us back. Bruce agreed but asked that the IT analyst be excluded from further sessions.

The rest of the day passed with no other exceptional events occurring. A few weeks later, Bruce picked up a multi-million-dollar commitment from this company and signed a corporate agreement. The lesson to be learned here is that, at some time during the sales cycle, your competition—whether internal or external—will make a mistake on which you have to capitalize. Are we advocating walking out of the room as a sales tactic? No. In fact, doing so was a very risky and brazen approach. The prospect could just as easily have left us in the parking lot. However, to give Bruce his due, he recognized the situation for what it was, unemotionally measured his response, and took action.

❖ ❖ ❖ ❖

The Generic Objection

Perhaps one of the most frustrating forms of objection is the generic statement or question that has little relevance to your solution. You sometimes wonder if people have been paying attention during your session. Often voiced by an uncertain prospect, the generic objection has no direct bearing on your proposal; rather, it is a diversion because the person is either unwilling or unable to make a decision. A classic generic objection is, "Your product is too expensive." Instead of cringing inwardly and sighing, take this objection as an opportunity to revisit your value proposition. Your sales partner should respond along the lines of, "So, you like our product, but you aren't yet convinced about the ROI we can bring to your organization." Should the prospect agree, you have an immediate opening to propose more face time to determine the true economics of your proposal.

Just as every SE organization has its top 10 objections list, so should the direct sales group have a list as well. Using this, the sales group should be able to respond deftly to and defuse any of the common generic, nonproduct-specific objections.

Basic Techniques of Objection Handling

Basic Technique 1: Listen

The most important thing before handling an objection is to listen carefully and observe the individual asking the question. A common mistake made by inexperienced SEs is to recognize the question and jump right into the answer before the prospect has even completed the sentence. Young SEs can be so excited about knowing the answer that they just dive in so they can look smart. This is exactly the wrong thing to do.

Look at the speaker as he asks the question and pay attention. Wait until he has finished speaking, then pause for a second or two longer. The benefits are as follows:

1. It shows that you are seriously considering the objection.

2. Someone else (from the intended prospect) in the audience may actually handle the objection for you.

3. Should the objection lie outside of your area of expertise, another sales team member has an opportunity to answer it.

Basic Technique 2: Coordinate

If several members of your sales team are present, be sure that your team knows who is responsible for answering certain questions. Salespeople are usually pretty good at this, but if you brought engineers or corporate staff along, or if you haven't worked with a particular salesperson before, you should take a few minutes before the session to discuss responsibilities.

Usually, simple ground rules can be established, such as, "Whoever is running the discussion will answer the question. If he doesn't know the answer, he will glance at the other team members." Multiple people speaking at once in response to a question is unprofessional and makes it more likely that you will contradict each other. Another common habit to avoid is the "pile-on" response, where a member of your sales team appends a "let me add one more thing" after the question has already been dealt with. In the event that the discussion is taking place entirely over the phone or via a webcast, ensure that you have set up an Instant Messaging backchannel to coordinate responses and change strategy on the fly.

Basic Technique 3: Clarify

When unsure exactly what the question is or what the prospect is concerned about, ask for clarification. This can be in the form of requesting additional information or a more detailed explanation. An off-the-wall objection can often be defused by asking, "Give me an example of how that would affect your business today," or a suitable equivalent. When possible, aim for specifics because this eliminates many hypothetical technical questions that may appear to point out weaknesses in your solution.

> *Hint: Make the Question More Specific*
>
> *Although SE's are taught to ask open-ended questions, you don't always want to be on the receiving end of them. For example, a software vendor might be asked, "Which versions of which operating systems do you support?" That question, especially if asked by a Seymour or posed as a competitive objection, can be very dangerous. It is perfectly acceptable to seek clarification and respond with, "What do you have installed within your company, and what are your future plans?"*

Never answer a question if you do not understand it or feel that you are missing the underlying reason for the objection. Clarify and restate until the objection has been simplified or divided into manageable pieces.

Basic Technique 4: Restate

Many professional presenters will tell you to always restate an objection or question. Our advice is more qualified and situational in nature. If you are dealing with a large audience and microphones are involved, then certainly restate it. With a smaller audience, it may not always be necessary and can at times be very annoying. Remember that the art of good objection handling is to make your technique natural.

Should someone raise a critical issue, then by all means restate the objection. (Bear in mind that a suggested response from your "Objection FAQ" may help you restate the question in a kinder and gentler fashion.) Otherwise, you can vary between restatement and inclusion of the objection in your response (i.e., "Yes, we do run under Windows Vista," or "No, we do not need a 220V power outlet").

Basic Technique 5: Answer

As a general rule, your answer should be short, simple, and to the point. A long, drawn-out, rambling reply will undoubtedly lose some of the audience and lead to confusion. Consider these points:

1. Where possible, if you know your answer will be complex, start with a yes or no, answer the question, and then summarize your answer.

2. To amplify a particularly important point, try to internalize it for the audience. Using a "What this really means to you is ... " type of summary can be very effective; however, you must be cautious with this technique. If applied inappropriately, you can come off as patronizing. When used properly, it is a great way to redirect the conversation toward the business benefits your solution provides.

3. "I don't know" is an acceptable answer, although you should be judicious in its use because you never know when you will reach your limit with an audience. It should always be followed up with the response, "But I'll certainly find out for you."

4. A picture is worth a thousand words. Sometimes a simple sketch can avoid a 5-minute monologue. Offer the person who raised the objection the sketch if you made it on a notepad. Whiteboarding can lead to unproductive discussion, so when you want to close out a discussion after handling the objection, erase the whiteboard so the audience isn't distracted.

5. Make sure your answer is understood. Finish with "Is that clear?" or "Did I answer your question?" for important objections or important prospect personnel.

Working With Consultants

Third-party consultants can be either a help or hindrance when handling objections. They rarely take a neutral stance. Some feel the need to display their intelligence and value in front of their clients by posing, Seymour style, numerous complex objections. Single-person or small, private consultancies are often angling for their next assignment. This is an unfortunate fact of life, but one with which you need to deal.

We recommend taking a few minutes before the meeting to brief the consultant or even hold a premeeting. In this way, the consultant is educated beforehand in a controlled environment. Selectively point out business and competitive advantages to them. Frequently, you will hear these same points echoed back by the consultant during the meeting. This approach may seem very transparent, but it has been highly successful.

Follow Up Leads to Closeout

Regardless of the meeting's outcome, follow up on all open action items, questions, and "I'll find that out for you" promises. Do this in writing, whether by e-mail, fax, or conventional letter. Maintain an audit trail to show that the objection was answered, so that it cannot be resurrected at a later stage in the sales cycle. We also recommend that when directing specific follow-up at one individual, you copy at least one other person (potentially your internal coach) on all correspondence. This way nothing gets "lost in the mail."

Summary

Listen and observe carefully. One of our former managers once noted, "You have two ears and one mouth—listen twice as much as you speak." Treat each objection with respect, and gain closure where possible. Maintain your professionalism and composure no matter what the circumstances may be. Categorize each objection, and make sure you understand it. Follow up on all outstanding issues, and ensure that no objections raised are left to trap you in the closing stages of the opportunity.

Skill Building

New SE	1. Learn the answers to the top 10 objections.
	2. Put the answers into your own words.
	3. Practice listening (your spouse or significant other will love you).
	4. Draw pictures and diagrams where possible.
	5. Attend Q&A sessions. Note all questions. Categorize them. Debrief afterward.
Experienced SE	1. Build and maintain answers to the top 10 objections.
	2. Coach the new SEs on responses.
	3. Conduct a "live" Q&A as a training exercise. Videotape the session.
	4. Use the prospect's terminology in your replies.
	5. Frame replies to emphasize your competitors' weaknesses.
	6. Build the answers to common objections into your presentation materials.

The Executive Connection

In the business world, the rearview mirror is always clearer than the windshield.

Warren Buffet

Meeting with higher-level executives can make many technicians very nervous. Once you realize that a different set of priorities drives executives, such meetings become easier to manage. In this chapter, we finally lay open the mystique surrounding how to deal with executives, both inside and outside of your company, and their decision-making process.

What They Think of You

Although this is a little stereotypical, executives usually think of technicians as people likely to get into far more detail than they want to hear. Technicians are not expected to be as polished as the salesperson in both dress and presentation skills and are commonly expected to be unsure of themselves. Many executives will use these impressions to their advantage and attempt to intimidate you. Others will be genuine "nice guys" and try to put you at ease.

An executive meeting occurs either because your own sales team or someone from the prospect believes that you have valuable information that needs to be provided to that executive. The executive is hoping that you have been prepared and briefed and can impart your value in a concise and professional manner. The executive is expecting that it is not going to be that easy. Your mission is simply to beat expectations.

Hint: Executives Are People Too

Although the prospect of meeting with a CIO or CEO may seem daunting, remember that he or she is as human as you are. Without resorting to clichés about imagining the executive naked or remembering that "he puts his socks on one at a time too," focus on the person and not the position.

We cannot emphasize enough how profit and investment oriented most executives are. Part of their job is to invest their corporation's resources in the way they believe will generate a solid return. After all, if a salesperson called on you at home claiming to be able to reduce your monthly expenses by 10%, you would want all the financial details.

Keep It Simple

The magic number for executives is two, plus or minus one. This means that, ideally, you should focus on two main points in any executive interaction. You can increase this number to three or drop it to one when the occasion arises, but two is a good starting point.

The "executive rule of two" applies to all forms of interactions—letters, e-mails, the spoken word, and especially PowerPoint presentations. Any slide or overhead with more than three bullet points is a candidate for immediate rejection. Applying a sharp focus to all stages of the sales cycle always pays dividends, but especially when seeking to gain executive commitment. Approached another way, executives are paid to make choices by distilling sizable amounts of data into meaningful and insightful decisions. By already summarizing key points for them, you are more likely to get their full attention.

Plan the Meeting

Setting the Stage

Your internal coach or a third party will often have sponsored the meeting. Presumably the meeting would not have been arranged if the executive had nothing to gain from it, but some advance press never hurts. Ask your sponsor to legitimately "talk you up," either personally or as a company, to get the meeting off to a great start.

Also, research the people with whom you will be meeting. See if they have published any papers or have had speeches published on the corporate Web site. In addition to "Googling" executives, check professional-networking sites such as Linkedin and Plaxo. Depending upon their generational profiles, you may also gain interesting personal information from Facebook, MySpace, and even personal blogs. Ask your sponsor about the executives' interests and if they typically spend a large part of a meeting on relationship building or if they have a straightforward business approach. Key pieces of information to discover are how long they have been (1) at the company, and (2) in their present position, and (3) where they have worked before. Many a meeting has started with the surprise discovery that the executive worked either at one of your company's biggest successes or failures.

Be sensitive to language, culture, and geographic location. Although it is not a hard-and-fast rule, dealing with financial-services executives anywhere in the world, but especially in New York City, is likely to be short and sweet with a minimal amount of time spent on introductions. In Asian cultures, in contrast, the first 20 or 30 minutes may be simple introductions, a series of compliments, and an exchange of business cards. You will also learn that executive attention span can vary quite radically by position. As a very broad generalization, CFOs and operations and security executives can remain on task longer than SVPs of sales or marketing.

Not only is it important that you have your two discussion points prepared, but the executive needs to understand why you are meeting. As with any other occasion, confirm the length of the meeting and the subject matter to be discussed. There is nothing wrong with launching the business part of the meeting with a statement such as, "By the end of our 15 minutes, I'd like to have your agreement to … " If the salesperson or sales manager is accompanying you, then this task can be left to him or her.

Hint: Always Budget for Less Time

Just because you have 30 minutes on an executive calendar does not mean you will get the full 30 minutes. In the best possible case, allow 5 minutes for introductions and 5 minutes for wrap-up, leaving 20 minutes. In the worst case, your meeting time will be compressed.

Always be prepared to conduct your meeting in half of the time you originally allotted for it.

Following the Dollars

Almost every executive you meet has some form of budgetary or profit-and-loss (P&L) responsibility. In fact, if he does not, this is a good sign not to expend too much time and effort with him. Although not a skill classically taught as part of SE training, we strongly recommend learning how to read a balance sheet and income statement.

This data is easily available from an annual report or from 10-K and 10-Q filings from the government's EDGAR database (http://www.sec.gov/edgar). Similar sites exist for most major stock markets. Another good step is to read the company's latest earnings press release or review the transcript for its earnings call (available at http://seekingalpha.com). Earnings announcements often highlight a company's key strategic initiatives, so, clearly, if your solution supports these initiatives, this will be to your benefit. We are not proposing that you become a financial analyst, but you should know if the prospect is profitable, what their gross and net margins are, and if any of their key financial ratios are markedly different from the industry norms. Ultimately, whatever you sell will either raise revenues or decrease costs. Knowing how and where to account for this can significantly help during both the discovery process and executive discussions.

Case Study: The Point of No Return

A senior manager at Ernst & Young related, "At one point, we were in the discovery process with a company looking to minimize their ballooning inventory. Their COO and CFO had indicated that this was their number one business problem, and if we could fix it, they would buy from us. A little investigation showed that their gross margin was several points lower than that of any of their competitors. Subsequent analysis determined that their cost of goods sold was so abnormal because of an extremely high return rate on their products. To make up for poor quality, they simply stocked more raw and finished goods so that their customers never had to wait for a replacement part. So, the problem was related not to the quantity of their inventory but rather to the quality of their finished goods. So, we instead proposed a few radical changes in quality control, which when implemented would save millions of dollars in inventory and scrapped returns. Had we sold them what they wanted, the system would have failed. A year later, they asked us to come back and single-sourced their inventory-control system to us."

❖ ❖ ❖ ❖

The second aspect of following the dollars is understanding how the executive is compensated for performance. Behavior is driven by compensation, so understanding the performance measurements, whether revenue, stock price, gross margin, or profit, can assist in finding the proverbial hot buttons for any executive. This is generally a more appropriate topic for one of your own executives to raise during a later executive bonding session, but it is valuable information nonetheless.

Determining the Goal of the Meeting

Technicians will frequently lose sight of the purpose of the meeting. Despite having two key points and all the preparation in the world, the meeting needs to have a purpose and at least one key goal. Write down the goal(s) on an index card and agree on them with your sales partner. Ideally, you should have a minimal acceptable achievement (MAA) and a best possible result (BPR) goal. Meeting the MAA means that your meeting is a success; achieving the BPR means that the sales team owes you lunch.

Some goals revolve around gaining executive agreement or approval on a future course of action. Others depend on removing a roadblock or objection from the boardroom or C-level executives. We recommend that you set up goals for an executive meeting just as you would a management by objective (MBO) by using the "SMARTI" acronym (see Table 16.1).

You Are the Expert

Above all, be confident in your approach and delivery—after all, you are the subject matter expert whom the sales team has decided is the appropriate

Table 16.1
SMARTI: Goal Setting with Executives

Specific	Each goal should have a specific key result.
Measurable	If possible, state the goal as something quantitative that can be measured. Qualitative functions such as behavior are difficult to measure. Avoid verbs such as know, believe, understand, and enjoy.
Attainable	The goal must be realistic. Having an executive agree to sign a contract upon first contact is not achievable.
Result-Oriented	The goal should be central to closing the sale.
Time-Limited	The goal should be traceable. Using "by 12/20/02" or "within 2 weeks" as the final phrase of the goal will ensure this.
Incentive	What is the executive's personal win if the outcome is what you wish for? Does this support a personal or organizational goal?

For a more detailed discussion of SMARTI, see the hint on SMARTI Goal Setting in Chapter 17.

person for this meeting. Some of our more delicate colleagues have likened some executives to ravenous dogs who can detect nervousness a half-mile away. However, now being classed as executives ourselves, we can assure you that this is not the case. Ask yourself this question: who are you more likely to listen to and believe, a nervous individual who can barely put two coherent sentences together or a steady, yet not overly confident, person who honestly believes in what he or she is saying?

If the occasion presents itself, we suggest actually giving the presentation to your manager or vice president beforehand to practice your delivery. As a matter of career advancement, it pays to have a reputation for being comfortable with the executive connection.

Execute the Meeting

Education Versus Selling

As part of goal setting for the meeting, you need to decide if your role will be one of education or selling. In our experience, you will accomplish far more and achieve a higher success rate if you intend to educate an executive rather than sell to him. Leave the direct selling to your sales counterpart, who can leverage your knowledge and abilities during the meeting.

Hint: The Magic Number Revisited

As a sports coach working with young children, one key you quickly learn is to make sure your players have a simple answer to the parental question "What did you learn in practice today?" Without stretching the analogy too far, apply this thought process to executive meetings too. Your executive should walk out of the meeting with a very clear idea of the lesson she learned by meeting with you.

Although it is possible to sell when educating an executive, it is very difficult to educate when selling to one. An educational example may be speaking about industry trends and how your proposal uniquely matches those trends and will give the prospect a competitive advantage and significant cost savings. A sales example is talking only about your company and product and why it is the best.

Presentation Ideas

Most executives are visual and tactile learners. This means that a picture or an action, as opposed to the traditional thousand words, best communicates a technical message. One standard exception to this is when you are demonstrating a product. Often you can tell an executive how something functions in response to a question rather than physically showing him. However, demonstrating a product early on in the sales cycle is fraught with danger and should only be undertaken if there is no other way to proceed to closure. No matter how well the meeting goes, you will not get a check that day, and there are so many other negative possibilities. The later in the sales cycle the executive is exposed to the details of your product or service, the more likely you are to get conceptual acceptance based on business conditions rather than some technical architecture. Refer back to Chapter 9, "Snap Demos," if you find yourself having to provide an on-demand demonstration to an executive.

CASE STUDY: THE FLYING PDA

One of the major competitive advantages of our product was the way it handled the workflow and accountability of tasks and action items. Traditionally, explaining this to an audience would take 10 to 12 heavily layered PowerPoint slides. Executives loved the concept but never grasped the reality of these functions.

One day I picked up my $400 PDA, stood in front of the VP of sales, and said, "Michael, this is a hot $2 million lead for your sales force." Then, I tossed the PDA into the air for him to catch—which thankfully he did. I asked him what would have happened if he had been out of the office, sick, or on vacation. "The lead would have dropped into the cracks," he replied. Retrieving the PDA, I handed it back to him and asked if he now had it safely in his possession. "Yes, I am now responsible for the $2 million sales lead."

I finished by stating that while our competition handled task assignment the first way, we did it the second way. "I prefer your way," Michael joked, throwing the PDA back at me. Our message had been internalized, and in the final analysis, we won the business, largely because of our workflow capabilities.

Presentation Technique

A relatively unscientific survey of over 50 executives we conducted a few years ago showed that more than 80% preferred an informal, one-to-one presentation, termed *shoulder-to-shoulder selling*, over a formal slide show. They recommended that you sit next to them and make your point using a piece of paper, brochure, or whiteboard. As an interesting corollary, executives within our own companies recommend this approach for employees trying to gain internal project approvals!

Another common theme, unanimously voiced during our research, was that executives want to feel that you have prepared for the meeting (even if they haven't). Expectations are that you understand their business, their terminology, and at least some of their processes. In short, a little research goes a long way. Even at the start of a sales cycle, you must prepare adequately for any executive session. If your salesperson cannot brief you before such a meeting or insists on doing so in the lobby 15 minutes beforehand, that is a major red flag.

Follow Up After the Meeting

Building a Relationship

Over the years, you can build up a Rolodex full of executives with whom you have had meetings. There is no reason, especially if you truly are a subject matter expert, why you cannot offer to make yourself available at a later date should an executive need more data or have more questions. Perhaps one time in five, you will receive a follow-up call, giving you the opportunity to build a relationship that can help both your immediate and your future career.

Remember also that if you are in the business long enough, all the managers and directors you meet with will eventually get promoted. One of the authors of this book remains on good terms with a programming manager he first met 20 years ago, who is now the CIO and executive vice president of a major U.S. company.

A Rational Decision

As an SE, one of the hardest things to accept is that, although you may have won the technical battle and the evaluation team tells you that you are their number one pick, the deal can still be lost. Many executive decisions are still stereotypically made on an exclusive golf course or over an expensive dinner. This is outside the realm of the average SE and can be very frustrating to watch. We can only advise that the deal is not done until the paperwork is signed—so be vigilant. This process can work for and against you. In a previous career, one of us won a deal at a financial-services corporation he thought had been lost because his company offered to move its 401(k) retirement accounts, which represented a sizable opportunity for the customer.

The Informal Executive Connection

Be prepared to encounter executives from all companies in various mundane settings, such as on planes, in airport terminals, at your children's soccer games, in line at Starbucks, and even at local parties (remember executives are people too!).

A social conversation may at some point include, "Whom do you work for?" or "What line of business are you in?" Whether you work for a Fortune 100 name-brand company or a small startup, always respond with your company name, followed by a short and catchy, one-sentence tagline. The subsequent conversation may then go anywhere and will usually result in a purely social interaction. If, however, you receive a response along the lines of "And how does your company do that?" you should have a short 60- to 90-second executive elevator pitch prepared, once you have ascertained who your conversational friend really is.

Don't be shy about waxing on regarding your product in this 60 to 90 seconds. It is socially acceptable for anyone to be an "alpha" example of his species for that period, and you may make a spontaneous connection with a decision maker. In the worst case, he may change the topic of conversation. Be prepared to exchange business cards and even agree to an e-mail follow-up. You should also be prepared to drop the subject and redirect the conversation back toward soccer or coffee as the situation dictates.

CASE STUDY: A BACK OF THE NAPKIN PRESENTATION

> I once worked for a company that sold hundreds of different enterprise software products and wasn't particularly well known as a market leader in any area. The company featured solutions in the arenas of IT infrastructure management, security, and governance. After several confusing attempts at explaining exactly what our company did, I settled on the analogy of a house—an object everyone is familiar with. While drawing a picture of a house, I explained that our management products monitored and measured utilities such as water, gas, and electricity, making sure, via thermostats, fuses, and suchlike, that the house continued to function as the owners required. Security products locked the doors and windows and provided an alarm system and smoke and CO detectors, thereby ensuring the safety of the occupants and their property. Our governance products ensured that everyday maintenance was performed, permits applied for, taxes paid, and so on. The analogy was an instant hit, especially when executives extended the story by drawing in security gates, closed-circuit cameras, and building extensions!

Summary

More than any other meeting, an executive session needs to be highly focused. Stay on message and on target. Use the executive rule of two to keep the presentation simple, and remember your two key talking points. Respect the person as well as the position, and value the executive's time. Avoid long demonstrations or presentations, and, in most cases, key in on the business benefits and return on investment executives will receive by purchasing from you.

Above all, prepare, plan, and prepare again for the meeting, keeping in mind your goals and objectives for the session.

Skill Building

New SE	1. Be prepared. Practice giving your presentation in half the allotted time.
	2. Try to avoid an early executive demo or defer to a senior SE.
	3. Remember the executive rule of two.
	4. Keep it simple. For a large account, practice with one of your executives.
	5. Set your meeting goals early.
Experienced SE	1. Examine the financials.
	2. Map your product benefits back to dollars.
	3. Focus on your key points.
	4. Focus on building relationships, particularly for CIOs.

The *U* in Technical Sales

No one can drive us crazy unless we give them the keys.

Doug Horton

The wonderful thing about being in technical sales is that no day, in fact, no task, is ever the same. Customers always want something new and different. You have the flexibility to do your job as you see fit, subject to actually getting the job done. This means you can inject a lot of your personality into the position in the way you deal both with prospects and with the rest of the sales team. This flexibility also makes it easy to become lazy about managing your career. In this chapter, we talk about technical sales as a career and how you can make the most of it. We also discuss ethics and provide reasons why personal ethics are critical to long-term success in sales.

Me, Myself, and I

You must always remember that you are the only person who can manage your career. Good managers know they can get more out of you if your career goals are aligned with what you actually do at work. Unfortunately, many sales managers are only concerned with meeting the quarter's number. Your challenge is to meet your quarterly revenue goal while still progressing toward your long-term aspirations. By striking a balance between meeting your own goals and those of the company, you will make progress toward your ambitions while satisfying your management.

What Are Your Goals?

Discovering what your goals are can be the toughest part of achieving them. In this chapter, we discuss a standard approach to becoming a leader in a product-focused SE organization. Work with your manager to determine how to best customize this approach to your situation.

You will also have long-term goals with which your manager will be less able to help. Based on the number of interviewers who ask, "Where do you hope to be in 5 years?" you would think more people would have an answer. Don't feel badly if you haven't developed a master career plan—yet. Being in sales provides opportunities to interact with senior management and, in turn, to refine your long-term goals. However, you should have a list of well-defined short-term goals. If you don't, build one based on your answers to the following questions:

▸ What do I hope to learn from my current position?

▸ What skills or experiences do I need to build for my next job?

Before proceeding, write down the answers to these questions, as well as any other high-level professional goals you have for the next 2 years. We will use these goals to establish your personal brand statement and to discuss developing a plan to achieve these goals.

Hint: SMARTI Goal Setting

Goal setting generally refers to developing a set of written statements that identify your aspirations, outline the necessary steps to achieve each, and finally motivate you as you go about the hard work associated with each goal. As you progress through the chapter and begin to identify your goals, keep the following criteria in mind. After you have written down your goals, consider rewording them based on the criteria. They will help you to develop an attainable plan. Goals should be:

Specific: Is each goal narrow enough that you can apply the criteria that follow to it? If your goal is specific, it may also detail some of the tactics you will employ to achieve it. For example, "Close three or four $1 million deals at Clorox, the Gap, Charles Schwab, and Ford Motor Company by December, overachieving quota by 20% and qualifying me for the club trip to Hawaii."

Measurable: Will you know when you have completed the goal? For quota-related goals, this is simple to measure. For career-growth goals, try to identify quantifiable characteristics by which to evaluate yourself. For skill-related goals, you can always use subjective benchmarking to help you compare your abilities to those of your competition.

Achievable: Given the skills and resources at your disposal, can you complete the goal?

Realistic: Is this a realistic goal for you? Do you need to break the goal into intermediate goals? Consider breaking big goals up into two or three portions. This will help keep the goals relevant and current.

Time limited: Assign a date by which you hope to accomplish the goal. This will help with motivation and with prioritizing the activities in support of the goal.

Incentive oriented: Mention the incentive or motivation for your goal in the goal statement itself. Make it something that really excites you. For example, "Read one industry or technical book every 2 months to improve my consultative selling skills and increase my revenue." If this is a subgoal, consider making the incentive a reward you purchase for yourself in recognition of the achievement.

Sometimes your goals will not fit nicely into a short statement that meets the criteria above. Don't try to force it; use whatever works for you. Used properly, goal setting can help you build concrete action plans, provide motivation, and improve your communication with your mentors and your spouse.

Your Personal Value Proposition: Self-Branding

Self-branding is the act of identifying what differentiates you from others like you and making those characteristics clear to the professionals with whom you interact. This means that you define and communicate the niche you fill better than any competitor. By doing so, you will be better able to compete with generalists and, therefore, to command a higher salary or get a promotion. Review your goals and think of three adjectives or characteristics that would be applicable to the person who could meet those goals.

A good way to think of this is as a *sound bite*. We will refer to this sound bite as your *personal value proposition* (PVP). The PVP should be specific and reflect how you add unique value, such as "sales engineer who knows the most about the automotive industry in the mid-Atlantic region." This statement is good because it clearly communicates how you add value (by better knowing the business of automotive manufacturers), as well as because it is specific enough that you can judge whether or not it is true. You could start with "the SE who knows the most about the automotive industry," but this may not be true. What about the German SEs who sell to BMW and Mercedes? You may later determine that you are the best or most knowledgeable worldwide, but you can only do this by first establishing your value or position at a more specific level. You may even have different PVPs for internal and external use.

Internal Branding

Think about the value of a PVP like "the SE who knows the most about the automotive industry." If you become known as the "go-to person" for automotive deals, then you are going to be the primary person for any important issue related to that area of expertise. In a sales situation, this will usually mean that you will get involved in the largest deals. Side benefits include being the person that marketing, engineering, and others call to discuss the needs of that particular market. This can be a valuable position because it gives you additional contacts in the organization.

External Branding

How do you want to be perceived externally? "Professional," "responsive," and "knowledgeable" might all be words you would like to have associated with your "brand." Every new customer is both a new opportunity and a new challenge to put your brand into practice. It can be difficult to find areas in which you add unique value for a customer, but it is certainly well worth the effort. Such areas may include anything from your grasp of technology to established relationships with systems integrators. Try to establish yourself as the person to go to if a customer has a specific need, be it for wireless applications or guaranteed project delivery within 90 days. Establish your position, and you will be in excellent shape the next time you need to use a customer as a reference to help you in a deal.

Your reputation will allow you personally to play a part that other salespeople can't. In reality, it can be very difficult to establish this type of reputation and credibility. If you are isolated within a specific geography, this is much easier because previous customers can help refer and promote you based on past successes.

If you cover a large geography, you will need more external validation to occupy such a space. Consider trying to speak at conferences or write magazine articles if your sights are set on extremely broad coverage. The larger the pool you are competing in, the better you must be. In most cases, it is better to be a big fish in a small pond than just another fish in the sea.

Communicating Your Personal Value Proposition

Once you have an idea of how you can brand and differentiate yourself, run it past the best people you know in that area. Even if you know these people well, take a few minutes to walk them through your background. Describe your achievements and capabilities, and ask them if they think your value proposition fits. If they don't, then they should be able to give you some good guidance on how you can become an expert in your chosen area. Ask them for specifics as to how you can improve your resume to justify that type of reputation. Also, they may think the fit is not right because you haven't done a good job of communicating your expertise in past interactions, so you must set about correcting that misperception.

After validating your branding statements, it is critical that you reinforce them in your dealings with other employees as well as customers. During introductions is a great time to do this. When you introduce yourself at the beginning of a meeting, you frequently have an opportunity to explain what you do or why you are present. Be sure to mention that you have been invited to the meeting not just because you are the local salesperson but because you are the local expert in your field.

- *Bad example:* "Hello, I'm Jim Doe from Acme. I'm your local SE, and I hope we will be working together."

- *Good example:* "Hello, I'm Bill Blank. I'm Acme's financial-services specialist in Sydney. I've helped some of your largest competitors improve the quality of service they deliver to their customers, and I hope I can help you do the same."

Don't be shy about sharing this valuable information. Not only does it help reinforce your stature, but you are also giving other people concise data about how you can help them. If introduced to the two salespeople described above, which would you call with a question about current products applicable to the financial-services industry? These introductions may sound a little "canned," but with some practice and feedback from the rest of the sales team, you can learn how to hit the right points in one or two sentences to start new relationships off on the best footing possible.

Delivering on Your Value Proposition

Put Together the Plan

Put together a list of the items necessary to make your PVP a reality. If you don't know what you need to do to get there, go back to your manager or mentors for advice. Table 17.1 shows a sample plan for the Bill Blank example above. The table lists claims, evidence, and actions. Bill is attempting to cover the entire spectrum of business, technical, and financial issues for his industry. This is probably more expertise than most individuals will have, but his example should overlap significantly with any sales position. For each area in which you seek to differentiate yourself, identify the evidence required to prove your superiority. Each piece of evidence may require different action items for you to complete. You may already possess many of the skills or experiences you identify. Write them all down and then compare yourself to your competition. Remember that you will be able to best differentiate yourself as a salesperson if you can articulate specifically how you are superior to the competition and how that capability benefits your customer.

Put Your Plan Into Action

Share your plan with your manager and begin building the skills and experiences you have identified. Most companies have programs that will subsidize the following:

▸ Training classes;

▸ Periodical subscriptions;

▸ MBA classes;

▸ Membership in professional societies.

Take advantage of the resources you have available. Work with your manager to schedule training appropriately throughout the year, and put the rest of the items in your *downtime file*. Work on the downtime file when you are traveling or have quiet periods. (See the "Using Downtime Efficiently" hint in Chapter 26 for further details.)

Hint: Prioritizing the Action Plan

When you are looking at the overall set of tasks you need to complete for your PVP, how should you factor in the items from your action plan? The obvious answer is that you should only consider an item important if it is part of the action plan for delivering your quota commitment. Many of the items that show up on your plan, and which are

Table 17.1
Personal Value Proposition and Steps to Achieve

Claim 1: **Deep domain expertise in financial services**

- *Evidence 1:* Understanding of financial-services business issues.

  Action 1: Research financial-services industry.

  Action 2: Interact with financial-services business executives to understand their concerns.

- *Evidence 2:* Understanding of legacy and technical issues in financial-services environment.

  Action 1: Research financial-services technical issues.

  Action 2: Consider joining relevant industry organizations dedicated to financial-services standards or technical discussions.

Claim 2: **Mastery of relevant technologies for total solution**

- *Evidence 1:* Mastery of technology required for products the company sells.

  Action 1: Master demonstration setup and delivery.

  Action 2: Pass demonstration certification.

- *Evidence 2:* Indepth knowledge of technology, standards, and architecture.

  Action 1: Take C++ class at local college.

  Action 2: Take developer class from the company.

  Action 3: Become a certified developer for the company's products.

- *Evidence 3:* Knowledge of the capabilities of competitive and partner solutions.

  Action 1: Attend at least one trade show per year.

  Action 2: Subscribe to relevant newsletters and magazines for the financial-services industry—both technology publications and business publications.

  Action 3: Write a one-page competitive summary of a primary competitor's product once per quarter as information is gained from the actions described above.

necessary to support your PVP, you will have to work on when business is slow. Does this mean that your PVP and plan are useless when you are starting a new job or working 70 hours a week? Not at all. You can use the goals and actions you have identified to help you decide between different courses of action or even different potential customers. The understanding of where your skills lie today and where they will be tomorrow is very relevant to what business you can win now and which client engagements may help you build the skills you need for the future.

Career Progression and the PVP

If you develop a PVP, break it out into an action plan, and diligently pursue those activities, you will find your skills progressing and maturing much more quickly than they otherwise would. At some point, you may even begin to become complacent and think about your next career steps. Use the method described above to put together a PVP for the person you would need to be to justify that new position. Work with friends and mentors to clarify the pitch and the steps you will need to take to develop the skills to back it up.

Hint: Seek Out a Mentor

If your company does not have a formal mentoring program, you should seek out a mentor to help you develop and grow. Identify potential mentors by observing those around you, looking for someone who has the right balance of technical and interpersonal skills. Do not limit your search to just presales, as you can also find a mentor in the ranks of sales and marketing. You may even find a mentor outside of your company if you are seeking guidance on skills such as leadership or creativity. A Catalyst report published in 2004 determined that those employees with a mentor were 40% more likely to be promoted over a 3-year period than those without one.

The difference between this type of planning and that already discussed is the need to position yourself for that future job. If you do not have management experience, you will not be the ideal candidate for a management position. Instead, look to substitute current capabilities for the holes in your background. In sales, lack of management experience is usually mitigated by past individual success and the promise that you will impart that success to the team that you manage. So, find out what the key substitutes are for the skills you cannot develop in your current position and work twice as hard to be outstanding in those areas. You should also remember that you are part of the sales organization and need to be prepared to convince someone to take a leap of faith to offer you your first management position.

Benchmarking

Once you have put together your list of claims, evidence, and actions, place an item on your schedule once per quarter to benchmark yourself against your competition. Your competition may be internal (e.g., other employees eligible for promotion) or external (e.g., other sales teams). Be honest with yourself. If you feel there is room for improvement regarding one of the skills you are working toward, focus even harder on that aspect of your development. You will find that this reasoned introspection will keep you at the top of your game and help you to articulate your strengths to others.

Ethics in Sales

At some point in your career, you will face an ethical dilemma. A typical issue would entail telling a customer the truth when doing so may hurt your ability to win a sale. It is helpful to think through these issues ahead of time to determine how you might respond to them. As a salesperson, you must maintain a high level of integrity in every interaction you have with customers, other employees, and even competitors. It is impossible to know when you will work again with or for someone whom you have treated poorly previously. So, even if you are the least ethical person imaginable, a definite cost is associated with any moral lapse you might experience as part of chasing a deal. Our first rule of sales ethics is this: *never, ever lie.*

If someone catches you in a lie, you should not expect that person ever to trust you again. Additionally, if another employee hears you lie to a customer, though he may sympathize with your current business goal, it will impact how he treats you in the future. No one would choose to deal with a dishonest professional.

But what is a lie? Most frequently, this issue comes up regarding issues of solution functionality. Perhaps you told the customer that something was available, then later found out that it wasn't or that the product had been canceled. In this case, you should definitely make a point of notifying the customer that you were incorrect in your earlier communication. Sometimes you inadvertently "lie" by telling the customer that your system does something, provided that some other activity happens. This other activity may include purchase of another product, payment for another service or implementation, or the availability of other resources. The tough question is how to determine which of these situations are trivial and which are significant and could impact your customer's ability to succeed.

In general, if it is going to affect their costs, time, or the probability of their project's success, you should raise the issue. If the issue means that there will be an extra $5,000 in costs for a $2 million project, then it is probably not worth mentioning. If, however, you end up with fifty $5,000 add-ons, then your credibility may be in danger. A good rule of thumb is that if your company would be willing to pay for the difference in cost (without penalizing your revenue contribution), it may not be necessary to raise the problem to your customer. The real issue is being able to operate without perfect information. Your job is to help craft technical solutions that solve real-world needs. Speak with your coworkers, managers, and even current customers to help you determine a reasonable level of information or certainty.

Your company, industry, and position will likely have other unique ethical questions. As you come across these problems, talk to your peers to find out how others have responded. In cases related to product issues, you should communicate the problems back to the engineering or marketing organization, which may be able to perform studies or cost justifications to help provide additional guidance to customers. For ethical concerns not related to your company's products, you should apply the second rule of sales ethics: *treat the people you sell to today as if they are the people you will sell to tomorrow.*

Remember these two rules, and you won't risk injuring your relationship with your customer or doing something with which you are not comfortable.

Summary

Regardless of what role you hold in an organization, you have much to gain by actively managing your career. Identify your personal goals and branding. Build a plan that will reinforce those points, helping you to add more value to your customer interactions and your corporation's abilities. Craft a personal value proposition that lets new employees or new prospects know exactly how you differ from other salespeople in your position. Use this pitch frequently and consistently, and watch your personal stock soar as you gain a reputation as the go-to person in your area of expertise.

If you plan on staying in sales long, ethical behavior is mandatory. By maintaining a high degree of ethics and pursuing your personal differentiation plan, you can rest assured that your customers and colleagues will hold you in high regard.

Skill Building

| All | Regardless of your level, the lessons of this chapter hold true. Define how you add unique value to your customers and to your company. Hold a personal review every 3 months, benchmark aggressively, and seek out a mentor. If you manage people, challenge them to rise to the same level of introspection and look for a junior-level SE to mentor. Share the concepts from this chapter and help that person build plans to reach his or her goals and identify unique personal value propositions. |

Selling with Partners

The most important central fact about a free market is that no exchange takes place unless both parties benefit.

Milton Friedman

Partners who resell your products and services can be the best of friends or the worst of enemies. Partners are one of the most effective tools in the SE's arsenal when you're looking to advance an opportunity through the sales cycle, but they bring an additional stakeholder to the table, whose needs must be satisfied if they are to help you in turn.

Partnership Defined

A *partnership* can be loosely defined as a functional relationship between two or more entities working toward the common good. An alternate view was expressed by Howard Sorgen, former CTO of Merrill Lynch, who once defined vendor partnership as "that large sucking sound when money is transferred from my wallet into yours."

There are many different kinds of partners: those who resell your products directly, those who build their products on top of yours, and those who do not directly sell but recommend your products to prospects. There is no question that partners provide additional leverage to the sales force. Instead of just having your sales organization selling, you also benefit from having another, potentially larger organization also selling on your behalf. For the majority of this chapter, we focus on channel/system integrator (SI) partners because they typically provide the most opportunity for additional revenue.

Hint: The Effective Partnership

As cynical as it may sound, very early in the partner-engagement process, you need to uncover the "what's in it for me" aspect for your technical counterpart. This is a relationship you need to build constantly, whether or not any more immediate sales opportunities are in the pipeline.

As an SE, having an engaged partner for an opportunity opens up a world of possibilities. You may now have access to demonstration centers, hardware, software, and other resources that were previously unavailable. On the downside, you may have to invest considerable time in the training and education of your chosen partner.

Particularly in small organizations, a disparity may exist between partners the sales representative may choose for an opportunity compared to your choices. Given the freedom to make the decision, a rep will select partners on the basis of account access (i.e., being introduced to the CIO), whereas an SE will select partners based on technical and business fit. For this reason, partner selection should be undertaken near the start of the sales cycle when you are conducting account planning and strategy, and most modern sales methodologies now support this. Selecting the correct partner will impact the outcome of the opportunity, and the entire sales team should approve the choice.

A third option is the political fit, based on the outcome of a meeting between two vice presidents who decide that they will partner on the next opportunity no matter what. Usually a fait accompli, this happens more often than you would expect, so make the most of the situation—at least you can count on some executive support!

Defining Account Ownership

Salespeople spend considerable time debating who "owns" an account. Ownership is determined by which organization sets the strategy, leads the sale, and has the final say on account decisions. This is traditionally based on who brings whom into the deal. For example, if you are working an opportunity and determine your cause would be better served by partnering with another company whose products or services amplify yours, then you bring them into the deal. When a large SI is bidding on a project and asks you to participate, then they are bringing you into the deal.

CASE STUDY: BE CAREFUL WHO YOUR PARTNERS ARE

> We were pursuing a large opportunity with an office-supply company on the West Coast. One of the "Big Four" consulting companies was running both the evaluation and the business-process analysis. The Big Four company was scrupulously neutral and treated each of the three vendors equally. We decided to partner with two smaller software companies that sold overlay products on top of our main system. One of these companies had an exclusive arrangement with us; the other worked with us because we were the first to ask and were probably the best positioned in the account.
>
> At one point during the sales cycle, it looked like we were being placed third out of three. One partner stuck with us, redoubled their efforts, and came up with an alternate strategy that proved very effective. The second partner, without the slightest hesitation, went behind our back and proposed their solution directly to the prospect, claiming it would work with whichever main vendor they selected.
>
> Thanks to the work of our first, loyal partner, we won the opportunity. The prospect issued purchase orders to the two of us but omitted the other partner who went behind our back. The prospect felt that this other partner could not be trusted and refused to do business with them.

The other general rule of engagement you need to be aware of is remaining faithful to your partner. In effect, once the partnership is declared, you should not work with competitors, submit independent bids, or take any action to break the partnership. Practically speaking, this engagement model holds until the prospect selects one partner but not the other. We cannot recommend strongly enough that you scrupulously follow these rules of engagement. "Cheating" on a partner can significantly diminish your reputation. Word will spread, possibly impacting your future sales and career.

During the research phase of writing this book, we discovered that everyone has a different opinion about the pluses and minuses of dealing with small or large partners. Many respondents warned SEs to watch their backs with smaller companies because they tend to be more opportunistic when a large opportunity presents itself. Others felt that larger companies are less trustworthy, either because multiple divisions are competing against one another politically or simply due to their size in relation to most vendors.

From an SE viewpoint, being the prime account owner gives you access to additional resources to complete demos, RFPs, discovery sessions, and so forth. Do not be afraid to ask for help or advice from your partners—just make sure you retain control over the timeline and final deliverables. A large part of your time may be spent coordinating third parties as opposed to actually selling. On a recent opportunity in which we participated, the SE had to coordinate 13 different companies—down to the level of deciding which PowerPoint format to use.

CASE STUDY: WHEN A PARTNER IS NOT A PARTNER

Midway through the sales cycle with a strategic account, we needed to participate in a full-day scripted demonstration and presentation of our software solution. The audience consisted of 20 staff members from the prospect and 3 or 4 consultants from the Big Four SI who was running the show for them. During the lunch break, one of our managers noticed that two members of the audience were equipped with an excessive amount of IBM paraphernalia. A brief discussion over coffee revealed that these two individuals were from IBM Global Services and were technology advisors to the client.

Later that afternoon, we came to a session on product futures that required a reminder about the legalities of the nondisclosure agreement (NDA) we had all signed. The sales manager, as per standard practice, asked if everyone in the room was both covered by the NDA and an employee of either the prospect or the Big Four consulting company. The two individuals at the back raised their hands. Not only were they not covered by the NDA, but they also actually worked for a business unit of IBM that implemented our competitor's product. A "partner" whose compensation was driven by selling the services of our number one competitor was actually advising our prospect!

If you are acting as the primary ("prime") point of contact, the customer will expect you to coordinate all facets of the solution, including project-managing all other partners. Running an opportunity as prime also affords you a tremendous amount of leverage with your partners, allowing you to stockpile favors for the future. Although the marketing department may release a horde of press releases announcing cooperative reseller agreements, this PR is turned into reality at the field level. No amount of "Barney marketing" (I love you, you love me) can build up the massive goodwill generated by a successful transaction yielding revenue for your partners.

Working the Relationship and Building the Infrastructure

The downside of selling with partners is that they need to be trained, supported, and updated on a regular basis. This is without doubt a high-maintenance activity. Mature sales organizations will have a dedicated partners group that includes specialized SEs and deals exclusively with external partners. Smaller organizations may have no such group or may only have business-relationship managers with no technical resources of their own. This places added stress on the SEs because they will be then responsible for all pre- and postsales activities with the partners at the field level.

CASE STUDY: THE LEVERAGED LUNCH

At Sybase, we owned the New York financial-services database market in the mid-1990s. One of the noticeable impacts of such a dominant market share was that *everyone* wanted to partner with us. We had so many requests for meetings, seminars, trade shows, and joint campaigns that Frank, the sales manager, and I were becoming overwhelmed. We instituted a program for Monday lunchtimes called the "leveraged lunch." Because Mondays were typically office days for handling conference calls and performing account reviews, a high proportion of the sales team was usually present. In return for providing lunch for our sales team, a (potential) partner would come into the office and present for an hour. We would exchange both sales leads and business cards, and joint strategies for penetrating new accounts would be put into place.

The sales representatives were rather blasé about the whole program until we suddenly got a $400,000 deal out of nowhere from one of our leveraged lunches. Within a week, we had lunches booked out for 4 months and partners begging us to be included in the program. Instead of putting off partners, our reps and SEs had a direction and a program to follow. I instituted an annual management by objective (MBO) for each SE to become an "application ambassador" for at least two third-party add-on products each year.

Frank and I still conducted our own partner relationships outside of the Monday events, but the leveraged lunch proved to be a great success and was copied in many cities throughout the sales force the following year. Our third-party revenue stream increased from less than 5% during the prior year to more than 20% during the leveraged lunch year.

As an SE, you need to balance the needs of local partners against the direct sales opportunities you are pursuing. We recommend that, unless one partner stands out from the crowd, you be opportunistic in nature. Look at your target market, identify likely partners, and proactively engage them before any sales opportunities arise. Remember that consulting companies live and die by billable hours, so you may need to build the relationship before and after standard business hours.

Hint: Beware of Multiple Partners Within a Partnership

Once you have engaged in an opportunity with an SI Partner, make sure you are dealing with the correct internal partner (or managing director). Focus predominately upon the partner (or senior manager) who is actually on the ground at the customer site and less on the corporate-relationship partner or manager of the SI. If you ignore the partner team making the bid, you will get lost in the corporate shuffle and politics of both the large SI and your own company.

It is likely that your partners have little knowledge of your product and value proposition. Handing over a pile of manuals and marketing glossies is useful for background material but serves no immediate purpose. For initial meetings with a partner, the SE should provide the following, independently of the sales representative:

- A personalized, one-page elevator speech that the partner can learn;
- A bulleted list of business problems solved;
- High-level technical requirements;
- A "whom to call" list;
- A summary of likely competitors.

You also need to set expectations about support and response time. As an SE, you lead a busy life and will be out of the office for long periods. It is unreasonable to expect you to respond like a support hotline, so it is important to set the ground rules up front. You will notice other partners doing the same with you. When asked to present your product internally, qualify the quality and quantity of the proposed audience. Aim for high-profile events such as regional or national sales meetings or even user-group meetings.

Partner relations make for an excellent MBO if these are part of your compensation package. You receive a short-term monetary bonus and also reap the benefits of the long-term relationship.

From a managerial aspect, the requirements of partner management can be overwhelming for a small SE team, especially if there is no corporate infrastructure on which to fall back. It is difficult for the field SE to see the benefits of a partner relationship, given the quarterly nature of revenue-rich opportunities. As the manager, you need to plan, in conjunction with the sales manager, your partner approach. Shutting out partners entirely until you absolutely need them will restrict long-term growth and, even in the short term, can cause fewer deals to enter the pipeline if you develop a reputation as hard to work with. Too heavy a focus can deprive the sales force of necessary SE resources at crucial times. For a young organization, this is a delicate balancing act. Within larger organizations, the politics around the partner channel often result in massive shifts in strategy every 12 to 18 months, causing a partner-friendly organization to become partner neutral or even partner hostile, then to swing back to accommodating partners in the next management cycle. As a business-savvy SE, you should maintain your partner contacts and relationships regardless of the current corporate strategy.

A common approach, whether a partner organization is in place or not, is to tier your partners—categorizing them as gold, silver, and bronze partners, for example. Gold represents your premier partners, who receive the bulk of available resources. Silver partners qualify for a quarterly update and invitations to local user groups and marketing events. Bronze partners only receive resources when a live opportunity is being actively pursued.

In the long term, almost every sales organization sets up a parallel partner-relations organization. Initially comprising business-development managers and a marketing manager, specialized SEs are rapidly added as the resource requirements climb and the field SE managers complain. Our advice, which we expand on in Chapter 23, is to set up a centralized SE group that handles both partner and analyst (business and financial) relations.

The Dangers of Dealing with Partners

As we have already discussed, partners bring their own agendas to any sales cycle. You must build specific concerns into the partnership to make sure that it remains a win-win proposition. First, we consider *share of wallet* and then the *hidden relationship*.

Share of wallet refers to the amount of the total capital budget your product is capable of capturing. An IT department may often have a fixed amount budgeted for a new system. From their perspective, the "system" will actually consist of multiple products plus the system-integration effort. A simple scenario might be as follows:

▸ *Capital budget:* $2 million;

▸ *Cost of Solution A:* $400,000;

▸ *Cost of Solution B:* $400,000;

▸ *Cost of system implementation and integration:* $800,000;

▸ *Cost of hardware:* $400,000.

If you are selling Solution A, you must be careful to ensure that your value proposition is strong enough to justify the purchase of your product and to prevent the partner from "stealing" the budget for your solution. A common example of this situation is one in which Solution A has a weak return on investment (ROI), and Solution B has a strong one. In this case, the salesman for Solution B can argue that the prospect should really spend $400,000 on Solution B and perhaps shift an additional $200,000 to Solution B add-ons in light of their superior ROI. Earlier in this book, we discussed the benefit a senior SE can bring to contracts and negotiations by discovering the true value added for all solutions. This is a perfect situation in which an SE's knowledge can help preserve sales margin.

Hidden motivations and relationships are another danger you must face when dealing with partnerships. Did someone on the partner's sales team go to school with a member of the competitor's sales team? Is there a corporate relationship or revenue-sharing agreement in place? If the answer to either of these questions is yes, you can be sure that the partner will not be acting wholly in your best interest. The only way to mitigate this risk is to perform the research to determine that it is absolutely in the partner's best interests that you win the deal. Research may consist of consulting other sales teams who have worked with this company or talking to the partner sales team to find out how they are compensated, what they expect to get out of the deal, and so forth. In the spirit of simplicity and directness, there is nothing wrong with asking your technical counterparts about any conflicts of interest.

CASE STUDY: THE PROBLEMATIC PARTNER AND THE POWER LUNCH

We were trying to sell to a major retailer who had hired a large consulting firm to handle the product evaluation. Our company had a corporate relationship with the consultants, but so did the competitor. We were extremely concerned that the partner in charge might favor our competitor and perhaps tip the recommendation to them because of that preexisting relationship.

The real situation was a bit more complex. As we began to proceed through the sales process, we were allowed more interaction with the customer. They had extremely complex requirements, and we had to fly some of our best people from corporate out to help the customer come up with an implementation plan. As we worked with the customer, the consultants also sent in a team to keep an eye on us and to make sure things went smoothly. Over the course of a few days, we began to develop personal relationships with these consultants. We learned that their Chicago and New York offices were jointly staffing the project because each had specific expertise this customer needed. This also meant that there were actually two managing partners (MPs) who needed to be sold on our solution. This complicated things quite a bit.

We found we were able to make good progress with one MP, whereas the other was more difficult to work with. During one of the technical-planning sessions, our team casually invited the consultant's project team to Wendy's for lunch. The team told us we were in hot water because the New York MP had signed a reseller agreement with our competitor. The MP would get almost 10% of the final cost of our competitor's product. Aside from being a huge breach of ethics, this would make it very easy for the MP to recommend our competitor's solution. In the end, we struck a similar deal with both the New York and Chicago MPs; plus, we threw in additional training to ensure that the partners would have sufficient staff to begin working on the project on day one. Though we won the deal, we may not have if we hadn't had that "power lunch" at Wendy's.

Summary

Handled appropriately, partners can give your sales force tremendous leverage. The initial investment of time and resources, although hard to justify, will be repaid in the long term as your partners find more uncontested business for you.

Utilize all resources available to you from your partners, operating on the principle that "if you don't ask, you don't get." Establish contacts within the technical and business ranks of your partners, and value them as you would customers. Develop a personal plan for handling partner requests, rather than dealing with them ad hoc or having them handed down from your manager. Remember that someone within your organization is probably being paid to channel business through the partners. Seek out this individual, and use his or her contacts. Above all, be honest and straightforward in your dealings with partners.

Skill Building

New SE	1. Assemble the key components for partner education.
	2. Develop a personal strategy for partner interaction.
	3. Cultivate technical and business contacts within partners.
	4. Set expectations for support response times.
Experienced SE	1. Adopt several key partners and become their "go-to" field person.
	2. When looking for promotion opportunities, propose to start up an SE partner team.
	3. Seek out speaking engagements at partner conferences.

19

Chapter Goals

Be able to identify, neutralize, and ultimately defeat your competition.

Develop a competitive strategy from a technology viewpoint.

Understand how your competition sells.

Competitive Tactics

An organization's ability to learn, and translate that learning into action rapidly, is the ultimate competitive advantage.

Jack Welch

Almost every sales opportunity involves some element of competition. Frequently, you are fighting your biggest competitor for the right to convert a prospect into a paying customer. Throughout this book, we have been preaching the merits of selling a solution and proposing the value of that solution to executives as high up the corporate ladder as you can reach. However, on many occasions, the competitive environment will resemble hand-to-hand combat, despite the merits of solution selling. Though we all like to think that the team presenting the best return on investment (ROI) will win, this is not always the case—and that is precisely the environment this chapter discusses.

Identify the Competition

Although you spend a significant proportion of the sales cycle developing and proposing your own solution, it is important to understand your competitors. Typically, you will compete against anywhere from one to three main competitors again and again, as well as against dozens of point solution competitors that you will encounter only once or twice a year. Just as no professional sports team would ever play a match without scouting the competition, any competent sales organization must do the same. Try one or more of the following approaches to help identify your competition for an account.

First and foremost, just ask the prospect for the names of companies against which you will be competing. On occasion, especially if a third party is involved, this request may be denied. It is then time to get creative and pursue other options:

- Check the cc: list on outgoing e-mails from the prospect.
- Check the visitor log at the customer site.
- Watch for literature, samples, or manuals from your competition on the prospect's desk.
- Keep asking every contact at the prospect.
- Request the information from any third-party consultants who may be working on site.
- Review the document property tags of any e-mail attachments you receive.

Sometimes, despite your best efforts, you cannot get a full list of competitors, so at that point you will need to make an educated guess.

Develop a Competitive Strategy

A competitive strategy must be both focused and consistent. Early in the sales cycle, you should know enough about the opportunity to develop a strengths, weaknesses, opportunities, and threats (SWOT) matrix for each major competitor. At the risk of stating the obvious, we remind you to complete one for your product too. The best approach is to gather the sales team, draw a matrix on a whiteboard, and then brainstorm. Keep all the ideas, no matter how poor they may be, and then pick the top three in each category.

It is important to sell your strengths, especially if your competitors are weak in those areas. Tie each strength back to its business or technical importance to the prospect. One way or another, every strength leads back to either the creation or saving of dollars—increasing revenue or decreasing costs. These strengths should have associated sound bites that each member of the sales team repeatedly uses throughout the sale. Think of this as a way to brand your own product solution set. Use power words such as "fast," "reliable," and "proven." Similarly, brand your competition with adjectives like "slow," "complex," "unproven," and "difficult."

Differentiate between financial and strategic benefits. Strategic benefits often appeal more to the technician because they are "neat and tidy." For example, your product or service might fit perfectly into the prospect's technical architecture and be an excellent long-term strategic fit. These benefits are often tough to quantify, and the high-tech industry is littered with wreckage of companies that chose to compete on the basis of open, scalable architectures. A financial benefit has immediate dollars associated with it. Bear in mind the old English hunting proverb "A bird in the hand is worth two in the bush"—a hard dollar saved today is frequently preferred to two soft dollars saved next year. Even when you are being drawn into a feature-function war, it is still important to stress the financial benefits, because your competitor is unlikely to be doing so. Somewhere within the prospect's organization there is an executive who cares about ROI. It is your sales team's job to find that executive.

During creation of the strategy, you must be brutally honest about your capabilities. Discard anything that sounds like "marketing drivel" or "corporate fluff" because an objective assessment of the situation is crucial. Should the opportunity really lie in your sweet spot, then attack it at full force—often referred to as the *frontal approach*. Knowing that you have the product, services, technology, and references needed to beat the competition, fully engage the prospect with the assumption that you expect to win the business. As an SE, your primary jobs are to keep the technical buyers on the prospect's side focused on how well your solution uniquely meets their needs and to determine any financial benefits they will derive from your solution.

Hint: Does It Pass the Sniff Test?

The best test for marketing drivel and corporate fluff is to ask yourself, "Who says so?," or, alternatively, "In whose opinion?" If the answer is, "We do," or "In ours," then you have uncovered corporate fluff, and that alleged fact should be removed from your competitive strategy.

When the opportunity lies in a competitor's sweet spot and outside of yours, then employ the flanking strategy. This involves driving up the importance of some other requirement you can meet and trying to negate those you cannot. As an SE, you play a crucial role because the new requirement is usually some technical feature turned into a business benefit. Again, although you may feel that you are in the trenches, translating that business benefit into cash is vital to the solution sale: "Most companies that want these features also consider these particular features to be really important because they end up saving much more money." This is why, when employing a frontal sales strategy, you need to keep the prospect focused, because your competitors will be attempting to flank you and destabilize your advantage.

Know Thine Enemy

Do you know the name of the competitor's sales representatives who cover your territory and the names of your technical counterparts? Do you know what they look like? Have you studied their sales strategies? Humans are creatures of habit, and everyone falls back into familiar patterns when under stress. Learning the habits of your competition can reap enormous dividends.

CASE STUDY: AN EXPENSIVE LESSON IN VARIETY

Early in my career, after more than a dozen wins, I once lost three successive deals to the same sales/technical team from the number three player in our market (we were number two). Their product had certainly not improved; nor had ours changed in any way. They had adapted to our tried-and-trusted sales techniques and were proactively handling our competitive bombs. It was not until the third loss, when the prospect's decision maker brushed off our ace-in-the-hole advantage by saying, "That's not a problem. They [the competition] already told us about that," did we realize what was happening.

For the next 6 months, we were constantly modifying our presentations, proposals, value propositions, and all other elements of the sales cycle to ensure that we did not exhibit predictable patterns. We had fallen into a rut, which had cost us three new customers, several months of quota, and an anticipated commission check.

❖ ❖ ❖ ❖

Based on the SWOT matrix generated for competitors, you should then game-play their anticipated strategy, asking the following questions:

▸ Will it be frontal or flanking?

▸ Will they sell at the technical, business, or executive level?

▸ Do they have success stories they can leverage?

▸ How will they counter your own anticipated strategy?

You cannot base your entire competitive strategy on the anticipated actions of a competitor because then you automatically grant them first-mover advantage. However, if you can neutralize some of their actions by proactively providing references, success stories, and documentation or by using sound bites, you should certainly do so. Above all, if you can discredit your technical competitive counterpart at any time during the sales cycle, you gain a major advantage for your team.

At this point in the sales cycle, you should also attempt to identify the competitor's coach. Remember that a competitor may have more than one coach and that one individual can actually coach several of your competitors. Having a "double agent" coach may sound like something out of a James Bond novel, but it can be very destructive to both you and your competitor involved.

CASE STUDY: THE DATABASE WARS—A FLANKING STRATEGY

In the early 1990s, Oracle was the darling of Wall Street and the number one vendor of relational database management systems (RDBMSs). However, Sybase, Inc., another young upstart company, had been gaining market share due to better performance and data-integrity features. In 1993, Oracle finally caught up to Sybase in terms of performance and feature and function comparisons and, with the exception of selling to the Wall Street brokerage community, was beginning to overwhelm its smaller competitor.

Sybase then released a product named Replication Server that enabled companies to copy and synchronize, in real time, data from multiple systems. It enabled a company to keep a database server in London, New York, and Tokyo and instantly pass a transaction made on one server to the others. Oracle, and the rest of Sybase's competitors, had nothing like it. Elegant, well designed, and easily understood, the product could be simply tied back to business basics. Almost every single sale Sybase made from that point on involved a flanking strategy with Replication Server—even small, single-site companies had a need for a real-time backup of their systems for disaster recovery.

For 18 long months, Oracle sales representatives had to sell around their lack of an instant-replication strategy until finally problems with the quality of Sybase's flagship database engine gave them an edge. At that point, however, Sybase had grown annual revenues to $1 billion and built enough loyalty in its customer base to survive.

The Art of Competitive Analysis

Broad-level competitive research is traditionally undertaken by the product-marketing group, synthesized into bite-sized chunks, and then passed onto the field. Remember that it is this group's job to make their product look good and to motivate the field. You need to apply some cynical realism and liberal use of the "sniff test" to any corporate analysis. In particular, you to need to be aware of the future-releases fallacy, where the next version of your product or service is favorably compared to the competitor's current version.

Assuming that product management has access to all public-domain material available on your competitor, nothing prevents you from going a little further in your research. The important caveat is that you must be fully aware of any material that may be marked as company confidential or proprietary as you cannot under any circumstances accept that material, no matter which source it comes from. Becoming a successful competitive expert is a good career booster for any SE and a major piece of value-add material for any sales opportunity. So, sign up for any webcasts given by your competitor, ask your partners for any legitimate competitive data they can pass on, and ask your trusted customer base for any input they may be able to provide. Also review any on-line chat, wiki, or public customer-support/user-group forums on the Internet. You will be astonished by the material you can find.

"Tell Me About Your Competition"

Somewhere in the execution of the competitive strategy, both the SE and the salesperson will be asked why your solution is better than the competition's. The prime directive is to stay positive, concentrate on your strengths, and remember the agreed-upon sound bites. Naturally, you should be ready for this question and have a 60-second "elevator speech" prepared with no more than two points (remember the executive rule of two!).

Hint: Speaking About the Competition
If in doubt about whether to slam the competition, don't!

This 60-second speech will rarely suffice, and the prospect will often remark that, while they appreciate your not wanting to slam the competition, they need to have some "ammunition" for an upcoming review or meeting. You now have a very important decision to make, and your options are as follows:

1. *Refuse:* Taking the moral high ground may be fine, but very often the prospect does have a need for this kind of information. Should your sales organization or the opportunity strategy forbid "dishing the dirt," you can try turning the tables by asking the prospect what they consider to be your advantages over a particular competitor. You can then reinforce those perceptions during the conversation. This is an act of high diplomacy because you can potentially look like you know nothing about your competitor.

2. *Use a third-party source:* You can almost always find a negative news story, chat room, industry analyst, or financial-analyst report about your competitor. Either referring the client to these sources or providing them with the material is a good approach. Third-party material is far more believable than anything you can say or do.

Note that there is no third option to "give them the information." In 20 years, we can only recall two instances when this has resulted in a win. Any response not backed by third-party information turns the discussion into a debate of opinions. Passing on irrefutable data from industry analysts or customer references supports your position and improves your personal credibility.

Frequently, your competitor will throw dirt first and give the prospect a list of the top 10 or 20 reasons why your solution won't work. Under no circumstances should you simply respond to the prospect's request to counter the list. Two highly successful and proven strategies are as follows:

1. Ask the prospect, "If we satisfactorily answer these questions, will you buy our product?"

2. Pick two or three items from the list that you can easily discredit. Briefly and verbally respond to these items, stating that the document is probably full of similar inaccuracies. Should the prospect

insist on continuing through the list, offer to reconvene in 24 hours and have the prospect pick their top two issues; in return, you will pick your top two. If possible, you should avoid a written response. The odds are high that the prospect will return your response to your competitor, perhaps in order to allow the competitor another response or to correct the competitor's misinformation. Either circumstance hurts your cause.

Case Study: A Competitive Leave-Behind Can Leave You Behind the Competition

Recently, we were competing for a sizable opportunity, going head to head with our largest and fiercest competitor. All of the preliminaries had been completed, and the prospect had narrowed the short list down to the two of us. Coaches, executives, and approvers had been identified, and we were preparing for a lengthy RFP process. Suddenly, via e-mail, we received a 450-item spreadsheet from a mid-level IT manager who we knew favored our competitor's solution. The sales team started to panic, especially as they had been given a 48-hour turnaround.

In fact, the spreadsheet, which our competition had provided to this manager, listed all the features and functions they believed would put us at a disadvantage. Recognizing this ploy and noting similarities in the spreadsheet to one we had seen in Europe a few weeks earlier, we undertook some further investigation. Opening the spreadsheet and using the File | Properties option, we could plainly see that the spreadsheet had been created by our competitor and passed on to us unedited by the prospect.

We strategized and decided not to confront the IT manager with this fact; instead, we set up a call with a senior VP to discuss some higher-level issues and pleaded for more time to complete the 450 items. During the conference call, we claimed that the spreadsheet was a competitive setup and that we were seriously considering withdrawing from the opportunity. The IT manager claimed that the requirements list was fair and had been generated internally. We had the senior VP load the spreadsheet on his PC and perform the File | Properties trick. Fireworks ensued at the other end of the line, and we were asked to call back in an hour.

The IT manager and his department were taken out of the picture for the duration of the evaluation. Our competition was discredited, and the prospect literally bent over backward to ensure we were given more than a fair shot at the business. Several months later, we signed a multi-million-dollar contract for a sizeable suite of our products and services.

The purpose of refuting negative claims is to discredit your competitor. Create the mental connection in the prospect's mind that if some of the information they have been given is incorrect, then how can they trust any of it?

Using Product Benchmarks

In almost every industry involving a product sale, there is always a way to measure your product against the competition. You see it every day in the media—a comparison of frequent-flier programs, checking account options, discount-brokerage accounts, automobile features, and so on. Similar comparisons apply to your industry in measuring speed, performance, productivity, price, or some other quantitative element. This is the marketing equivalent of an arms race.

Comparison tables are sometimes useful in a business-to-consumer model but are meaningless in a business-to-business environment, especially if the benchmark has been conducted by, or on behalf of, one of the interested parties. A published and audited benchmark is usually the result of months of carefully engineered work designed to show your product in the best light. After all, have you ever seen a company release data showing that its product to be inferior? The only qualification is that if the benchmark shows that you are markedly superior—almost to an order of magnitude—then it may have some effect. The downside of a benchmark is that a competitor can always find something that is artificial, not reflective of the real world, a hack, or just plain wrong. However, if you have a performance benchmark and the competitor does not, that plants the meaningful and insightful question "Why?" into the back of the prospect's mind.

Continuing the flanking-strategy story of Sybase versus Oracle, the Sybase claim to fame for years was that their database was faster and cheaper according to artificial benchmarks called TP-1 and TPC-A. Oracle finally published a faster figure than Sybase's and then had egg on their face when it was claimed they had turned off a major feature in their database to get their superior numbers. This just goes to show that while competitive benchmarks sometimes work, using them is a gamble fraught with risk. Your competitors can dissect and analyze the results you publish and eventually use them against you.

Summary

As the technical representative, your credibility is key to any sale. You know your product very well; it is unlikely that you have the same level of knowledge about your competitor's product. Just one misstatement can cost you months of work. Take the high ground and refrain from bashing the competition—even if asked to do so. However, there is no reason why you cannot focus on those areas of your product that are superior.

Know your enemy and anticipate their moves. A great chess player can look ahead several moves on the board based on his opponent's history. Develop a strategy and stick to it. Above all, never do or say anything that you feel is legally or ethically incorrect.

Skill Building

New SE	1. Learn your product before trying to learn about your competitor's.
	2. Know against whom you are competing.
	3. Learn and rehearse a 60- to 90-second elevator pitch on your technical advantages.
	4. Attend a competitor's seminar or trade show.
Experienced SE	1. Learn your competitor's product.
	2. Create a demonstration or presentation that highlights your strengths and the competition's weaknesses without explicitly talking about them.
	3. Learn and rehearse a 60- to 90-second elevator pitch on your business advantages.
	4. Be prepared to counter your opponent's top 10 list.
	5. Never use the same strategy twice in a row.

Chapter Goals

Understand the benefits of CRM for you, your company, and your customers.

Learn how to support your sales processes with CRM features.

Know how to get the most out of your corporate CRM system by accessing organizational knowledge.

Using the CRM/SFA System

If you have knowledge, let others light their candles with it.

Winston Churchill

Almost every sales organization now utilizes either a customer-relationship management (CRM) or a sales-force automation (SFA) system in an effort to track their customer interactions and sales opportunities. Typically, the software is tied to a sales methodology that may be homegrown, or it may be a standard off-the-shelf type, such as SPIN[1] Selling, Solution Selling,[2] Customer Centric Selling,[3] or any variation thereof, designed to support and reinforce the standard corporate sales process.

Throughout this chapter, we use CRM and SFA interchangeably—although this is not technically correct. A CRM system encom-

---

1.   Huthwaite, www.huthwaite.com.
2.   Sales Performance International, www.solutionselling.com.
3.   Customer Centric Selling, www.customercentric.com.

229

passes all interactions with a customer, whether they are inbound support calls, outbound telemarketing calls, literature requests, product shipments, or even legal discussions. An SFA system only tracks the sales interactions around a specific revenue lead or opportunity and is therefore a subset of CRM.

We are also making the assumption that your organization has a well-supported and highly utilized SFA system, which is viewed as the system of record for sales activities and metrics. Unfortunately, over the years, some SFA implementations have devolved into simplistic pipeline tracking and forecasting systems that offer minimal support for any form of team selling. Should that be the case, you have our sympathy—a key internal sales tool has been taken away from you!

Why CRM Is Your Best Friend

As an SE, it is important that you accept the mind-set that any CRM system, especially when coupled with a sales methodology, is your best friend. Think through some of the advantages it offers you:

> It establishes a common language to avoid misunderstandings.

> It injects a repeatable discipline into the sales process.

> It helps you leverage other people's knowledge and account history.

> It provides a quantifiable form of measurement and revenue contribution.

A CRM system can act as the "nervous system" for a sales organization, coordinating activities among the different participants in a sales process. Progressing through the sales cycle as described in Chapter 2 becomes less stressful once a CRM system is superimposed upon each opportunity. When correctly executed, it ensures that no step is forgotten; plus, it aids the SE and his management in ensuring that the dash to demo (see Chapter 8) and other shortcuts are avoided.

As previously discussed, every sales methodology divides the sales cycle into stages, although each measures and defines the stages differently. Two common measurement schemes are a simple percentage relating to progression through the cycle or a letter tag relating to a discrete step in the cycle. These are correlated in Table 20.1.

The forecasting aspect of the SFA system also provides a further data point for decision making. Transactions entered into the system are

Table 20.1

Sales Methodology Correlations

Milestone	Shortened Milestone	Generic Solution Selling Milestone	Typical Activities in this Stage
Unqualified Opportunity	10%—Unqualified Lead	T—Territory	Lead Generation Develop Lead
Qualified Opportunity	20%—Qualified Opportunity	S—Suspect	First Call(s) Initial Discovery
Business Drivers Confirmed	30%—Drivers Confirmed	D—Development	Follow-Up Calls. Detailed Discovery. RFP response
Understand IT Need and can map it to our solution	40%—Need mapped to Solution	C—Execution	RFP response. Proof stage w/demo-presentation(s)
Architecture created, delivered and agreed	50%—Architecture or Solution Agreement	C—Execution	Further evaluation and Competitive Positioning
Purchase Cycle confirmed by customer	60%—Purchase Cycle Confirmed	C—Execution	Initiate POC/Trial
Successful technical evaluation	70%—Technical Win	B—Acceptance	Conclude POC/Trial
Successfully Delivered Formal Proposal	80%—Proposal Accepted	B—Acceptance	Quote , Miscellaneous Technical Q&A
Customer has agreed on pricing and contractual terms	90%—T & C Agreement	A—Negotiation	
Customer signed contract (Closed-Won)	100%—Contract Signed	W—Won	
Closed - Lost	Closed—Lost	L—Lost	

commonly marked as "forecasted," "upside," or "pipeline." "Forecasted" implies that the salesperson commits that the deal will close in the current month or quarter, "upside" suggests that it might close, and "pipeline" indicates that it will happen in the future.

Time and Resource Prioritization

Salespeople are often regarded as believing that SE time is an unlimited resource and that an open checkbook exists for SE hours and efforts. A well-regulated sales force, combined with a disciplined SE team, can use the SFA system to prioritize resources and set time and resource boundaries. This allows both sales and SE management to make decisions based on time, money, and commitment rather than pure emotion and the "buddy network."

CASE STUDY: IF ONLY I HAD MORE PRESALES RESOURCES

> One of our account managers, who was distinctly middle of the pack, worked a remote territory in upper New York state and New England. During each quarterly account review with our VP of sales, he bemoaned his lack of local presales assistance and stated that he could sell more if only the presales team would travel into his territory more often. In effect, he threw me and my small team of SEs under the bus each quarter, stating that our group wasn't contributing appropriately in his territory. After 6 months of operating an internal SFA system, my presales director ran a report listing activity hours by account manager and brought it to the next meeting. When the standard complaint arose, my boss went to the whiteboard and wrote the following numbers on the whiteboard: 41, 9, 25. He explained that out of 41 account managers, this account manager ranked 9 in presales time utilization in our entire region, yet ranked 25 in terms of quota attainment. This eliminated further argument.

For example, SE management can place boundary conditions upon where in the sales cycle an opportunity needs to be before an RFP can be answered, a customized demonstration can be created, or an on-site trial can be entered into. Providing such guidelines gives the individual contributor SE the ammunition to say no to requests that, as defined by the standard corporate process, represent a bad use of time or are at least premature relative to the life cycle of the opportunity. We have provided some guidelines in Table 20.1, although you may need to modify these based on your specific sales cycle and solution-set requirements. Leaving aside the special conditions of widely different deal sizes, a forecasted deal should always get resources before an upside deal, which, in turn, has priority over a pipeline transaction. The most common resource conflicts occur between a large pipeline deal and a smaller forecasted deal. The salesperson handling the larger deal will plead for help, saying "I know it's going to close," which yields the perfectly acceptable response, "Well, why aren't you forecasting it yet?"

The Art of Repeatability

Active use of a sales methodology in conjunction with a CRM system can lead to the desired state of a repeatable sale. This allows you to reuse materials and tactics from prior sales, with only minor adjustments, to close additional opportunities at new accounts with fewer resources and in less time. A sports analogy would be that of the professional golfer: With comparatively little effort, a pro can hit a golf ball over 300 yards with a basic swing of a club. Small changes in the grip and stance allow the player to hit the ball higher or lower or to fade or draw the ball around obstacles. The key to this, other than hours of practice, is developing a repeatable system of addressing the ball, holding the club and starting the swing, which the human body remembers. An undisciplined, amateur golfer approaches each shot in a different manner, with no set routine, and struggles to improve—often driving the ball out of bounds or totally mishitting the shot. An undisciplined sales force pushes the sales-engineering organization to approach every opportunity as a one-off, with little chance of learning from or utilizing past successes and failures. The chance of a failed sales call or demo is far higher when every activity effectively starts from ground zero.

Gain Advantage by Tapping Organizational Knowledge

The true power of CRM is that it enables you to effectively leverage the knowledge and interactions of other people (and even partners) within your organization. An old heuristic from the late 1990s was the "3 to 1 rule," which stated that in order for a CRM system to be both effective and usable, you needed to gain three times as much knowledge out of the system as you put into it. So, entering call reports, customer interactions, and even product architectures may prove useful to you in the long run as a form of electronic and corporate memory; yet, it is likely that others within your company will benefit from it more than you will. Conversely, you need to look into the system to see what useful data you can extract and how to apply it. You can make the case that it is the overall account manager's job to access this data, but since you are responsible for the technical side of the sale, you should not absolve yourself of this responsibility purely as a point of principle.

One natural starting point is interactions with customer or product support. You don't need to be in the business for too long before you experience being blindsided during a supposedly friendly customer visit by someone complaining about the quality and quantity of product support and problems in your product. Before you make a sales call on a customer you have never seen before or haven't visited for a while, you should always run a customer-support report and, if you are selling hard goods, an on-site field-service report. In addition to determining how many support calls the customer has made, you may gain an indication of a training mismatch (i.e., many callers ask, "How do I . . . ?"); plus, you should know the number of open calls or problems and the average response time. You can derail many a complaint session by placing a pile of call reports, with an executive summary, on the table in front of you as soon as the issue rears its ugly head. This summary should include a chart listing dates, the parties involved, and all topics addressed.

Hint: Who Owns What?

It is also worthwhile checking what products your company thinks the customer owns and their level of support and maintenance rights for those products. You can proactively remind companies that it may be time to upgrade from an old release before their support contact expires.

The corporate memory function of the CRM system may show you how many RFPs, trials, and proofs of concept have been run at the company. Plus, you can see which campaigns have been targeted at which contacts, as well as who has attended seminars, webinars, and user-group meetings. For larger accounts, which may span geographies or even business units, you may be able to see other active opportunities. In short, the more you know, the less likely you are to step on someone else's deal or commit some other faux pas.

Hint: Sign Up for Alerts!

As a side note, many CRM systems allow you to sign up for alerts when a high-priority or system-down call is made. We would recommend that if you have access to this capability, you sign up for each of your major accounts, as well as for any large current deals you are working on. Sign up the account representative, too, while you are at it!

CASE STUDY: THE INTERNATIONAL CONNECTION

A large, multinational publishing corporation issued an RFP from both its U.S. and U.K. headquarters directly to both of our national offices, requiring the installation of software and use of services in both locations. Of course, because of commission-split issues, neither national sales team informed the other, assuming that only one RFP had been issued to our company. It was only because an enterprising junior SE looked into our CRM system 2 days before the submission date and noted that one of his peers across the Atlantic had been logging time against an RFP that we managed not to bid against ourselves! One proposal had been 15% lower than the other and specified a different set of products. We regrouped and submitted a single, final joint proposal to the publishing corporation.

Many companies use the CRM repository to hold documentation for the handover of a successful sale from the pre- to the postsales functions. We highly recommend this as a best practice (or else set up a common file share or intranet site) to ensure that the delivery side of the organization knows what sales promised and has access to all call notes, architecture diagrams, demo scripts and screens, and so forth.

Look at the Numbers

Measurement is, of course, a two-edged sword; yet, the data points within a CRM system can work very effectively to your advantage. First, CRM provides historical data, even to the point of telling you how you spent your time each week (most SE's would overestimate the amount of customer face time). You can also see which account representatives utilize most of your time and upon which functions. Second, you receive a current view of your activities: by seeing which of the active deals in your pipeline are supposed to close this month or quarter, you can prioritize accordingly. Third, you gain a perspective on the future: by seeing the pipeline over the next 3 to 6 months, you can plan around any bottlenecks or resource constraints.

Using this baseline data, you can now gain a perspective on how others in the organization view the way you spend your time. Should you be spending a higher proportion of your time answering RFPs and a lower proportion giving presentations? Identifying such trends can be an early signal for a personal-skills upgrade. As an experienced SE, you may find yourself typecast as a subject matter expert in one business area or solution set yet struggling to become engaged in newer technologies or opportunities. Unless this is where you wish to spend the rest of your career, expand your talents!

Annual Review Time

One advantage of CRM to the competent SE is that it retains a historical record of your activities with each client. About a month before your annual review, we suggest that you run a report showing which revenue transactions you have been involved in, the conversion rate of trials/POCs and RFPs, and how many postsales items, such as support escalations, you resolved. While your direct manager will undoubtedly remember the larger and more spectacular deals, he may need prompting on the smaller ones. By showing that you were the lead SE on 20% of an area's revenue, yet were part of a 10-person team, you make the case that you were twice as productive and deserve a larger raise or promotion.

The natural caveat to this advice is that the activity needs to be both legitimate and realistic and not the result of gaming the system or artificial deal inflation (i.e., being attached to every deal in the pipeline). Although the practice of tying SE bonuses to general or specific customer-facing activities is now regarded as passé, several smaller companies now reward sales teams who fully document their sales activities such that they benefit others within the organization. These reports can also be helpful if you have MBO bonuses tied to extending your competency in certain areas.

Summary

A CRM system, coupled with a repeatable sales process, can be the best friend of any competent SE. By taking the emotion out of the sales process and providing a true and relative measurement of one opportunity against another within the company, prioritization and resource management become more of a science and less of an art. You will also learn to leverage the knowledge and activities of other personnel within your organization and become more effective for this. Finally, CRM measurement capabilities will allow you to identify perceived skill gaps and acknowledged personal strengths, as well as to capitalize on that knowledge. Remember that with a successful and repeatable sales process, coupled with SFA compliance, you want history to repeat itself.

Skill Building

New SE	1. Use the system as a way to make your sales efforts repeatable.
	2. Search for similar opportunities and similar competitive situations.
	3. Learn the bells and whistles and interfaces of the SFA/CRM system.
	4. Use the system to track your activities against your development goals.
Experienced SE	1. Automate reports and alerts from other, nonsales departments.
	2. Use the system as a repository to pass on your expertise to others and as a way to identify mentoring opportunities.
	3. Use the system to document account history to highlight the resources your firm has applied to each client.
	4. Gain an understanding of how the organization views your skills and improve or train accordingly.

Chapter Goals

Learn how to position yourself to make the change to being a salesperson.

Understand what you should expect as you make the transition.

Discuss how to make the change work successfully.

Crossing Over to the Dark Side

It's just a job. Grass grows, birds fly, waves pound the sand. I beat people up.

Muhammad Ali

There comes a time in every SE's career when, after watching a series of sales representatives stumble through the sales process year after year, he or she decides, "I can be a salesperson too." This process is known as "crossing over to the dark side," and some SEs will be highly successful, while others will not.

What Is Your Motivation?

The first action to take is to conduct an internal discovery session to determine your motivation for wanting to make this career change. Is this something for which you have already been planning and preparing? Or is it an act born out of frustration with either your current position or the salespeople with whom you work? In some cases, SEs become fascinated with the financial rewards, which is exactly the wrong reason to cross over.

A significant portion of this book has dealt with building up both technical and business skill sets with a future career path in mind. When it is posed to them, every SE should be prepared to answer the question, would you like to sell? The opportunity may be the result of careful planning, or, as happened to one of us, a matter of stepping up to fill the head count for the greater good of the company. Either way, you need to assess periodically both your skill sets and your career aspirations to determine if this is the right move for you. Do not view such a career move as either a promotion or demotion but more as a lateral step. It certainly opens up a wealth of career opportunities for you, but it also closes down some others.

The phrase "crossing over to the dark side" comes from the famous *Star Wars* film directed by George Lucas (Paramount Pictures, 1977). We do not want to imply that SEs represent the good side and that salespeople are evil; instead, we are saying that make this transition is a life-changing event with many ramifications.

Positioning for the Change

A cynical colleague of ours suggested a short, but effective, four-step program:

1. Learn to play golf.

2. Buy several very expensive suits.

3. Lower your IQ by 20 points.

4. Forget everything you learned about the product.

Although we would certainly agree on at least three of these four points, there is a lot more involved when positioning yourself for a career in sales! In addition to developing the standard sales skills, you must make major psychological adjustments.

First and foremost, following all the other advice in this book, you need a plan. Make a list of all the sales-related skills you believe you will need and then grade yourself from 1 to 5 on each. Next, speak with your local sales manager, several of the more successful sales representatives, and, of course, your SE manager about what it would take to make the move. Emphasize that you are only thinking about this course of action.

Hint: Create a Mission Statement

Build a mission statement for yourself, such as "Within 12 months I see myself as a quota-exceeding salesperson selling our core products to existing accounts in Seattle."

As a result of these preliminary conversations, you will have more skills to add to your list and an indication of how the organization thinks you rate in connection with those skills. Armed with this list and other feedback, you are now in a position to start planning. Look ahead over the next 6 to 12 months—whatever your immediate timeline may be—and see if you can attend any courses (internal or external), sales meetings, or special training sessions that will help you pick up these missing sales skills. Go back to the sales manager and salespeople and ask for their help too. Ask to become involved in pricing, contracts, and negotiations as a silent observer. When working smaller opportunities with a salesperson, volunteer to take on more of the sales-related tasks.

Hint: Expand Your Network

Networking is a vital activity for anyone involved in sales, regardless of job function. Once you have decided to move into sales, make a conscious effort to reach out and expand your network at twice the previous pace. The more contacts you have who are willing to help you out, provide leads, give favors, and so on during your first months, the smoother the transition will be.

Psychologically, becoming a salesperson is much harder to prepare for than being an SE. Even as a highly experienced SE, you are still essentially a follower, whereas as a salesperson, you need to lead the charge for each and every sales opportunity. You also need to be prepared for plenty of rejection and for repeatedly hearing the word "no."

Hint: Handling Adversity

Ask yourself how you handle adversity and rejection in your private life. When turned down for a date, a car loan, or membership in some organization, how have you reacted? This is a solid indicator of how you may handle similar situations in your professional life.

All of the SEs we have known who have attempted a transition to sales have been taken aback by the level of rejection, cynicism, and almost out-right distrust they have faced in their daily routines. You should also know that the success rate of SEs making the move is low. Based on our experience over the years, we believe that approximately one in three SEs successfully accomplishes the transition. We define success as both achieving quota in year two and still being in the job after year three. You can mitigate the risk of failure by being well prepared and having a plan.

With all of this planning comes the realization that you will need to commit to this position for at least 1 and possibly 2 years. During that time, your cutting-edge sales-engineering skills will steadily dissipate, making it harder to cross back over from the dark side to a technical position. It is also fair to point out that if selling is your lifelong dream, you don't want to reach the end of your career regretting that you never tried to accomplish it. Remember the words of Jimmy Johnson, a famous U.S. National Football League (NFL) coach and TV personality: "Do you want to be safe and good, or do you want to take a chance and be great?"

What You Should Expect

You should expect to be treated differently. You are no longer a knowledge-able SE who can make the product stand on its head; you are now a sales-person. You can no longer expect prospects to believe almost every word you say; you are now a salesperson. You can no longer expect to answer technical questions, even when you do know the answer; you are now a salesperson. You should expect to spend a lot of time with your sales manager. Without the support and advice of your immediate manager, your chances for success are small.

In our experience, converted SEs need to pay particular attention to the follows areas:

> *The forecast:* Once you accept a sales position, you will be given a quota. Usually, you have a 3- to 6-month grace period with no quota and then ramp up to a full quota. From day one, you need to adjust to forecasting opportunities and build a pipeline. The simplest way to think of it is that you are now running your own business unit of one. A forecast is a commitment to the company that you will bring in revenue, and most converted SEs are either wildly optimistic or incredibly conservative during their first year. Seek your sales manager's guidance before committing to any large deals and also run a reality check with the local SE manager to ensure you have not missed any steps.

> *Cold-calling:* Potentially one of the least pleasant parts of sales, cold-calling is the act of calling a company and asking to speak to buyers with whom you have had no previous contact. Most SEs have no experience

with cold-calling into an organization chart. Make a few friends in the telemarketing group to get a feel for what you will face. Although most mature sales organizations now have massive lead-generation programs headed by corporate and field-marketing groups, sometimes working the telephone is the only way to break into a particularly stubborn account.

▸ *Leads:* A new salesperson will typically have few leads and even fewer opportunities with which to work. In this position, it becomes easy to follow up aggressively on all leads, whether qualified or not. Although it may be a good training exercise for you, wasting other people's time on unqualified practice calls is a surefire way to burn through a lot of goodwill.

Hint: Smile Before You Dial

One of the most intimidating acts for a new salesperson is making sales calls and cold calls by telephone. Try smiling as you are dialing the prospect. The act of smiling relaxes your facial and upper-body muscles and will actually help relieve some of the stress you may feel.

▸ *Discounting:* Competing on price alone, especially in smaller transactions, is a common mistake. SEs, because they have rarely had to deal with contracts and pricing in the past, tend to be more price sensitive than experienced salespeople and may discount heavily as a sales strategy to gain traction within an account. Remember that discounts usually increase, rather than decrease, over time, so be mindful of setting precedents.

▸ *Saying no:* It is extremely difficult, when pursuing your first possible sale, to say no to a prospect. You are so eager to please and build the relationship that you will give away products, services, and other benefits far too early in the sales cycle. Converted SEs often forget their bad memories of trials and evaluations and offer these to get the deal instead of focusing on solution selling.

How to Make It All Work

When you are a salesperson, you assume the majority of the risk and accountability for the sale. Although the financial rewards compensate somewhat for this grueling and emotional experience, it can be a nerve-wracking ride. Being on quota is stressful; it is a constant measure of your performance. Every converted SE we interviewed noted that you should double whatever emotional highs and lows you are expecting. They also mentioned that they wished they had been better prepared psychologically. Your work—getting the deal, making quota—can consume you. Your family and friends will see less of you and will have to live through your emotional swings too. Forearmed with this knowledge, you need to get as many people pulling for you as you can. As the next chapter describes in more detail, accepting a hybrid sales role as a product sales specialist within an overlay group can be a less stressful introduction to the classic sales role if you believe you need to "learn the basics" before making the jump. Regardless of the path you take into sales, you should take certain steps to make the transition smoother.

> ▸ *Get buy-in:* The more people, both inside and outside the company, you can make part of your team, the better your chances of success. Creating a network of friends, advisors, and mentors who all feel they have a stake in your new career also gives you a support system when times are hard.

CASE STUDY: FROM TINY ACORNS, MIGHTY OAKS CAN GROW

Joel was my first hire as a new SE manager at Oracle. Within an hour of our first meeting, he had managed to spill coffee on me, and within 2 months, he had caused early-morning shopping trips in Indianapolis and Toronto due to forgotten dress shoes and an ink-stained shirt. Technically, he was brilliant, but he had a long way to go on the business side of things. I knew early on that Joel had a long-term desire to cross over to the dark side, and he made no secret of that ambition, telling everyone who would listen. Many of his peers and colleagues humored him, feeling that he was totally unsuitable for sales, but Joel persevered.

Almost 3 years later, Joel's opportunity arrived, and he jumped at it. He then proceeded to make almost every mistake in the book and invented a few others during his first few months. Gradually, he began to find his rhythm and, with the help of a very patient area sales manager, made his first few sales. Over the following years, Joel became very successful, making his quota 6 years in a row and being promoted up the ranks, until he was finally in a position to hire an SE as a rookie salesperson. We are both older and wiser now, but behind the successful businessman with the polished appearance and confident demeanor, I can still see the young SE telling me how much he wanted to sell.

❖ ❖ ❖ ❖

Hint: Get Buy-In at Home First

If you have a spouse or significant other, be sure he or she is behind your career change 110%. You should expect a lot of long, emotional hours. Without that person's support, you will have a difficult time succeeding.

▸ *Help the SEs:* Do not forget your roots. Take care of your SEs, and they will take care of you. Respect their position and allow the SEs to answer the technical questions. Do not be tempted to "step in front" of technical questions to show off your knowledge. Junior SEs will appreciate working with a salesperson who can gently bail them out if necessary. Senior SEs can usually help you out of a tough situation using their experience. In fact, the positive relationships you have with your former peers may provide you an advantage over the rest of the salespeople for your first 6 months if you reinforce those relationships.

▸ *Work the account base:* Having viewed many SE conversions over the years, one overriding similarity seems to stand out among the successes. The SE was initially asked to sell into the installed base of customers or was given one high-profile, but very happy, account on which to focus. Rarely have SEs succeeded when asked to prospect, generate their leads and opportunities, and operate in "hunter-killer" mode as opposed to "farmer" mode.

Hint: Sell to Happy Customers

Ask for a territory that contains a large number of existing customer accounts, not necessarily even the largest accounts, just those that are already familiar with your company and its services.

▸ *Keep an open mind:* Always be willing to learn and ask questions of everyone on your sales team. Almost every salesperson we have ever worked with was more than willing to provide advice, solicited or not, on "the art of sales." Remember that you have moved from near the top of the class as an SE to almost the bottom rung on the sales ladder. It is better to learn from the mistakes of others than make your own when dealing with your pipeline.

Summary

If your ultimate goal is to move into sales, start preparing early—but do not neglect your technical skills. Inventory your sales skills and be prepared to ask many people for help and advice. Let local sales management know of your intent, and be ready to seize the opportunity when it presents itself. Remember that salespeople love to be sold to themselves, so sell yourself hard for the position you want. Set your expectations for a tough first year, both financially and psychologically, and rely on your network of friends for support and guidance. You are traveling a road many have journeyed along before you, so if you persevere, you should succeed. In keeping with the theme of the chapter, "May the Force be with you."

Skill Building

All SEs	1. Create your mission statement.
	2. Objectively, and via third parties, evaluate your sales skills.
	3. Work on alleviating your weaknesses and improving your strengths.
	4. Ask for help and advice—constantly.
	5. Volunteer for sales responsibilities now, such as pricing and configuration.
	6. Attend training classes on topics such as solution selling and handling objections.
	7. Practice handling rejection and distrust.

Chapter Goals

Define the role of the hybrid sales/sales engineer position.

Analyze organizational structures covering overlay positions.

Introduce specialized skills required by the position.

Discuss necessary considerations for presales management dealing with this position.

The Hybrid Sales Specialist Position

If we all did the things we are capable of, we would astound ourselves.

Thomas Edison

As the breadth of products and services offered by a vendor steadily expands, so do the difficulties for a single account manager and sales engineer in effectively covering the product set. For a company to grow, it must often move into adjacent market spaces, either by organic growth or by acquisition. A sales force that cannot adapt to this growth can end up sending a dozen people to a single customer meeting (known as the multilegged sales call). The rationale for this approach is, "We want to make sure that we can cover all possible questions in as much depth as possible." How then, to prevent this inefficient and costly use of valuable corporate resources?

In this chapter, we will examine the changing role of the account manager, the sales engineer, and the creation of a new, hybrid, technically-oriented sales specialist. In

247

particular, we examine how the "classic" presales teams deal with this new position. We note that this chapter (1) primarily applies to larger multiproduct and multimarket vendors; (2) is also relevant for sales organizations far removed from headquarters, where it is often necessary to play multiple roles; and (3) is somewhat of a hybrid itself as it deals with both individual-contributor and field-management issues.

The New Role of the Account Manager

The new mandate for the account manager within a large vendor can be defined as "relationship manager" or "account director" (AD). The major responsibilities of the AD are:

  ‣ To identify and perform preliminary qualification of sales leads;
  ‣ To be the primary face of the company to the customer;
  ‣ To understand the customer's business, issues, and future plans;
  ‣ To serve as "trusted advisor" to the customer;
  ‣ To conduct or participate in sales pricing and contract-negotiation meetings;
  ‣ To deliver the solution purchased by the customer and ensure it is successfully implemented.

In truth, as many of the larger technology companies, such as IBM, SAP, and CA, have discovered, it is unreasonable to expect an AD to be deeply knowledgeable about an entire product set. It is, however, reasonable to expect an AD to understand at a high level what each product does and to be able to ask a few qualifying questions. At this point, where does the AD turn to for assistance in further qualifying and progressing the opportunity? In a small company, this would be the responsibility of the AD himself, in conjunction with a generalist sales engineer. In a larger company with multiple business units and several hundred individual products, the problem is far more complex.

Introducing the Hybrid Technical-Sales Position

The logical course of action is to fill this void formed between the classic sales-engineering teams and the account directors with one or more positions that are hybrid in nature. We use the term *hybrid* as the job requirements and expectations of these positions possess aspects of both camps. The position frequently carries an individual quota; yet, it also requires the ability to present and even demonstrate certain products, plus possession of considerable subject matter expertise. One defining aspect of the quota is that it is rolled up into another person's or department's quota; thus, the hybrid becomes known as a form of "overlay" position.

From a managerial viewpoint, the hybrid positions are difficult to fill from outside the company, as the potential pool of candidates with the correct blend of technology and sales skills is even smaller than that for traditional presales positions. In the majority of large companies that have implemented such a position, the most likely candidates are either current presales engineers or professional-services engagement managers who want to pursue a career in sales and view the hybrid as a lower-risk starting point. Indeed, such positions are often the only entry point offered into sales for existing SE's for precisely that reason. Refer to Chapter 21, "Crossing Over to the Dark Side," for more details about the expectations and realities of a sales career.

In terms of engagement within a sales opportunity, Figure 22.1 shows an expanded representation of the classic software sales cycle detailed in Chapter 2 with suggested roles and tasks outlined. We stress that this is a sample sales cycle, as culture, geography, politics, and compensation all serve to influence a real-world corporate model. The important factor for the SE is to determine the roles and responsibilities of each member of the sales team with the introduction of these new players. Issues such as who coordinates the use of outside resources, who is responsible for RFPs, who takes the lead in sales calls, and so forth need to be laid out very clearly right at the start of each engagement. Experience has shown us that the SE will now interface far more frequently with the overlay teams and less so with the primary account director.

Parallel Sales Forces

The first step most companies take is to create a separate sales force for a new product. This may be via natural growth or forced through an acquisition. Microsoft, for example, has used both strategies—constructing a parallel sales force for each major product line, while maintaining a core team focused upon sales of the various flavors of Windows.

	Account Director	Primary Account Sales Engineer	(Product) Sales Specialist	SE Technology Specialist
Account Management/Go To Market Planning	- Own overall account strategy - Understand customer core initiatives and map to solutions - Identify key players responsible for executing initiatives and manage org. chart - Identify areas of opportunity and map resources to the plan - Leverage existing relationships to identify opportunities stakeholders	- Own overall Technical account Plan - Collaborate on overall account Plan - Execute to Plan - Involve Specialists as needed - Establish roles and responsibilities	- Collaborate with AD on their specific solutions - Define key plays for key accounts. - Establish sales methodology for their solutions	- Involved in Account Planning Sessions as needed.
Lead Generation	- Conduct cold call into contacts - Support lead generation activities -seminars, lunch & learns, partners, etc. - Roadmap Reviews	- Identify New Contacts - Deliver or Identify Resources for Roadmap Reviews and Product Updates - Support lead generation activities -seminars, lunch & learns, partners, etc.	- Conduct cold call into contacts based on overall account strategy. - Initiate and support lead generation activities (seminars, lunch & learns, partners, etc.) - Integrate strategy into overall account plan - Provide and educate the account team on how to excute key plays.	- Provided support for overall lead generation plan.
Lead Qualification	- Enter lead into SFA system - Complete customer research - Send appropriate documents (whitepapers, etc.)	- Engage with technical contacts to determine requirements - Ask questions - Discover roles - Define expectations	- Qualify business drivers & technical fit	- Ask probing questions
Opportunity Qualification	- Update SFA opportunity - Follow qualification process	- Create and update Technical Decision Status in SFA - Determine if solution is appropriate fit - Collaborate on message	- Qualify funding and timeframes - Qualify decision process and key players - Identify competition - Follow qualification process - Request SE Tech Specialist	- Collaborate on message
Opportunity Development	- Provide continuous touch to the customer with high value information - Engage key resources as necessary - Engage Support/Customer Care/Services	- Develop technical acceptance plan - Execute overview presentation - Link solution to customer need - Set strategy with account & specialist teams, further level of qualification	- Drive sales strategy - Manage/influence requirements to gain competitive edge - Formulate required solution components, including 3rd party partnerships	- Plan session with account team & sales specialist - Execute technical presentations and demos - Provide specific product/solution info - Set strategy with account & specialist teams - Drive further level of qualification
Evaluation Process	- Lead start of deal structuring - Define budget requirements - Define success criteria - Provide budgetary pricing - Lead and Coordinate RFP effort - Lead competitive positioning	- Execute joint call with SE Specialist and customer to understand decision making process - Coordinate resources with extended team - Ensure follow-ups are handled in a timely manner - Drive acceptance with technical team - Update Technical Decision Status in SFA - Record customer questions and follow-up - Setup, Frame objectives & expectations - Setup, Training of technical business drivers (also/or Specialist Rep) - Present and drive POC pre-install doc - Manage tech involvement of all participants - Reassess consistently the project objectives and strategy - Lead technical coordination for RFP's - Coordinate timelines - Review overall response - Perform final review through OOT	- Support RFP's - Strategize competitive positioning - Leverage PM and engineering resources as appropriate - Secure references - Coordinate POC development	- Conduct joint call with Account SE and customer to understand decision making process - Execute detailed product demos - Manage POC - Update POC activity and milestones in SFA - Participate in POC pre-meeting - Validate POC pre-install document - Execute POC according to plan - Participate in status calls - Follow-up as needed, on-site or otherwise - Investigate competition - Own weekly touch points with account team to progress the opportunity - Provide assigned technical responses - Participate in RFP/RFI activities - Reassess consistently project objectives and strategy
Solution Approval	- Obtain/send legal contracts and software agreements - Determine any special terms & conditions - Obtain verbal agreement of contract terms - Negotiate final pricing - CLOSE	- Enter Win/loss analysis for Technical Decision Status in SFA - Coordinate of technical resources - Briefing of resources	- Secure technical decision - Leverage AD relationships with key decision makers and execs - Assist AD with executive visits - Provide config and pricing info to AD - Lead or assist in proposal generation - CLOSE	- Act as touch point for all team members to understand the customer's decision - Engage Consulting and other business units as needed - Review consulting deliverables
PO & Process	- Track PO through appropriate internal systems and compliance - Monitor order processing		- Assist AD with pricing negotiations - Assist AD with pricing or licensing questions	
Booked	- Verify order has been processed - Record order number in SFA		- Hand-off to Customer Care/Support - Transition to Professional Services for design/deployment - Monitor/ensure reference-ability	

Figure 22.1 Sales engagement model.

The questions of compensation, account control, and customer confusion then rear their ugly heads because, unless the primary AD is paid upon all sales made by the parallel teams, major conflicts arise. This is often quickly resolved by making the parallel sales team an "overlay team" as previously described. This means the AD carries a full quota for the customer, and the overlay team is only responsible for part of the quota (refer to Table 22.1). The price of conflict resolution then becomes paying more people for a single transaction. One large, U.S.-based software vendor calculated that this change resulted in their paying 122 staff on one particular transaction instead of 14, when rolled up to a national level and including sales and presales management.

To introduce some new organizational job positions, the overlay team will consist of a salesperson we will name the product sales representative (PSR) and a sales engineer we will name the technology specialist (TS) to differentiate their responsibilities. Their only focus is to sell a particular product or product line as that is all they will be paid for. It is therefore up to the AD to watch for cross-selling opportunities as no other individual contributor in the company has that incentive.

Hint: The Optimal Time to Be Part of a Sales Overlay Team

The best career and financial opportunities within a sales overlay team occur within the first 12 to 18 months of formation. Usually, commission rates are higher, corporate muscle is placed behind the product set, and particularly if part of an acquisition, retention incentives may be in place that can prove to be very lucrative. You also have time to judge both if the overlay time will be successful and where the most visible corporate positions are located in the case of transfer.

Table 22.1
Quota Options for Overlay Sales

Quotas	Parallel Sales with No Credit for Overlay Sales (million)	Full Credit and Overlay Roll Up (million)
Core products	$4.0	$4.0
Overlay solution A	$3.0	$3.0
Overlay solution B	$1.0	S1.0
Overlay solution C	$2.0	$2.0
Total account quota	$10	$10.0
AD quota	$4.0	$10.0

This structure, although still popular, runs into scaling problems. Imagine the poorly qualified sales call where the AD decides to bring along his generalist core SE, plus three full product-overlay teams. Now add in a few managers, and the attendee count from your company is in the double figures. This provides smaller and nimbler competitors, who may be operating in a niche market, to position the larger company as ponderous, complex, and difficult to do business with. Note that if you work for the smaller company, it can be very effective to deliver a comment such as, "I can't believe it takes 10 people to cover a simple explanation of how their products work. They must be very difficult to integrate."

The role of the PSR in this organizational structure is to pick up and further qualify a sales lead, eventually progressing it through the sales cycle until it can be turned back to the AD for negotiation and closure. As the PSR deals with a restricted product set, he or she is expected to have more business and technical depth in the solution set. This covers gathering in-depth business requirements, initial product presentations, and a good portion of the final proposal. Technology skills may extend to architectural sessions and a product demonstration.

Depending upon the product's complexity, the technology specialist may only be responsible for complex demonstrations or on-site trials or proofs of concept. This in itself poses a problem in a blended SE organization, where the "desired skill state" is often more business oriented, creating career-progression issues for a technology-heavy technology specialist.

CASE STUDY: REVERTING BACK TO POOR HABITS

Our company had just acquired a full product line that provided product portfolio management (PPM) capabilities—in effect an IT project dashboard for the CIO. It also contained rudimentary help-desk-style ticketing to cope with the reporting of resource conflicts. One of our company's core products was a full-function, full-service help desk. An opportunity naturally arose at one of our major-named accounts for both help-desk software and a PPM system. The product specialist overlay team engaged first, as they had been accustomed to doing before the acquisition, and pitched their PPM solution and its help-desk capabilities in direct contradiction of the AD, but in true alignment with their compensation plan. What should have been a multisolution sale turned into a single-product sale plus an option, depriving the company of $300,000 of revenue and providing our customer with a less-than-optimal solution. Ironically, a year later they received the help-desk software for free as the other product option was discontinued.

❖ ❖ ❖ ❖

Complexities of the PSR Model

The challenges of the PSR model can be encapsulated in the three C's of compensation, communication, and cross-selling. Each of these areas also proves to be a skill set well worth developing for overlay hybrid salespeople as they need to sell their products both externally to customers and internally to the account directors who control the major accounts they need to penetrate.

Compensation

As the PSR and TS within each overlay team are only compensated on their product, there is a natural conflict between teams as they compete for limited customer budgets. It is bad enough to deal with traditional competitors without having to deal with internal competition as well. In the case study above, the overlay team maximized their commissions based on the behavior dictated by their compensation plan to the detriment of the overall corporation. Correct behavior can be driven by incentives (i.e., a 25% bonus or multiplier if multiple products are sold) or by penalties (deducting lost revenues from attainment). In our experience, there is rarely any disciplinary action taken against rogue overlay organizations.

Nevertheless, PSRs are forced to fight for the attention of the AD to get introduced into the account and commence a sales cycle. This leads to the "shiny new toy" syndrome, where the newest and easiest-to-sell overlay product is preferred over established core products. In particular, using the previous example, if an AD has a $10 million quota, which can be filled by any combination of solution sets, this will drive different behavior than if he or she has three or four smaller-product quota buckets to fill that must add up to the $10 million.

The built-in organizational assumption is that the AD is really *the* account director and serves as the central coordinator for account strategy and penetration. If the company operates on an entrepreneurial model, where any rep in any business unit can call on an account, then the strategic discipline rapidly disintegrates into a fight for available dollars. One of us was in the embarrassing position earlier in his career of sitting in front of a CIO who was waving five separate quotes from five salespeople for the same set of software from his company. Incidents like that make you appreciate the value of having a single point of accountability somewhere in the sales organization. Although the rank-and-file SE can have no impact upon the compensation model, it is important to understand how and why the sales force is paid so that you can understand the behavior models created by the compensation system.

Communication

From a presales management point of view, overlay organizations can be problematic as these teams either report directly to sales or have a totally different and independent reporting structure aligned within their own business units. In the instance where several concurrent opportunities are occurring within an account, it usually falls upon presales management to coordinate all of the RFP, demonstration, and on-site activities. Since there may not be a great deal of synergy at the product-engineering and -development levels, different solution sets from the same company, but written by different engineering groups, usually have radically different technical specifications. This may manifest itself in conflicting patch levels, application or Web server requirements, DLLs, security, and authentication. We were recently made aware of a situation within a large financial-services company that was offering a suite of financial instruments (sales engineers are not confined to high technology) to its largest customer and discovered that the regulatory requirements of at least two products were mutually exclusive!

Moving past technical configuration issues, you now need to coordinate the activities of personnel from different teams with undoubtedly different objectives and different policies and procedures for trials, demonstrations, and even basic discovery meetings. To prevent mundane, but necessary, logistics from bogging down the AD and presales leadership, larger companies employ full-time certified project managers or trial managers just as they would implementation managers after the sale.

As a guideline, we employ a worst-case heuristic guideline named the "Square of Complexity." Two products from different business units or product lines entail four times the complexity of a single product. Three different products equal nine times the complexity, and so forth. As an exercise for the reader, note that running a five- or six-product worst-case scenario is beyond the realm of presales and requires professional assistance from a consulting organization.

Planning for meetings can also present a challenge when several overlay teams, or even channel partners, are involved. You and your sales partner need to be very clear as to the boundaries and no-go areas for each attendee. Many a sale has been delayed or lost as a result of internal competition for the same collection of dollars or euros.

Hint: Career Progression Thoughts—Supply and Demand

For an experienced SE looking for the next career challenge, joining an overlay team in either a PSR or TS role can be very rewarding as you become one of a small number of people within the company who understand the complexities of the product or service being offered. Should you decide to stay within a core SE role, it is still worthwhile to obtain more than just a cursory knowledge of the new product line as you can be viewed as the expert within the core team. This proves to be a valuable skill as the overlay team cannot be with you on every sales call, and it is a major benefit to have salespeople view you as able to advance the sales call instead of their having to say, "I'll get back to you on that." Being in demand by the sales force is always a positive force in your career.

Cross-Selling

Untold millions of sales are lost each year as cross-selling opportunities are left by the wayside. This may be due to either a lack of knowledge or a lack of financial incentive. Recognizing such opportunities falls upon the core sales team of the AD, the generalist SE, and their management. It is therefore imperative that this team can identify and prequalify such opportunities. This may involve sitting down with each overlay team operating in your territory (particularly immediately after an acquisition) and brainstorming every possible link between the two products. Once the cross-sells have been identified, it is then incumbent upon the local sales and presales management to drive that knowledge into their staff and not rely upon corporate training and white papers. Cross-selling additional products with the help of a product specialist can also improve your win rate as part of a classic flanking, or $1 + 1 = 3$, maneuver.

CASE STUDY: MAKE IT RUN FASTER, AND THEN SECURE IT

For example, CA (formerly Computer Associates) has a suite of security products that can lock down Web-based applications and even individual transactions within those programs. In 2006, CA purchased Wily Technology, a company with a suite of software for monitoring application servers and modeling customer transaction times. There were obvious cross-sells and integrations available with the rest of CA's comprehensive monitoring tools. However, a successful cross-sell of "if you have an outward-facing application server for customers, you must need to secure it" was field-developed by an insightful presales director and rolled out across the company. This was all driven by a post mortem after an initially disastrous trial at a customer site in which the two products conflicted. The two product-marketing teams, to their credit, then jumped on this theme and released an integration pack within a few months, formalizing the field-created cross-sell.

Summary

The expansion of product lines and target markets eventually necessitates the creation of parallel sales forces, overlay teams, and hybrid technical-sales positions. However, the primary challenges are organizational, centered on communication, compensation, and accountability for overall strategy and cross-selling. As a member of an overlay team, your prime directive is to support the sale of your product, which, in the long run, is more likely to happen with the cooperation of other internal groups than if you take an antagonistic position. As a presales individual contributor or manager, your primary task is to integrate the overlay teams into your everyday planning to minimize account surprises and maximize revenue.

Skill Building

New SE	1. Develop a relationship with the overlay teams.
	2. Understand the basic positioning and competition for the overlay products.
	3. Volunteer for training if it is a natural extension for your skill sets.
Experienced SE	1. Learn enough about each overlay product to answer introductory questions credibly.
	2. Learn the integration points between the core and overlay product solutions.
	3. Examine the business model to determine if it offers both a lucrative and educational career opportunity for you.

Chapter Goals

Understand the different structures used for SE organizations.

Review examples of the different roles that need to be played in an SE organization at different stages of a company's growth.

Understand the career implications of different organizational structures.

Organizational Structure

We must open the doors of opportunity. But we must also equip our people to walk through those doors.

Lyndon B. Johnson

This chapter examines the advanced topic of how to structure a sales-engineering organization. The first section will be of interest to SEs who desire to better understand the different roles and opportunities within their organizations. The second section will be of little interest or value if you are not currently at the director level or above.

When considering organizational issues, remember this rule of thumb: "Does this help make the field more successful?" As you read this chapter and think about how these concepts relate to your company, always apply this mantra. If a position or investment fails the test, do not devote resources to it. This chapter will introduce you to several elements of sales-organization construction theory. Although this subject could consume a book in its own right, we will try to present you with the most relevant details. If you are an individual contributor, this chapter may be a good one to remember and refer to later as need dictates. If you are a manager, you should familiarize yourself with the subject matter and be ready to pull this book off the shelf at the first sign of a reorganization. For members of either camp, an understanding of organizational structures will help you work more effectively within your company and also give you insight into your company's internal political landscape.

Most companies have SEs as part of the sales organization; the question is, at what level do they report? Many startups have SEs reporting to the local sales manager, which may provide some local management structure but does little to help the SE develop. Classic SE organization provides an SE management structure up to the director or VP level. Usually, the top SE manager, hereafter referred to as the SEVP, reports to the VP of sales.

In multinational companies, the sales organization may be split into North America; Europe, Middle East, and Africa (EMEA); and the rest of the world. Each SEVP position reports to its respective local sales VP or general manager. These structures are pretty intuitive when you are working in them. It is important to understand the different types of structures because they will have significant implications for your career and advancement options. As such, we will discuss the structure and roles separately. The roles in an organization are the "jobs to be done." The structure is the aggregation of those roles into positions and individuals. Ideally, the structure is well laid out based on careful thought and consideration. As often as not, however, it is actually the result of careful politicking, corporate history, and influence peddling.

Structure

Why does structure matter? Who cares who reports to whom? If you are a line SE, this is actually a good attitude to take. You should keep your head down and focus on generating revenue. Let the managers preen and position themselves. If you are a manager, it will immediately become keenly important whom your organization reports to because that point of intersection will determine how much attention and focus your team is able to get. Attention and focus ultimately resolve themselves into money and resources. Here we consider two different organizational structures. For each, we will discuss the political and career issues and opportunities.

Structure 1: Separate SE Structure

This structure involves a separate SE structure with an SEVP who reports to the regional VP of sales. In this situation, the SEVP will be heavily focused on raising the level of play of the SEs across the group.

Corporate Support

There will typically be a good, bordering on overindulgent, focus on "corporate support" or centralized resources under the VP's control. These folks provide the training, help desk, sales operations, and field-escalation functions defined later. Because the SEVP allocates total SE head count, a higher percentage of resources will be allocated to the corporate function. From a political and career-advancement perspective, being part of the corporate team can be an outstanding position in which to find oneself.

The overlay structure implies that there will be one or more levels of management into which you can move, although, as a support person, it may be more difficult to transfer into marketing or engineering because you will lack the history of direct customer experience that those groups value. We know of one promising young manager who was able to get a job in marketing but failed miserably. She had spent 4 years in sales-operations handling the logistics of sales training. By the time she left, she had lost her understanding of the market and products her company served. When her group needed to reduce head count, she was one of the first to go.

SE Management

In this type of environment, managers can be seen as being "commoditized" or simply filling a box on an organizational chart. They are not responsible for their team's revenue numbers, so their ability to maintain appropriate staffing levels is frequently perceived as the basis of their worth. This may seem counterintuitive to those who have been SE branch managers. We assure you that from the perspective of your company's management, 95% of the time, any good work done in a branch is associated with the efforts of the sales manager. If things are going badly, you may share some of the blame, but usually the sales manager is the one to be replaced.

This model involves significant SE organizational overhead, so you will have good prospects for advancement. Your advancement, however, is more likely to be tied to political connections and general management ability than to your ability to manage and motivate field SEs.

Field SEs

This structure benefits you because the increased focus on corporate support means you will have better access to training, marketing materials, and demonstration materials. Unfortunately, these resources come at a cost. Usually, the overall head count for an SE organization will be based on a fixed ratio of SEs to the number of sales representatives. So, if an organization has 100 sales reps, and you have a 1.0 ratio, there will be 100 SEs. This total head count is then split among supporting staff. So, if support comprises 15% of the total, there will be 0.85 SEs for every sales executive. This is justified based on the expectation that you will be working more efficiently with the additional support, but it does result in a greater need for multitasking on your part because you will be supporting more than one sales rep.

If you correctly utilize the support structure, you will be more likely to hit your number and make more money, probably with less effort. You should spend some time thinking about the corporate resources available to you and how you can make the best use of them.

Structure 2: Strong Branch Management

On the opposite end of the spectrum, SEs could report to sales branch managers. "Corporate functions" are allocated and staffed by engineering and marketing, with a small SE operations group reporting to the sales-operations group. In this case, the field SEs have greater visibility, but the corporate functions usually get short shrift. As branches grow, branch SE managers may be hired or promoted, and they then report to the sales branch managers.

Corporate Support

Marketing and engineering will frequently skimp on their supporting role because it is not their core business. Because the support positions are seen as secondary, weaker candidates will fill those jobs. Frequently, compensation will be in line with engineering or marketing pay, which is normally less than sales compensation. Career opportunities will probably lie in other parts of the organization. Movement into product management or marketing is common.

SE Management

You will live or die based on your interactions with the branch manager you support. How well this works is a function of your relationship with that person as well as your current success. You are more likely to be assessed based on your real contribution to the organization because the sales manager will likely be able to evaluate how effective you are better than some distant SE manager. Because the corporate functions are run out of different organizations, it will probably be more difficult for you to get the corporate support group to react to your business needs in terms of training and sales materials. Your career opportunities will be limited in the SE organization because there is little hierarchy. You are also likely to feel more pressured to perform as a "player-coach" and still conduct your own demonstrations and presentations instead of focusing fully upon the development and performance of your team.

Field SE

You will be closely tied to an individual sales rep. Expect most growth opportunities to be either in the sales organization or branch SE management.

Roles in the SE Organization

Enough with the politics and on to getting the real work done. This section describes the major roles that support your field SEs. Some of these roles are very straightforward and intuitive: training, for example. Others, like mentoring, may be played by different people in different organizations but must be fulfilled for your organization to function properly.

Review the different roles, and see if you can identify any that are not currently filled in your organization today. Can you see how filling that role would have a positive effect on sales? You can transform yourself into a highly desirable sales engineer by filling in these gaps. You should understand clearly, however, that these are roles and not job descriptions.

Training

Product training is the most important element of training, but presentation and sales skills are also critical components of a good training program. Training will also require a project manager to coordinate course development and delivery as these programs should include both internal and external courses.

Demonstration Preparation

Depending on the type of product or service you are selling, demonstration preparation can be very time intensive. Giving a single group responsibility for developing and maintaining the demonstration is a great opportunity to eliminate inefficiency. The most leverage can be gained when such a group (or even a single individual) is associated with each market into which your company is selling.

CASE STUDY: DEMO SUPPORT STRUCTURE EVOLUTION

Our company grew from 30 to approximately 300 SEs worldwide over the space of several years. Being a software company, we frequently had to customize product demos to make our prospects believe the solution would meet their needs. We initially had a core group of two people who handled most of the "hardcore" customization efforts. As the company expanded, that group grew to six and would frequently fly anywhere in the world to support different sales efforts. Although this was great in terms of knowledge sharing and being able to bring an "old hand" along on a deal, it became difficult to get these scarce resources on a timely basis when a new deal came about.

Over the course of a few years, regional managers would each assign one or two individuals to this function as their groups grew. Frequently, one out of every eight SEs would be hired to a "technical expert" profile. These experts would learn the trade from the central group and could still call on the central group when dealing with new technologies or requirements that were too vast to staff locally.

Bid Support

A common function in medium-sized or larger organizations is the centralization of responses to requests for proposals. This is a good opportunity to bring new people into the sales organization by giving them a smaller scope of responsibility consistent with a previous job. Frequently, a bid-support person will have a strong writing background as well as a good understanding of your marketing pitch and, ideally, the customer's requirements. This can also be a good role for someone who has not been successful in a field position.

Mentoring and Skills Development

Managers need mentoring too. Any individual who doesn't report to someone capable of providing career guidance is likely to be at risk. This is one of the major arguments for the establishment of the SE management structure reporting to a VP. This role is especially important to track when promoting from within. Frequently, strong individual contributors who are promoted to managers will not have great mentoring skills. Such new managers can be paired with strong lead SEs who have a talent for mentoring. This is really a skill, not a position, and should be part of the training program for any SE identified as having management potential.

Motivation

Who rallies the troops after a bad quarter or when competitors are beating your sales teams? This is a key role that absolutely must be fulfilled, either by sales or SE management. Sales managers often do not have the time to keep the SEs going, which can result in higher turnover. This role can also be fulfilled by strong product marketing or other visionary groups in the organization.

Product Expertise

The SEs are the product experts, aren't they? Well, they are, but whom do they call when they are stumped? A large SE organization is likely to have a hierarchy of product experts who are SEs themselves. Alternative structures rely on field-marketing or product-marketing managers who provide credibility and depth during customer engagements. In startups, don't be surprised if the president or CTO of the company fulfills this role for the first year or so. We have worked in and are familiar with multiple environments where the product was changing so quickly that only the founders could really articulate the benefits as they changed from week to week. Being an SE in such an environment is a great opportunity. At first, you will be keeping quiet for the most part, but the understanding you will develop will make it worthwhile.

Point of Escalation/General Management Support

SEs always need someone to represent their interests. This may involve career, compensation, or dispute arbitration within the office or with a sales rep. If the SEs report directly to salespeople or sales managers, it is unlikely that anyone will be able to fulfill that role. As such, this concern usually justifies the existence of the SE manager. Frequently, however, these activities are not perceived as valuable relative to revenue generation. It is important to impress on the financial analysts and sales VPs the benefit of reducing employee turnover as well as the need for managers to improve their SEs' skills. Ironically, SEs are frequently the most vocal critics of their managers. Until an SE experiences a problem in his or her work situation, that SE may simply see the manager as an expensive administrator. Good SE managers need to remember this and be sure to add value during the sales cycle.

When designing your organizational structure, be sure to build in options for career growth. Consider which positions or skills are key to the success of your organization, and provide options that make filling those positions attractive for top-quality SEs. For example, you may wish to have special career tracks for individual contributors with great technical skills or domain expertise.

Review of Sales Support Functions

Supporting organizations should base their goals on how well they support the needs of the individual SEs, not on how well they build a demo or training program. There are many examples of supporting functions that have been excellently managed and implemented but have had little impact because they misunderstood how their group contributed to making a sale. In this section, we will discuss the primary functional groups that will be filling the roles we just discussed.

Hint: Mantra of Sales Support Personnel

If you are a manager, sales support employee, or sales overlay, you should qualify all of your activities with the following question: How does this help the field? If it does not help the field, should you be doing it?

SE Manager

Often, in new branches or geographies, there is no formal SE manager. Even in a "heavyweight" SE organization, remote offices may have no SE management. Classic examples include new offices in Europe or Asia (where the headquarters is based in the United States). In such a situation, the sales manager implicitly plays the role of the SE manager. If you are reporting to such a manager, you should lower your expectations about the typical areas in which a manager would support you.

Trainer

Someone needs to train your SEs. If the organization has more than five or six SEs, someone also needs to project-manage the logistics of the training. We will highlight common problems with training programs to help you decide how to approach the issue in your organization. This may constitute a brief detour from the primary subject of the chapter, but it is worth the trip.

Training is frequently skimped on. Many managers simply assume that good SEs can work with marketing to develop and deliver a training program. This approach introduces two areas of risk: poor content and poor structure. Poor content will often result if you ask your best SEs to develop training. First, many good SEs don't really know what works for them. Worse, they may have a certain style that works for them but not for others. Second, those top-tier SEs may not have the time to put together good content. If they do have extra time, they should be selling.

Poor structure results when someone not skilled in developing training programs is put in charge of running one. We have been to many SE training programs that devolved into company-sponsored beer busts because the trainers did not complete their materials, tried to do too much, or fell afoul of logistical problems.

A good training program should be equipped to provide multilevel training as described elsewhere in the book and summarized here:

- A 30-day corporate overview;
- A 30- to 90-day product-expertise training program;
- A 90- to 180-day presentation-skills and general training program;
- New product training (quarterly or perhaps yearly);
- Periodic technical refreshers (facilitated via conference call or Web enabled).

The good news is that training staff are fairly cheap if you can have the lead SEs and field-marketing teams provide the content. If your organization cannot justify a full-time person, try working out a joint arrangement with the marketing department to "split" a person with the events group. Typically, the skill set required for trade show and event planning works well for training programs.

Lead SEs

As your organization grows and matures, certain individuals will naturally develop who are superior to the rank-and-file SEs. "Make them managers" is the knee-jerk response. Sometimes this is entirely appropriate. At other times, the individual may not have the desire or aptitude to manage. You may also find yourself in the position of not having a management spot available at a given moment. In these situations, your organization should have a formal lead SE position. The position should represent a higher level of individual contributor and be given perquisites similar to those enjoyed by management.

Mature organizations also have a principal SE position analogous to that of an SE manager and a master SE position almost at the director level. This gives the really outstanding SE with no managerial aspirations a career path, with status and money attached. The principal SE position is a good one for long-time SEs who have been with the company for "ages" (however your company defines that). The principal SE may evolve into a sales overlay position as described later.

Once a lead SE position is established, it can be used to define success for those who are at the top of your organization. Do not tie a position like this solely to revenue. Executing toward your quota should represent its own reward. Individuals aspiring to this position should be top producers as well as leaders in the organization. This leadership may often take the form of nonsales activities related to marketing, product development, or even strategy. Lead SEs who take part in these corporate activities will be better able to mentor other SEs and will likely be more effective within a sale. They will have less time to devote to selling and should be teamed with more junior SEs. Lead SEs are excellent candidates for filling most of the roles described earlier. As the reader may have noticed, this role provides the benefit of many of the interesting parts of management without the administrative headaches.

Infrastructure Support Groups

SEs need to have standardized hardware and software setups. Some organizations force the SEs to set up their own equipment, while others have a centralized group perform the configuration. Which option should you use? This can be a complex trade-off based on factors such as frequency of updates, time to set up, number of centralized resources required, and relationship with IT. In general, centralizing any software configuration reaps many benefits. The recent proliferation of virtualization software, such as VMware, lends itself to the rapid setup and distribution of standardized demonstration environments. Some argue that an SE should be technical enough to perform the installation. This requirement places an additional burden on the hiring manager and decreases the SE's available selling time.

Overlay Sales/Market Executives

As your organization grows in complexity, you will reach a point at which you will not be able to maintain a high level of industry expertise in each field office. In our experience, this occurs somewhere around the $150 to $250 million revenue point. These domain experts are particularly relevant if your products address end markets with strong regulatory requirements or complex functionality. You may even have certain sales team members with advanced degrees or certifications, such as a CPA, to enable you to better speak your customer's language.

Also, your company may decide to enter new vertical (or horizontal) markets where your product has not been sold before. You can shore up gaps in your organization by hiring individuals experienced in the area in question. These individuals are generally considered to be regional executives who are responsible for developing relationships with the executives at the customers within their industry. Overlay salespeople are more effective at selling into these markets because they know the buzzwords and relevant issues. They can then work with marketing and with individual sales teams to tailor your presentations and proposals to the needs of that market.

As your company gains proficiency in the new market, the need for these types of roles decreases because your local sales teams will build up this experience. The overlay team members can still serve a useful function by acting as regional executives and staying abreast of the latest industry trends. There is some question as to whether these market executives are salespeople or SEs. The answer is that they have the requisite skills from whichever discipline to sell into their chosen market. For the purposes of this book, we consider them to be largely separate from the SE organization, but you should be familiar with the utility of this important role.

Field Marketing

Field marketing is usually responsible for bridging the gap between product marketing and sales. Smaller organizations may have only product marketing. As the sales organization grows, individuals will be identified who act as "the voice of sales" within the marketing organization. In addition to being a point of communication for product-related issues, field-marketing personnel frequently assist with regional marketing events and trade shows. If your company does not have a field-marketing group, you should expect that your communications with corporate will be less effective. You should also be prepared to bear more of the burden for supporting trade shows and marketing events with the field SEs.

Advanced Topics: Five Models for SE Organizations

In this section, we present five possible models for head count allocation at four different sizes of company. Some of the key items to notice are the ratios of different types of employees and the different issues facing each organization. Given that SEs are usually viewed as a cost of sales rather than as a driver of them, a trade-off will always exist between cost and perceived benefit.

The most important concerns are to make sure that the sales force is supported appropriately and that any positions or roles that are not funded don't end up being casually fulfilled by other organizations. For example, if you don't have centralized demonstration developers, then the SEs will end up performing this task, and their available selling time will drop. This is acceptable if you have factored it into your model; it is not acceptable if it is happening in an ad hoc fashion, and the sales managers are complaining to the VP of sales because "your SEs aren't working hard enough!"

Ratios: 2 to 1 or 1 to 1

When looking at potential organizational structures, it is important to know that SE head count is usually allocated as a percentage of sales head count, which is to say that for every quota-carrying salesperson, there will be some multiple of support staff, including SEs. Generally, for this purpose, the support staff is broken out between SE-related roles and generalists, including training, sales management, and administration. The ratio is based on how much of a sales engineer a given salesperson will usually need. The ratio can be any number, but in our experience it usually varies between a 1-to-1 and a 2-to-1 ratio. So, in a 1-to-1 situation, the goal is to have a single sales engineer for every sales rep, whereas in a 2-to-1 organization, each sales engineer is expected to support two sales reps.

The next ratio worth considering is the amount of SE support staff to field SEs. A reasonable rule of thumb is that for every 10 head count, 1 should be allocated to support and 1 to management of the 8. Good arguments can certainly be made for additional support staff, but it is important to remember that the total head count number is usually fixed by the first ratio discussed. So, if the SEVP determines that another bid-response specialist is needed, then there will be one less field SE and that much more work for each of the other SEs in the region from which the head count was pulled.

Model 1: A New Organization—Five SEs and $0 to $20 Million in Annual Sales

Personnel:

> ‣ One working manager;
> ‣ Four SEs.

As the manager, you will be responsible for hiring, human resources (HR), equipment logistics, and general administration. You will also probably be responsible for doing training and a lot of field work as well. You have a hard job and should be rewarded appropriately for it. A discussion of the successful manager at this level could consume a book in its own right. Our best advice for you is to share the pain with the other groups in the organization. In reality, the SEs will report to the sales branch managers on a daily basis. The SE manager's role is still critical to making the SEs successful and establishing the groundwork for team expansion.

Expect that marketing, engineering, IT, and HR will provide support in any area not directly related to sales. Work with the managers in those other functions to build "sales-friendly" behavior into their processes. An example would be asking the engineering group to work with you to develop test cases or test data that match your requirements to demonstrate a product. Doing so will let you demonstrate the product with minimal rework.

One of the major issues in this size of organization is motivation and esprit de corps. Sales is a tough field, and when you are one of a few people doing it, and all of the others are located hundreds or thousands of miles away, it can be difficult to stay focused. Fight to establish generous commission plans to encourage individual achievement. Supplement this with weekend trips for achievers and their spouses when the group as a whole reaches its quota in order to bolster teamwork and build the relationships necessary to grow the team. At this point, it is even more critical for you to build relationships with marketing and the other support organizations. Even a small team will be able to get great leverage out of your internal network.

Model 2: Getting Off the Ground—20 to 30 SEs and $50 to $100 Million in Annual Sales

Personnel:

- One director of SEs;
- Two to four SE managers;
- Two to three SE support-team members;
- Between zero and two lead SEs (individual contributors);
- Balance: SEs; 15 to 25 SEs;
- SE trainer (if you are going to be hiring frequently).

The major variables to consider in this situation are geographic dispersion and product complexity. The greater the geographic area covered, the more senior team members you will need because they will frequently have to operate independently of a manager. The number of products you have and the frequency with which they are updated will determine how many support staff you will need. If your products are static, it will be easy for the SEs to keep up with infrequent training. If your products are rapidly becoming more complex, you may have great difficulty maintaining expertise in each product in each geography. In this case, you should establish centralized product experts who will need to plan on traveling frequently.

The SE manager jobs are similar to those of the SE manager described earlier in Model 1. They will be working managers. The organization should provide them with specific guidelines for hiring and employee skills development to help ensure a consistent level of quality in the employee base.

Another concern of the SE manager is succession planning. If the organization is to continue to grow, a backlog of candidates must be available to fill managerial slots as they become available. It can be quite difficult to time the arrival of such a job with SEs' expectations. Most of them will feel that they helped the company get where it is and deserve to be rewarded with prestigious positions. Be sure to promote only those who have the skills and training to be managers. Consider promoting the others to lead SEs and having your corporation provide them with managerial training. At this stage in the company's life, you cannot afford to lose people because they don't see opportunity internally.

Model 3: Economies or Diseconomies of Scale—100 to 200 SEs and $350 Million in Annual Sales

Personnel:

- One SEVP;
- Three or more SE directors (approximately 1 for every 30 heads);
- Twelve or more SE branch managers (approximately one for every six to eight heads);
- A dedicated trainer;
- Two bid-response specialists;
- Seven product and industry experts;
- Two demonstration-preparation and -support personnel;

‣ Ideally, at least one lead SE or candidate for each branch manager to mitigate management turnover.

Notice that the numbers above correspond generally to the ratio of one manager and one support staffer for every eight SEs. One number that may vary extremely widely is that for demonstration preparation and support. We suggest two heads because we assume that either the marketing or the engineering unit owns much of the work to prepare your solution for demonstration. If those groups simply "throw product over the wall," then either you will have a larger group, or the field SEs will have to spend more time configuring their demo kits.

A group of this size should also have significant support resources within the marketing department. A common challenge faced by this size of organization is a proliferation of product lines. Each new product line or vertical market will result in additional overhead. This overhead will take the form of modifications to the demo or sales kit, additional training, and customized value propositions. Such a proliferation of markets can be impossible to support. You should be realistic about how you invest your support resources. For instance, if you are targeting 20 verticals, you may be better off doing an excellent job in 5 than doing a poor job in every market.

You should align your resources around the major markets identified by your sales and marketing strategists. At a minimum, have a product or industry specialist, and consider outsourcing some of your training-content development to a specialist in that area. Also consider moving back to a peer-led training model. Have the most successful sales team in each market develop the course outline and potentially some of the course material as well.

Model 4: Over \$500 Million in Annual Sales—Splitting the Business Unit
At this point, the business unit will usually split up based on a vertical, horizontal, or geographic focus. Depending on the nature of your business, you may split the SE organization much earlier. In this case, refer back to Model 1 and have fun with the new, more entrepreneurial organization.

CASE STUDY : PREFLIGHT TRAINING BEFORE THE PRODUCT LAUNCH

Our company was an amalgam of two similarly sized companies as a result of a merger about 18 months previously. The first release of the new, fully integrated product set was due in about 3 months. The presales-operations and training team worked with engineering, product management and marketing, and support to put together a series of 16 preflight lectures before the product launch. As a result of this highly innovative program, a worldwide team of 300 SEs was prepared to demonstrate and sell the product. As an added bonus, only those SEs who fully completed the sessions were eligible for a special new-product bonus incentive.

Model 5: Differences in the SaaS SE Organization

If your company sells "software as a service," or SaaS, your SE organization likely looks markedly different. Part of your software's value proposition is its ease of customization, implementation, and maintenance. As such, you will probably have a lower SE-to-sales-rep ratio and a group of SEs more focused on doing basic demos and responding to RFPs than engaging in complex customizations and product trials.

Making the Models Work in the Real World

When applying a model like one of those discussed here to a real-world situation, you should know that no matter how you structure an organization, most people will be unhappy with it for purely political reasons. If you keep the mantra in mind ("Does this help make the field more successful?") and establish clear ratios for field staff to support staff, we believe you will have the most success. The major variables you will have to work against that are out of your control are total head count and alignment with other organizations (such as marketing and engineering). When your organization is very small, it may be very difficult to justify some of the centralized support positions. In such a situation, try to work with part-time contractors or jointly fund a position with another department.

Cross-organizational alignment can be very challenging. If the other organizations are not staffed appropriately, your team will have to pick up some of the slack. This will decrease the number of feet on the street that you can field and thus decrease your revenue numbers. As such, you should work hard to make sure that each of the other organizations has accounted for your needs when building their own organizational charts. Consider the following organizations:

- HR;
- Product marketing;
- Engineering.

Is each of these groups delivering appropriate results to your organization? As we have already said, if they aren't, then your ability to sell is impacted.

Work with your sales management to communicate this message effectively.

> ### Hint: Tie the Support Groups' Compensation to That of the Sales Organization
> *This may be politically difficult to manage, but try to get your sales VP to authorize some quota-based compensation for key support staff in marketing. There is no better way to ensure that the marketing team will return your calls than to pay them for doing so.*

Summary

Understanding organizational structure is necessary for a variety of reasons. If you are an individual contributor, understanding the organization will help you manage your personal career path. As a manager, you must understand when you will reach a critical mass that will make it more efficient to add supporting staff members. The structure you put in place will be critical to making your SEs effective. Finally, establishing a good intellectual understanding of organizational structures will help you better interact with the finance and HR team members in your organization who are responsible for validating and funding organizational changes.

Skill Building

New SE	Understand how the structure of an organization is likely to impact your career and ability to succeed.
Experienced SE	Plot your organization's power structure and circles of influence. Think about your future career path. Who in the organization has the ability to get you what you need? Among those people, who do you have the ability to influence? Are your activities supporting and benefiting those people? Think of ways to start building relationship equity with appropriate individuals.
SE Manager	Familiarize yourself with the different organizational models. Understand the arguments for the different positions and the different structures. You should prepare yourself for two contingencies: 1. *You are caught in a reorganization from above.* You must be prepared to determine and defend your position in different areas quickly. 2. *You are asked to help design or coordinate a reorganization.* Given that you are in charge, you will have more time to think and build a defensible proposal.

Chapter Goals

Understand the role of
initial and ongoing
training.

Explain demonstration
and equipment support.

Learn about knowledge
management and
retention.

Understand general
sales-engineering
processes.

Building the Infrastructure

I have nothing to offer but blood, toil, tears
and sweat.

Sir Winston Churchill

Designing and then building the infrastructure to support a growing presales organization from the ground up is a daunting task. An
SE organization's development requirements
are varied and complex, as represented by the
technical-sales hierarchy of needs shown in
Figure 24.1. The typical ad hoc systems and
processes that work with small, 10-person organizations do not adequately scale to even 50
individuals. However, the foundation you lay in
these early stages can impact your growth in
later years. This chapter is intended for technical-sales management people, and we recommend skipping this chapter unless you have
such a scope of responsibility.

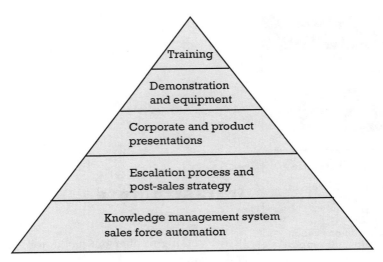

Figure 24.1   Technical sales hierarchy of needs.

A Little Philosophy

From day one, whenever your organization is asked to create a new demonstration, presentation, or white paper, the next question to ask, after qualifying the request, is, can my staff reuse some of this work? Just as you build a strong foundation for a house to withstand the elements of nature, so you need to build a strong foundation for the SE organization that can handle both growth and sudden shifts in direction.

During the life of a company, its technology infrastructure may change several times, but the process of capturing content (including intellectual capital) remains a requirement. For the nascent SE organization, the top three infrastructure actions it must undertake are capturing content, demanding reusability, and formally defining processes. In fact, by having processes in place early on, the remaining two items can be institutionalized into corporate culture. Of course, for most of us, that opportunity passed by many years ago, and we are forced to retrofit into "the way things are done around here." However, at some point in an SE organization's life, a transition takes place from ad hoc field-created processes to a central support organization responsible for infrastructure. The art and effort of building the structures of a small company can dictate the success of the larger corporation into which it ultimately evolves.

We realize that not every SE manager reading this book is in a position to effect material organizational change. Perhaps your company has grown to a sufficient size that a sizable infrastructure is already in place, or maybe you consider yourself too far down the corporate food chain to be able to implement any ideas. We would encourage you to examine which areas of process and infrastructure you have some influence over and which are sacred cows that can cause political heartache.

In an established organization, some of the most effective changes come when line managers co-opt current procedures and change them to fit their needs. Some of the most effective managers filter out red tape and administrative paperwork for their staff, take the corporate heat for not adhering to processes, and then deliver exceptional results. After all, in sales, overachieving revenue targets creates forgiveness for most sins.

Training Techniques

However, first things first: after you have hired all your winners, you must now train them, hopefully based on the 30/90/180 plans discussed in Chapter 14. The first SEs in any company are typically trained by engineering, marketing, and anyone else who has useful information. After this first wave, it becomes the responsibility of the SEs themselves to develop a process to train new hires and further develop their own skills. We can divide this process into three components: initial corporate training, initial technical training, and follow-up/update training, all three of which are discussed next.

Initial Corporate Training

By the time the SE organization is born, a small sales force is usually already in place, and someone has taken the initiative to create a new hire "boot camp." The smart SE manager will piggyback on this training, even creating an alternate track when topics like pricing, contracts, and revenue recognition are on the agenda. In the event that a boot camp is not in place, seek out your sales and marketing counterparts and put one together.

A classic boot camp, usually held at corporate headquarters, features presentations from each functional area executive, corporate and product overviews, competitive data, contract and pricing information, plus some basic sales strategy, and possibly a sales role-play session. Lasting from dawn until dusk for a week, a huge and numbing volume of material is thrown at attendees in a format affectionately known as "death by PowerPoint."

Should you be placed in the position of creating or revamping a boot camp, we recommend plenty of interactivity, including short presentations by the participants, quizzes and tests, and a restriction to using only six slides per presenter.

Initial Technical Training

Within a high percentage of organizations, the generic boot camp is the only formal training provided. On completion, you are shipped back to your branch office, where your manager and peers are expected to train you. Although the mentor-apprentice relationship is a great way to learn, it ensures that there is no consistency within the SE ranks. We recommend that you create a technical boot camp course (TBC) with certain entry requirements. For example, if your company has public classes on its products and services, you should sit in on several to gain introductory, possibly even hands-on, knowledge of the basic modules or services. This can then be followed up by some required reading and possibly even some homework before the TBC (such as installing software or preparing a short presentation).

The TBC can be narrowly defined, for instance, teaching SEs how to use and demo the product, or it can be broadened to include many of the topics covered in this book, such as presentation techniques, handling objections, and executive interaction. We recommend that you take the broader scope, mixing technical, business, and personal skills over a 2-week session. The ultimate goal is to return all SEs to their branch offices with a central skill set such that they can work with their SE manager to become certified within 90 days.

A classic certification process is a "demo day," at which the hapless new SE is forced to present and demonstrate a variety of products to a small group of account managers, senior SEs, and some technical managers. The SE is given a scenario/role-play document to follow that typically details a real-life sale the company has already made. Certification is basically a checkpoint both for the SEs and their management. Success should be very simple and objective—everyone grades the SE on a variety of criteria, and the score needs to exceed some fixed total with a pass in each major subject. Passing the certification should be made a major cause for celebration, failing one or two subjects should result in a retest, and a more drastic failure could be grounds for termination.

The demo day/certification process can be viewed as a crude approach to training, but it certainly does focus the new SE's mind on what is important. This places the burden on you as management to ensure that the certification really does reflect real-life requirements as opposed to being another form of ritualistic hazing.

Follow-Up/Update Training

Right from the beginning, set aside a certain number of days each quarter for ongoing training. This is an important metric we discuss further in Chapter 27. Fixing these days well beforehand prevents account reps from inadvertently scheduling SEs to be elsewhere (for example, set aside the first 3 days of the second week of the calendar quarter) and allows for advance planning. These training sessions can be a mixture of technical training (a new technology or system), business training (an introduction to certain industries for vertical markets), or personal training (communication and writing skills). The days do not include any training sessions set up by corporate for the major rollout of some new product or service.

> *Hint: Stick to Your Ongoing Training Schedule*
>
> *Remember that goals are rarely missed due to a single act of surrender; they usually slip due to a series of small compromises.*

It is all too easy to give up these training days due to the necessities of a sales opportunity, but we would recommend that you draw the line and push back very hard on the topic of any SEs not attending these updates. Your commitment to your staff is to train them and equip them with the right tools so that they can be as effective as possible in the field. At the end of any update or ongoing training session, a test of the SEs' knowledge should be given to ensure attendance and attention.

CASE STUDY: REDIRECTING SALES TRAINING

Given the rapidly changing nature of the business and our go-to-market message, our sales department used to hold regional quarterly training sessions and meetings labeled "QUST" (Quarterly Update Sales Training). Initially, these 2-day meetings focused predominantly on the account representatives, and any technical content was too high-level to be of use to the SE community. With the enthusiastic support of our regional sales VP, we prevailed upon the QUST organizers to group all the material that would be useful to the majority of attendees into a single day; then, we conducted breakout sessions with engineering, marketing, or product management to provide a deeper level of training for the SEs during the second day. We usually managed to work in a half-day of business or sales skill training before or after the main sessions to further enhance the productivity and value of these sessions. By the time the next QUST rolled around, every sales region in the Americas and Europe had duplicated our initiative.

Demonstration and Equipment Support

Very quickly you learn that there is no such thing as a generic presentation. (We define *presentation* here as an all-encompassing term covering any media-driven session in front of a prospect.) Although every prospect has unique needs that should be emphasized within the sales cycle, the key to productivity is the reusability and recycling of prior work. When there are only a few SEs, you are more likely to know what has already been created and how it was done. As organizations grow, the "watercooler" approach does not scale, and people resort to the e-mail blast directed to the "Sales–All" alias in the hope of a reply.

Step 1 for the presentation infrastructure is to provide a repository for content. Current technology usually takes the form of a server on the network with a Web-based front end for searches and easy categorization—in effect, an SE portal with discussion boards and wikis fully enabled. A standard process within the SE organization should be to post *all* presentations, demonstrations, RFI/RFP responses, scripts, and any other bodies of work on the SE portal, together with a description and installation/usage instructions. Posting can be encouraged simply as part of corporate culture, as a requirement for management by objectives (MBOs) and promotion, or just with monetary rewards.

CASE STUDY: THE INFRASTRUCTURE TAX

We were called into a sales situation at the last minute due to an executive change at the prospective customer's headquarters. We rapidly qualified the opportunity and discovered that we indeed had a good chance of winning. The major red flag we uncovered was that each of our competitors had several weeks to arrange a large demonstration, while we only had 4 days of organization time. About a year beforehand, our technical director had imposed an "infrastructure tax" on every sales activity that demanded an extra 10% of time and resources for documenting and testing any modification we made to the base product. Thanks to his foresight, we were able to go through a central code repository and look at demonstrations given to similar companies. A template and at least 75% of the modifications we needed already existed. We finished in 3 days and spent the extra day working on an innovative and attention-getting format for the next day's session. We were informed later that while our content closely matched that of our opponents, our delivery and responsiveness won the prospect over. The infrastructure tax paid for itself with that one sale.

Once there is a central place for demonstration software and scripts, conflicts inevitably arise over differing release levels, code quality, varied user interfaces, and so forth. Appoint a demo champion within the organization, or even regionally, to be responsible for building a demo environment that everyone can use, over and above the base product. Be aware that once you have a customized environment on your laptop, it is unlikely that corporate support will assist you, and you then need to look at setting up an SE hotline to deal with demonstration and configuration issues. Each small step you take toward sharing and centralizing content has infrastructure implications—in this case, head count and equipment. Over the past few years, the use of virtualization technology from companies such as VMware has made the life of the SE somewhat easier by providing a means to easily segregate and store multiple versions of a demonstration on the same system. Use of such technology does require that SEs be trained in basic usage, best practices, and some advanced tuning and setup—proving that there is still no such thing as a free lunch.

An obvious technique that can mitigate the support implications is ensuring that all SEs have the following:

- The same equipment and configuration;
- The same (fully licensed) software;
- The same environment;
- Copies of all software, including Microsoft products;
- A backup device;
- A spare hard drive;
- A "work" drive (for e-mail, etc.) and multiple "demo" drives;
- All standard content already downloaded.

Knowledge Management and Retention

Much of this chapter describes how information is shared within the organization as it grows. Knowledge management (KM) refers to the active capture, cataloging, and distribution of knowledge across a group or groups. Take a few minutes to consider how information adds value in your sales process. Knowledge management systems improve organizational effectiveness by supplying ready access to information, reducing the time and effort required to find key data, and retaining and promoting best practices.

Although an entire industry is devoted to developing knowledge management systems, you can achieve quick wins by implementing a simple Web server–based system. Free groupware and document-management packages are even available if you have no budget for a commercial package.

Key Requirements for a Simple Knowledge Management System

When implementing a KM system, focus on the following:

- Maintenance of a searchable index of documents;
- Ease of administration;
- Ability to review and approve submitted documents.

The ideal system allows all users of the system to contribute documents easily, such that a central expert (from sales or marketing) can review and approve those that will be deemed "best practice" documents. In addition, the system must be simple enough to interact with that it does not impose significant organizational overhead to use or maintain. The commercial packages available today can accomplish much more than our simple requirements but incur both up-front and ongoing administrative costs. If the effort required is too great, the information in the system will not be kept current, and there will be little value in using it.

Hint: Quantifying the Value of a KM System

Count the number of "Sales–All" e-mails sent out before and after the development of a KM system. Each of these e-mails will represent time wasted by the sender and recipients. This quick metric can also be used to identify holes in your knowledge coverage.

Implementation Suggestions

KM systems can be very effective if a few basic principles are observed. The process for entering and accessing information should be simple and well documented. If the instructions for a salesperson cannot fit on a single sheet of paper, the process is too complicated.

Someone must be responsible for maintaining and administering the information within the system. At a minimum, this individual should be held responsible for determining how effective the system is, maintaining the process documentation, and identifying improvement over time. For a small organization, you may be this person, or the process may be delegated to a top performer as a bonus opportunity. A power-user sales-operations person could also handle this task.

Finally, you must develop a culture of collaboration in which everyone benefits from contributing information to the system. This is most frequently developed within sales with payment of a bonus for capturing and submitting information to the system. Over time, as you learn where the weak spots are in your portfolio of sales materials, you can work with marketing to identify "hot spots" or high value-added areas to which your team can contribute content. Sales will often have to respond to a customer issue before marketing can build an official response. Your marketing organization will thank you, as will the rest of the sales force who can use that particular response.

Case Study: The Three-to-One Rule

At our company, the KM system was a complete disaster. Everybody wanted information out of it, but no one bothered to input new data. The entire deployment failed, not because of technology, but because of the corporate culture. Salespeople hoarded their references, marketing was too busy to update product information, and the executives only wanted forecast data. After some additional needs analysis, the system was relaunched on the basis that everyone had to contribute to the KM repository before they could pull data out. The three-to-one rule, stating that "in order for sales to use a system, they must get three times as much useful information out of a system as they put into it," was born.

Driven by the COO, high-level corporate executives were forced out of the mind-set of being net consumers of information. Even the legal department responded to the three-to-one challenge and posted contracts, frequently asked questions (FAQs), and acceptable wording changes on the Web site. Engineering posted preliminary product design in return for feedback from the field. The entire company got the message that although sales is ultimately responsible for making the sale, every other department can be part of the sales team.

Using SFA software to track the sales opportunities showed that the average sales cycle was reduced by nearly 5 days because the KM system allowed information delays to be removed from the sales process.

Engineering and Technical Support

Most products and services sold have a development and a customer-service department behind them, although some professional-services and consulting groups may be the exception. Establishing a communication channel among all of these disparate groups is essential to the presales organization. Any product or service invariably has problems. Once these problems start to escalate, the sales team starts to hear about them from the angry customer, and the presales engineers get dragged into postsales issues.

Set up an escalation procedure with customer service so that you are notified proactively of any top-priority issues and their status. In the event that a customer calls, the process should be for the sales team and customer service to take care of the customer jointly, but with customer service serving as the primary point of contact. A weekly call between senior customer-service and SE managers to review escalating problems is also highly recommended.

A pipeline into engineering is also vital. In the early stages of a product release, this is often the only way to get information on features, functions, and the real how and why of things. By volunteering to accept prerelease versions of a product, the field SEs get an early look at what is coming as well as a chance to debug or user-test a product before the customers. This provides the double benefit of training for the SEs and the ultimate provision of a better-quality product. In short, although you may know everyone in support and engineering if your organization is small, or just the senior managers if your organization is larger, your new hires and even your replacement may not know everybody—so get the process in place now.

As a senior SE manager, you know precisely what information your staff needs to be effective. Set up agreements with other departments to provide this information on a regular, or even real-time, basis. Using your sales training, you can position this as a win-win proposition. For example, with a small amount of effort, marketing can provide product-availability reports, analyst reports, references, and competitive updates. In return, the number of e-mails, voice mails, and calls the product managers receive will decrease by at least 50%. This is a surefire productivity gain for all involved.

General SE Processes

One of the delights about the SE job is that it is different from day to day and never routine because each sales opportunity is different. However, the SE routinely performs the same kinds of tasks on a weekly or monthly basis, so that is where processes and structure are useful. Every organization and its resultant processes are different, but here are our top 10 SE processes to build, phrased as questions, for your consideration:

1. How do you train new hires?

2. How do you conduct ongoing training?

3. Is the SE's role in the sales cycle defined?

4. Do you have a certification program for SEs?

5. Is the HR side, such as compensation, promotions, and so on, covered?

6. How do you capture content?

7. How do you distribute content?

8. Who supports the software, hardware, and paperware?

9. How do you handle specialization when the product line expands?

10. How will you handle industry or product verticalization?

This may seem like a flurry of questions, but if you can answer them and reach agreement on the processes to back them up, your infrastructure will always be 1 year's growth ahead of where it needs to be.

Hint: Using the Compensation Plan

Some of the best infrastructure ideas will come from your SEs. Ask them for input as to what processes would make them more productive. Use this input to have them create the system to support these processes by using the compensation plan to pay out based on objectives or spot bonuses. Pay for results, not ideas.

Summary

Start planning at the beginning as if your organization will double or triple in size each year. Pay close attention to training, presentation libraries, hardware and software support, and building relationships early on with other key departments. The best time to put processes in place is when no one has yet become set in his or her ways.

When working for an established company, choose your battles carefully and, assuming compensation drives behavior, use monetary rewards for contribution to the infrastructure. Use SE MBOs to create small infrastructure pieces, and put them together as part of your annual objective.

Finally, make reusability and content capture your goals for SE work within the sales cycle, always taking time to throw out the failures and refine the successes.

Skill Building

High-Level SE Executives	1. Define standards for almost everything—equipment, software, sales calls, presentations.
	2. Gain agreement from other departments to support these standards.
	3. Build a specialized SE training class to parallel boot camp.
	4. Create a new technical training program for new hires.
	5. Encourage quarterly technical and business update training.
	6. Store and index all relevant content.
	7. Start seeking head counts for central functions.
	8. Document promotions and compensation criteria.
	9. Support a sales methodology and automate it where possible.

Chapter Goals

Complete a hiring profile based on a job description.

Build a preinterview worksheet.

Develop a strategy for interviewing and checking references.

Make the hire.

Hiring Winners

If I have seen further, it is by standing on the shoulders of giants.

Sir Isaac Newton

We now examine exactly how to find and then hire the best possible SEs for your organization. We will focus on SE-specific tips and techniques rather than suggesting how to run a generic interview. This chapter is intended for the hiring SE manager.

As discussed in earlier chapters, the best SEs are schizophrenically talented in nature. The blend of technical knowledge, business acumen, and the capability to converse in complete sentences makes for a unique hiring profile. The ideal candidates are usually people who have done the job before, but they are in short supply. Any competent organization fights to retain people like that. So, how do you ensure that the right person is hired? Mistakes are expensive—both in terms of time and money. According to the Corporate Leadership Council, it costs 176% of base salary to recruit and train an IT professional and 241% for a middle manager. An industry rule of thumb for an SE is 1 year's total compensation (base plus bonus and commissions).

Our advice is to treat hiring and recruitment just like a regular project: know what you want to achieve and create a project plan with a scope of work. In this case, the scope is the job description and potentially a profile of the ideal candidate.

The Job Description

The human resources (HR) department or even a fellow manager may have already completed a job description, in which case, use that as a starting point. However, we will assume that you are starting with nothing. Create a simple two-by-two grid on a piece of paper (see Figure 25.1). Label the left column "Technical" and the right column "Business," and then add a "Requirements" row and a "Pluses" row. Then, fill in each quadrant with aspects of the job profile.

Once you have constructed the profile, you can use it as the basis to build a set of discrete job requirements for the position. This is definitely an area where you should rely on either an HR professional or a friendly recruiter to help you. You can also research job descriptions posted on online recruiting Web sites and view the official U.S. Department of Labor

	Technical	Business
Requirements	Three years as NT administrator Oracle background	50% Travel Strong communication skills
Pluses	C/C++ Javascript	Foreign language Prior knowledge of marketplace

Figure 25.1   The job description matrix.

definition of a sales engineer.[1] One starting point we have always found useful is to write down what you would expect an SE to do during a week. Because there is no such thing as a typical day for an SE, you need to use a period of a week or even a month to encompass the full range of duties. Examples will vary depending on the product being sold and supported, but generally they will run along the lines of "Be able to clearly present the product to an audience of 50 people" or "Be able to perform systems analysis during the discovery phase." You should be able to list at least 8 to 10 such items in a prioritized order. Table 25.1 shows some samples, and you can find a comprehensive list of job descriptions on the Mastering Technical Sales Web site (http://www.masteringtechnicalsales.com/resources).

Using the Hiring Profile

At this point, you can look in for candidates internally or externally by advertising, by using references, or by word of mouth. Depending on company policy, you may have to post all open head count positions internally before looking outside the company for candidates. Internal applicants can appear from the strangest places, but we have had the greatest success rate

Table 25.1
Sample SE Duty Statements

Work directly with customer prospects to learn and document their major business challenges.
Credibly describe and demonstrate solutions such that prospects see their top-of-mind problems being resolved.
Develop customer-specific demonstrations.
Provide a technical overview of product architecture, functionality, data requirements, and integration with other enterprise applications.
Develop presentation scripts that illustrate the needed functionality, benefits, and implementation approach to company's products.
Act as principal sales liaison to global services, decision engineering, product engineering, and marketing departments in communicating customer requirements and information.
Become a trusted advisor within each named account.

---

1. U.S. Department of Labor, Bureau of Statistics, www.bls.gov/oco/ocos123.htm.

looking at employees from the customer-service and product-engineering departments. Transfers from a services or marketing department seem to have less success. We rationalize this by assuming that hotline personnel have people skills and some product knowledge, whereas engineers have product knowledge and some people skills. Both have a strong desire to meet the people who are purchasing and using their software.

CASE STUDY: THE RED-HOT HOTLINE AGENT

Every 3 months, Elsie, an agent from the customer-service hotline, would call me asking if I had any job openings. Every 3 months, I would tell her no and that she wasn't qualified anyway. After a year had gone by, Elsie cornered me on a trip to corporate headquarters and presented a booklet describing all the courses and training she had taken, a list of a half-dozen internal references, and a proposal to create a new position—an associate SE. By coincidence, the day before I had been given authorization to hire another SE. The rest of my highly experienced and qualified team promised to help bring Elsie up to speed. In return, they would eventually travel less to cover West Coast accounts, so everybody would win.

I hired Elsie. It was the best hiring decision I have made in my entire managerial career to date. Within 6 months, she was confidently handling accounts by herself and had developed a superb rapport with our corporate salesperson. Together, they closed millions of dollars of business and enjoyed considerable success. Over the years, Elsie rose through the ranks before deciding to retire and become a full-time mother. She applied to medical school and was accepted, starting yet another phase of her remarkable career.

What makes this story so amazing is that Elsie was really unqualified for the job. Looking at the SE requirements list we had at the time, she barely scored 50% against a passing grade of 80%. The moral of the story is that no matter how much paperwork and science you have behind a profile, sometimes the right candidate just finds you regardless of what the numbers say. Trust your instincts.

External candidates enter the pipeline either via some form of media (newspaper, corporate Web site, job hunter Web site) or through a recruiter. Our advice is to set up a service-level agreement with the HR department to receive all submitted resumes within 48 hours and to acknowledge their receipt immediately. In the modern point-and-click economy, waiting 1 or 2 weeks to contact a potential employee means that a more organized and "hungrier" company competing for the same talent will beat you to the punch.

An open head count indicates that you have a defined need and that tasks within your organization are not being handled optimally. Filling head count ranks equally with revenue generation for the smart SE manager balancing long-term gain against short-term pain.

Hint: Use the SE Grapevine

The SE grapevine and rumor mill is one of the most efficient in the company. As soon as you know that a position will be opening up, put the word out to your peers and your staff before contacting any outside sources.

Referrals and word-of-mouth programs provide the most productive source of qualified candidates. If your company does not offer a referral bonus to employees for nominating candidates, push this issue up your management chain to get one established now! Not only will this save the company money, but who better than your current employees to know who would be a good fit for the position and the company? Many smaller startup companies, conscious of their expenses, recruit almost exclusively through their employees and venture capital partners.

CASE STUDY : THE POWER OF REFERRALS

The practice of employee referrals appears to be more common in the United States than in Europe. For example, at Ernst & Young (UK), 18% of new employees are referrals; yet, in the United States, the figure is almost 50%. The accountancy firm says the reason is that, like many large U.S. organizations, it relies heavily on its alumni association for recruitment.

Dealing with Recruiters

There are two major kinds of recruiters: retained search (known as executive recruiters) or freelance (known as headhunters or contingency firms). A retained-search firm will assist you in writing a detailed job description so that it can fit the best candidate. Providing a job description to a contingency headhunter will prevent a lot of false starts and random resume submissions. However, because contingency firms get paid only when their candidates are hired, they have a vested interest in pushing resumes into the system to stake their claim on the candidate.

For a retained search, the external recruitment company is paid up front to find suitable candidates for a client's specific requirements. Retained-search companies are working in your best interests, and although they are looking to fulfill their contract with you, they will be relatively impartial concerning which candidate is ultimately offered the job. Unfortunately, a retained-search effort is rarely conducted for an SE position unless it is part of a large expansion effort, requires extremely rare subject matter expertise, or is a VP-level position.

Contingency firms (headhunters) are a different story, however. They are paid only when a placement is made, usually 15% to 25% of the first year's salary, and are competing against the rest of the marketplace. Despite their reputation, many such recruiters have been in business for years and provide a valuable stream of qualified candidates for SE positions. We recommend that you develop relationships with a number of freelance recruiters, who can both help complete your head count and keep an eye on what is happening in the marketplace on your behalf. Some larger organizations insist that all headhunters sign a contract with corporate HR, specifying payment and placement terms. So, if this is your first hire, immediately check with HR to see if this is the case.

Regardless of your hiring needs, you should always keep the lines of communication open with external recruiters. In times of need, either personally or corporately, they will remember who always took the time to speak with them.

Screening Candidates

Each candidate should be treated just like a lead that needs to be qualified before it becomes an opportunity to pursue. Successful managers who value their time develop a quick 10- to 15-minute telephone interview to screen candidates before bringing them in for an interview. This proves to be a very efficient use of time and resources for both sides of the job search. Unless a hiring manager implicitly trusts the HR department or the recruiter presenting the candidate, a screening interview is an absolute must. In many countries, your HR department will insist that you keep records of such interviews to prove compliance with various antidiscrimination requirements.

Hint: Treat Every Candidate with Respect

Treat all prospective employees as if they were prospective clients. Be professional and courteous and follow up on your promises, even if the candidate is totally unsuited for the position. The SE community is a small one, and at some point, your paths will cross again.

The purpose of the interview is to ensure that the candidate understands the job responsibilities, travel commitments, broad compensation plans, and any other deal breakers that typically arise. In return, the hiring manager gets an early sense of communication abilities and that all-important first impression. Our experience with phone screening is that you can eliminate up to 60% of candidates through this simple process. This represents an enormous time savings for the hiring manager and potentially the loss of a half-day or day for the candidate.

Once you have decided that a candidate is qualified and viable for the position, respond quickly. Follow up and set up a second interview, preferably in person. If you feel that this person is a very strong candidate, then remain in constant contact with him because your competitor may be after him too. Send an e-mail every day with some preparatory material, or have an HR consultant call to see if she can answer any questions. Do not let a prolonged period of silence occur between first and second interviews.

The Interview

Setting Expectations

One effective tool for an interview is the 30-/90-/180-day plan introduced in Chapter 14. This document, which can be given to the candidate, outlines your expectations for training and accomplishments after 1, 3, and 6 months on the job. The plan serves many purposes. First, it provides a candidate with a sense that much thought has gone into professional development (a great tool for recruiting ambitious young candidates). Second, it serves as a benchmark with measurable objectives in case of a future performance issue. Third, it may bring to the surface any surprises or misconceptions about the position. Be prepared to spend considerable time with a candidate when reviewing this document. It can serve as a solid foundation for the flow of the interview and the basis for many insightful questions.

Be Prepared

We encourage you to reflect on some of the worst job interviews you have ever endured and the mistakes your prospective employer made. Remember that because you are selling the position to salespeople, you need to execute the hiring process flawlessly in order to hire the best—treat them as multi-million-dollar opportunities. With that in mind, ensure the following:

1. The candidate knows the place, date, time, suggested attire, and duration of the interview.

2. The front desk is expecting the candidate and has a name badge prepared.

3. The candidate knows whom to ask for. Very often HR is the initial point of contact for the first meeting.

4. An agenda is prepared, showing the names and titles of the interviewers.

5. Each interviewer is assigned a specific area of questioning. When five successive interviewers ask the same question ("Why are you leaving your current employer?"), it makes your organization look unorganized.

6. A scoring/feedback sheet is provided to each interviewer clipped to the resume.

7. You are on time.

In short, and forgive the pun on one of our names, "Act Like You Care"[2].

CASE STUDY: NO FREE LUNCH

A senior SE director at an enterprise software company relates, "In the early 1990s, I interviewed with a major PC hardware vendor looking for an SE manager. The interview was scheduled for 10 a.m. to 3 p.m. at a large Washington, D.C., hotel. I had a skimpy, half-page job description plus the results of some personal research. The day was a comedy of errors. The interview started 20 minutes late, the interviewers were all HR personnel except for one sales manager, and they never fed me lunch. I was asked repetitive questions for 4 hours—it was not an interview but an interrogation. Before the final interview session, I and two of the other candidates declined to participate any further and left.

Why is this important? Six years later, I was in the position of casting the deciding vote for which brand of laptop would be globally deployed to an SE organization. With nothing to differentiate between the two proposals, I selected the company that hadn't wasted my day and forgotten to feed me lunch."

---

2. John Care, "Act Like You Care," *CIO Magazine*, December 1997/January 1998, 106–108

Questions and Answers

As a hiring manager, your primary task is to determine if the candidate can (1) do the job, and (2) fit into your team and organization. You must delegate important functions, such as specific technical qualifications and general requirements, to other staff on your team, including HR, so as to not spread yourself too thin. Although the ultimate yes or no decision may be yours, that does not mean you need to do all of the work.

Hint: Asking for References

Every candidate can supply positive and prepared references. Ask for someone who would give a negative reference and some background as to why.

Continuing with the analogy of treating the hiring process as if it were a sales opportunity, frame all your questions in an open-ended manner—as you would in a discovery session. Take careful note of the manner in which the candidate asks her questions too. We strongly advise you to use situational questions that can bring out real-life examples. Phrases like "Give me an example of a situation when ... ," "Tell me about ... ," and "Describe a recent sale you assisted with in the area of ... " are excellent open-ended lead-ins.

In the event that the candidate has no direct experience, try hypothetical questions. In all cases, avoid the classics, such as "Where do you want to be in 5 years?" and "What would you say your biggest weakness is?" Frankly, if any candidate you interview is not prepared for these questions, he should not be in front of you anyway.

Some of our personal favorite questions are as follows:

- Describe a situation in which a salesperson claimed that your product did something that it couldn't. What was your reaction, and how did you set the record straight?
- Tell me about a sales call that went really astray.
- Give me an example of how you would set up a competitive trap.

Hint: Asking Nonstandard Questions

Two personal favorites to use during a final interview are, "Tell me about the last three books you read" and "How can you estimate how many gas stations there are in the United States?" By taking candidates out of the work environment in a nonthreatening and legal way, you gain some insight into their backgrounds and hobbies. Find something that makes them passionate, and use that to gauge how they will communicate passion to your customers.

Judging the Candidate's Performance

In our experience, one of the critical components of an SE interview is the presentation, or performance, phase. Typically, this involves asking the candidate to present for 10 to 15 minutes on a subject of her choosing. Assuming that a viable candidate will select a topic in which she has domain expertise, this process allows the hiring manager to focus on presentation and communication abilities. Over the years, we have witnessed presentations on topics ranging from the workings of the internal combustion engine to the merits of the 4-4-2 soccer formation.

Bring three or four people into the room, preferably including at least one salesperson and a potential SE peer. Encourage the audience to ask questions without being too aggressive at first. Every interviewee should be hit with at least one "zinger." A nervous or highly confident candidate should be stress-tested with several challenging questions or objections. The purpose of this session is to determine real-life behavior as a predictor of job performance.

Hint: Engage Sales in the Hiring Process

As long as the hiring process is not slowed down, engage your sales counterpart in the interview. Whether or not this person actually attends the presentation and meets the candidate, you will receive "buy-in" from sales—which makes both your job and that of the new hire considerably easier for the next few months.

This is the section of the interview that the candidate cannot "fake" or bluff his way through, and you should base a significant part of your decision on this 10- to 15-minute performance. Answers and statements can be practiced and rehearsed, but the live give-and-take of a presentation cannot. Pay particular attention to the nonverbal components of the presentation, as outlined in Chapter 7, as they will reveal the "real" candidate.

Hiring

Just as the perfect SE has a balance of technology and business skills, the perfect candidate elicits a balance of quantitative interviewer feedback and qualitative emotional gut feelings. Many of our best hires have been SEs missing one or two key items from the 'requirements' quadrant of the job description, who nonetheless convinced us that they could learn those skills. We credited them for having these persuasive abilities and showing them in the interview process. This is when intangible gut feeling and instinct are factored into the decision-making process. Although we can cite no serious scientific studies on the subject, gut feelings measure all the aspects of nonverbal communication. The fact that the candidate can put you at ease and strike up a relationship indicates a strong probability that she can do the same with customers and prospects too.

Having spent a significant portion of this chapter detailing a careful, measured approach to hiring your team, we are not advocating that you throw away all logic and rely on instinct as your ultimate guide. However, we both firmly believe that instinct is one way of externalizing knowledge and experience. The gut feeling is just a method your mind has of connecting the dots based on prior events in similar circumstances.

CASE STUDY: CLOSING THE CANDIDATE

> Shortly after assuming command of a regional SE team, I realized that I needed an experienced manager to handle the southeastern district of the region. After plowing through dozens of resumes, I received an internal referral for Kevin, who seemed to be the ideal candidate. We conducted a long phone interview on a Monday, during which I discovered he was speaking with several other companies. We set up an in-person interview and presentation for that Wednesday for Kevin and several other candidates, which resulted in an agreement to have dinner on Thursday evening to further discuss the position. During the next 24 hours, I walked a provisional job offer through the system and brought the formal offer letter with me to the restaurant. After a great evening, I told Kevin I wanted to hire him and handed him the offer letter. That act made such an impression upon him that we shook hands on the deal then and there; he came to work for me and did indeed turn the southeastern district around.

Once the decision is made, act quickly. Briefly discuss terms and conditions with the candidate or his agent, stressing that you are not an officer of the company and cannot officially or unofficially offer a position. Have your HR officer poised to process the paperwork, and both express mail it for next-day delivery and send an e-mail copy. Just as in sales, once you have gotten to yes, be quiet and close the deal.

Summary

Start with a job profile and create a functional job description from that. Use existing SEs as a basis if no such document exists. Once you have created this profile, post the job internally and externally, having first asked for personal recommendations. Screen all candidates, preparing carefully for a face-to-face interview. Use open-ended situational questions, and if the SE profile dictates it, ask for a short presentation on a topic of the candidate's choice. Once you decide, act quickly and get the offer letter delivered to the candidate as rapidly as possible.

Skill Building

New SE Manager	1. Attend a legal/HR hiring course.
	2. Ask for help.
	3. Create a job profile and build a job description.
	4. Look for internal or referred candidates first.
	5. Build a relationship with at least a half-dozen recruiters.
	6. Create a 15-minute phone-screening script.
	7. Prepare a list of open-ended, situational questions.
	8. Prepare your team for the interview.
Experienced SE Manager	1. Mentor your junior managers through the process.
	2. Ensure that your staff is trained regarding all legal and HR issues.
	3. Continue to build both your recruitment and referral network.

Chapter Goals

Be able to develop a prioritization scheme with your sales partner.

Build strategies to deliver even when you face time constraints.

Learn how to manage your sales representative's expectations.

Time Management for SEs

You can ask me for anything you like, except time.

Napoleon

The life of an SE is one of managing fixed time and infinite demands. This chapter will supply you with a framework for qualifying and quantifying sales activities. Delivering on commitments is the hallmark of the professional salesperson. You can use this structure to help you prioritize tasks across opportunities, increasing the effectiveness of your efforts, lowering the stress of time management, and improving your reputation as someone who "gets things done."

Fixed Time and Infinite Demands

How do you begin your day? Some SEs begin their day by booting up their machines and either continuing work on the previous day's task or rummaging through their e-mail and looking for new directives from their sales reps or customers. This can lead to a carefree lifestyle, working only on the most critical issues at a given time, with occasional overloads resulting in long nights and weekends. If something else comes in, it is handled based on how loud the customer or sales rep yells. Long term, this ad hoc approach will result in an abusive environment and an ineffective sales organization.

SEs frequently experience changing priorities, which can negatively affect their work. Customers will see half-finished responses to requests for proposals (RFPs) and demonstrations that fail because they have not been properly tested. Salespeople become accustomed to raising red flags to get instant attention, increasing the level of stress across the sales organization. Given the fluid nature of sales, many managers accept this state of affairs as a given.

Running Your Schedule Like a Business

Instead of handling requests on an ad hoc basis, a well-organized sales team should work together to load balance customer demands across all available resources. Tasks that require more resources than they justify should be declined or renegotiated. Long-term tasks, such as training and demonstration development, should be prioritized appropriately and only deferred when absolutely necessary. For most sales organizations, the real issue is accurate qualification and prioritization of customer requests. It is management's responsibility to help establish guidelines for the both of these policies. At the same time, your sales rep is really the ultimate determinant of your success.

This chapter provides you with the tools to establish the priorities among different tasks. These priorities should support the account strategy your rep has developed. By having a clear set of criteria to guide you in investing your time, you will deliver better results for your customers, spend less time working on low value-added activities, and lower the stress level at the office.

Hint: The Payback of Being Organized

According to a study by Day-Timer, maker of the popular personal organizer, "One-third of American workers (32%) never plan their daily work. While 45% make a daily plan at least once a week, only 9% accomplish everything they set out to do. The higher the income, the more likely the worker is to make a written schedule and prioritize tasks."

The Procrastination Problem

Before we get into the details of our recommendations for time management, you should first ask yourself if you are a "proactive" person. Many engineers, especially software engineers, come from a culture in which procrastination is endemic. This will not work in sales, where a missed deadline could mean the loss of millions of dollars in revenue. If you are a procrastinator, you need to change your approach before any time-management system can help you. Consider not only the additional risk to your sales effort but the burden you place on your management and the rest of the sales team. Without any visibility into whether you are going to get the job done, they will not be able to schedule or perform their portions of the workload accurately. Many will turn to developing bogus internal milestones to help you drive to completion.

In short, this is a frustrating and nonprofessional mode of operation, and you should strive to change it. The first time you show up for a presentation or demonstration without having stayed up late the night before, you will be sold on this concept. During the presentation you will do a better job and feel more energetic. This comes in part from being well rested and in part from the security of knowing that you had the time to think through your pitch and the flow of your presentation fully. Try it; you'll like it.

Prioritization

As an SE, you are responsible for translating the strategy the sales rep identifies into a discrete set of tactical activities. Your prioritization should reflect the sales rep's strategy and goals. We begin by presenting a framework for handling incoming customer requests. You can also apply this to internal, administrative, or training activities. We first identify two characteristics of the request. We will *qualify* the request to determine how appropriate it is to move the customer forward to a revenue opportunity. We will also *quantify* the request to determine an approximate level of effort for that activity. Table 26.1 provides a visual representation of this mental process.

Qualification

For each task, ask yourself, will this request advance our sales cycle? Will it benefit the decision makers within the account? If so, by how much? Pay special attention to requests that benefit the customer but do not advance your sales process. You should either avoid these gracefully or refer them to

Table 26.1
Task Prioritization Process

Receive Request
Qualify
Does this advance the sale?
Is this from a decision maker?
How much of an impact will this have?
Quantify
Determine a response commensurate with the impact to the sale.
Break the response into tasks.
Assign likely durations for each task.
Group tasks into 1-hour segments.
Schedule or Renegotiate
Assign tasks to others if necessary.

another internal or external group paid to handle such requests. Assuming the request does move you closer to a purchase, continue on to the next step.

Quantification

Next, break any requests or "to-do" items into a list of the tasks required to complete that request. Estimate the time necessary to complete each step. Group them into 1-hour segments. If you have three to four items, each of which should take 15 minutes, group them together into 1 hour. By grouping items, you lower the mental "overhead" associated with getting into a task, remembering the account background, and so forth. Now that you have a list of tasks and know which ones you will be performing, we can discuss how you can best manage them.

A Simple Structure for Managing Your Time

Plenty of companies out there will be happy to teach you how to manage your time. If you have never been through a course on time management, take one if it is offered through your company or if you can get reimbursed for it. Our structure is much more basic, but it has a few benefits. First, it is easy to use. Second, it is compatible with Microsoft Outlook and other popular scheduling tools. Third, it is designed to establish rules for your decision-making process. This will allow you to negotiate priorities with your manager and the sales reps with whom you deal.

Start by taking your current list of tasks. We have already determined that these are qualified activities, and we have a general sense of how long they should take to perform. Now we need to consider three other dimensions: importance, impact, and timeliness. You should assign each task a rating. These ratings can be 1 to 3, 1 to 5, or *a* to *z*. We recommend you use a rating system that your calendaring software can handle. For our examples, we will use 1 (high), 2 (normal), and 3 (low).

Importance

Importance refers to how important the customer decision maker considers the task to be. A customer may ask you for assistance because they cannot complete a critical step in their sales process until they get your help or because something you said caught the customer's attention, and they are curious enough to want additional detail. Note that this refers to the decision maker, not the individual. In many cases, you may wish to defer time-consuming requests from customer team members who are not critical to the process. Also consider whether this is an internal or an external task. If the task is externally oriented, it will usually be more important than a purely internal task.

Impact

Impact refers to the potential impact the activity has on the probability of closing your opportunity. This essentially refers to how important the task is to you and your sales team. If it is a critical step in the customer's purchase process, such as responding to an RFP, then it will likely be important and have impact.

Timeliness

You must also assign a completion date to the item. This date should be when the customer expects a response. If the customer has not given you an expected date, you should propose one based on your current schedule and your estimate of the task's importance and impact. When prioritizing, timeliness is a yes or no issue. If you are committed to a date or time, you must either meet or renegotiate the commitment.

Table 26.2 shows an example of how an SE might manage a schedule based on the three characteristics just discussed.

Table 26.2

Example of Managing a Schedule

RFP response: You have received a formal response for RFP, due in 2 weeks. In most cases, this would merit a "1" for both importance and impact, and has a clear due date.
Request for technical follow-up: If an engineer at a demonstration asks you to follow up on a technical point, this would likely receive a "3" for both importance and impact. If the decision maker asked a question about one of your references, this might warrant a "1" for importance and a "3" for impact. In some cases, the opposite might be true. If a decision maker has shown no interest, but asks for more information about a key differentiator, this may represent an importance of "3" in that person's mind, but the task would have a potential impact of "1" if it helps generate real interest on the part of the prospect.
Assistance with a trade show: This would probably be ranked "2" for importance and "3" for impact. Trade shows are really internally focused activities that are unlikely to drive sales for your sales team. This may vary depending on your industry.
Training session: You should only be engaging in training that is important, because it takes you out of the field; therefore we will categorize this as a "1" for importance. Training has no direct impact on sales, so we'd give this a "3." It does have a significant element of timeliness that we must consider. Generally, it is impossible to arbitrarily reschedule a training session.

Prioritizing the Tasks

Now you have a list of tasks that you must complete in a given period. Use the following rules to help with prioritization: timeliness, then impact, then importance.

Prioritize timely activities first, then work on the items that have the greatest impact, and finally work on the items that the customer believes are important. Why this order? Timeliness is critical for two reasons. First, certain items may only have a narrow window of opportunity for completion. Second, meeting your commitments is mandatory in order to maintain your credibility in sales; you must either be on time or formally request an extension from the customer. Your managers should understand and agree with this, although situations will arise in which you jointly attempt to change or negotiate the timing on a task. This will allow you to reprioritize the more impactful items. Impact should be favored over importance because impact is a measurement of the revenue related to the task. Schedule the "important" activities into any time remaining after you have scheduled the impactful tasks. Table 26.3 shows an example of how to prioritize the sample tasks from Table 26.2.

Note that in Table 26.3, although the trade show did have an element of timeliness, it was our lowest priority. In fact, we would probably work hard

Table 26.3
Example of Prioritizing the Sample Tasks

	Timeliness	Impact	Importance
Training	Yes	3	2
RFP	No	1	1
Meeting with standards group of customer	Maybe	2	2
Technical follow-up	No	3	1
Trade show	Yes	3	3

to avoid working at a trade show at all. If attending the trade show were a legitimate way to meet prospects, or if it constituted implicit training, then the importance of the trade show would increase, and we might rank it over the technical follow-up. The meeting with the standards group would be prioritized below the RFP because it is not as important (it is necessary but not truly critical to the evaluation process). If the standards group had limited availability, that task would be prioritized over the RFP.

You might observe that some important tasks are never prioritized, which means that perhaps they are never completed. Consider whether an important task with no deadline and no impact on sales is really that important after all. Good examples of these types of tasks include helping marketing on internal activities and working with customers who have no real compelling event.

Hint: Using Downtime Efficiently

Relax and retool. Sales is a cyclical job, so don't feel too guilty if you find yourself on the golf course on the first Friday of a quarter. Industry reading, technical updates, and computer-based training are excellent examples of tasks you should have ready and waiting when downtime happens. Keep a list of to-dos ready for when these opportunities arise. In addition to having an outbox and an inbox, keep a separate file for when you have surplus time. You will probably want to have both a physical file and a folder on your computer. Place all discretionary reading, new technical material, and corporate-policy updates in your file. Before a trip or anytime you expect to have downtime, take a folder with 50 pages of material with you.

A good rule of thumb to apply when prioritizing tasks is always to prioritize tasks that are dependent on other people. That is, if making a phone call is a dependency to scheduling a meeting, prioritize making the phone call over doing research or demo preparation. Any time you have to rely on someone else's being available or delivering something to you, it is in your best interest to enable the other person to complete his task as quickly as possible. Thus, phone calls and other communication activities will often be your highest-priority items.

How to Run Your Day

At this point you should have established your priorities and renegotiated any time-specific conflicts. Begin by reviewing your schedule for the day (see Table 26.4). You may wish to schedule 15 minutes every day for just this purpose. Check that you have allowed sufficient travel time between any appointments. Then validate that you have given yourself enough preparation or wrap-up time so that you will be mentally engaged in the topic at hand as you enter a client meeting. Travel and preparation time would have figured into your original schedule, but take this opportunity to give yourself additional time if you feel it is necessary.

Table 26.4
Schedule (Previously Scheduled Tasks Are Shown in **Bold**)

Time	
8:00 a.m.	Read e-mail.
8:30 a.m.	Handle phone calls from task list.
9:00 a.m.	**Review account materials for customer conference call.**
9:30 a.m.	**Conference call—dial-in information here.**
10:00 a.m.	**Conference call continued.**
11:00 a.m.	**Weekly conference call with branch manager.**
11:30 a.m.	Review demo kit checklist, confirm logistics with sales rep for afternoon.
12:00 p.m.	Lunch with Pete from marketing (set up during morning phone calls).
	Goal: Understand new product position and related ROI.
1:00 p.m.	**Drive to customer location for demo.**
	Review account profile and further customize sales pitch if early.
2:00 p.m.	**Demonstration.**
3:00 p.m.	**Demonstration.**
4:00 p.m.	**Travel home.**
	Send outbound e-mail.
	Do follow-up e-mail from day's meetings.
5:00 p.m.	Handle other tasks from task list such as demo prep or research using Internet.
	Daily close: Review activities for tomorrow.
5:45 p.m.	

Now begin filling in the blanks on your schedule. Review your list of unscheduled tasks or "to-dos." First, see if you must complete any of your tasks today. If so, you should have put them into your schedule earlier. Either book the task into your schedule or schedule a phone call to renegotiate your delivery of the task.

Next, look to see if you have any high-priority tasks to complete. If so, place them as appropriate into any free blocks of time. Remember the suggestion about prioritizing communication tasks first to allow the other party sufficient time to complete the activity or make time for the communication.

Your next step is to group the types of tasks you are performing together. Try to handle certain types of tasks in a group. Good examples are phone calls, outbound e-mails, or visits to other groups within your office. By doing so, you reduce the overhead of beginning each type of task. Making phone calls, e-mailing, and doing Internet research are good examples of tasks that benefit from being grouped and having time limits applied. It is very easy to end up spending too much time on e-mail or researching on the Internet. By setting aside a certain time for each activity, you will increase your chance of completing your goals without becoming distracted.

As you proceed through your day, if you complete a task early, begin working on another unscheduled task from your list. Sometime you may choose to begin working on the next scheduled set of tasks, but if you find yourself constantly revising your daily schedule, it is more difficult to keep all of your planned activities on track.

The Daily Close

You should always set aside 10 or 15 minutes at the end of your day to close out your schedule and plan for the next day. You should complete three major tasks. First, review any travel plans or conference calls to ensure you have captured all of the necessary logistical information. Second, be sure that you have already completed any presentation preparation that you will need in advance of tomorrow. Third, check off the tasks that you completed today and reschedule any items that you did not finish.

This is also a good time to reflect on what went well and what did not during your day. If you have a spouse or will be seeing any coworkers that evening, pick a couple of successes to share over dinner. It is a nice motivational technique for you and a good way to share what matters in your professional life with those who are close to you.

Hint: Keep Your E-Mail Under Control

Many firms issue Blackberries or other remote e-mail devices to all field employees. When using such a device, you need to be especially diligent regarding managing your mailbox. One of us had several junior employees who failed to respond to e-mails because they opened them on their Blackberries, planned to respond later, and then forgot (because the e-mail was no longer flagged as new). It is a good idea to respond to, delete, sort, or flag for follow up all of your e-mail on a daily basis. By keeping as few messages as possible in your inbox and flagging them appropriately for required action, you can be sure you are not dropping any balls. Remember the acronym "OHIO," meaning only handle it once.

Designing Graceful Fallback Plans

As you prioritize your tasks, situations will arise in which you must do more than the available time will allow. You can use the approaches described next when you either cannot complete your activities or do not have the time to maintain an acceptable quality of work.

Get a Little Help from Your Friends

Talk to your manager about when and how it is appropriate to engage other SEs. Most SEs' compensation plans are constructed to encourage collaboration within a branch or a region. If this is the case in your company, you should definitely leverage the other SEs within your group. By supporting each other, your hours of work per week will become more consistent. When your sales are slow, you will help others and work more. When you are busy, others will help you, lowering your hours worked per week. The net result is higher-quality work and less stress for the whole team.

Apply the 80/20 Rule

The *80/20 rule* states that 80% of the value is generated by 20% of the effort. In sales, this is frequently the case. You can often repurpose an existing sales tool to meet a customer request. Generally, you must also balance the quality of your deliverables with the responsiveness desired by the customer. Be careful that by applying these techniques you do not develop a reputation for shoddy work. If you believe that your customer expects a higher quality of work than you are able to produce, you should consciously make a decision either to disregard that individual's opinion, to renegotiate the deliverable, or to put more effort into the task than you intended. In some cases, it is appropriate not to meet the customer's expectation if they are unreasonable. Remember that you may damage either your relationship with customers or your personal "brand" if they communicate their dissatisfaction to their peers.

Hint: Avoid Being Too Interrupt Driven

If you need time to do focused work, turn off your phone, disconnect your e-mail, and check messages every hour. Too many interruptions make it difficult to focus and lower your effectiveness. Check your e-mail package to see if it can be set to only connect and download e-mail once per hour.

Attaching Caveats

If you have determined that you must complete a deliverable but do not have time to handle it with your preferred level of quality, you can always highlight this in the introduction to the document. Be careful that your disclaimer does not sound like an excuse. Your customer does not care that you were not able to bring sufficient resources to bear on the problem. A good practice is to inform your customer that you did not have enough data to fully complete the deliverable. Identify the portion of the deliverable that you do think is reflective of your best efforts and assure the customer that, given additional access to appropriate information, you can provide the same high quality throughout the rest of the deliverable. This is especially effective with demonstrations and RFPs.

Hint: Don't Follow Their Format

If the customer has given you a 500-line RFP and asked for a detailed description of your support for each line, it could take days for you to provide an adequate deliverable. Another option is to provide a summary document that you think covers the range of material asked for in the RFP questions. You may have such a document available from a prior RFP response. This will allow you to provide a reasonable answer within a faster response time. You can take a similar course with other deliverables, especially demonstrations. Generally, you should work with your sales rep to ask your customer if this is acceptable or not in advance. If the process is informal, such variance usually will be acceptable. If the customer has previously stated that you must follow all standards provided, you should certainly ask in advance.

"Be Prepared" Prioritization Tactics

Could you give a presentation with 1 day's notice? What information would you need to be able to do so successfully? Would you need additional resources? What if a demo were involved? Use Table 26.5 as an example for building your own list of tasks you are commonly called upon to do with little or no notice. Fill in the preparation time and resource requirements as well. By creating this table, you can establish expectations with the rest of the sales team for how much advance notice you will need to perform these tasks. Additionally, your sales rep or telemarketing rep will know what the minimum set of information or access you need is and can negotiate getting that access before committing to the customer.

When discussing the list with the sales team, explain that some fixed preparation time is necessary to get ready to do each item. This fixed time may relate to training or to readying demonstration equipment. This becomes overhead that you need to build into your quarterly schedule to ensure that you are ready to respond to appropriate ad hoc requests.

Long-Term Time Management

So far, this chapter has discussed approaches to managing daily or weekly time constraints. You should also establish strategies that allow you to continue to function in the long-term sales environment and at the same time keep your sanity. Opportunity-driven salespeople are notorious for burn out because they try to do too much. If this happens as a result of a short-term windfall of great deals, go for it; the commissions will make up for those sleepless nights. If this keeps up for much longer than a year, most

Table 26.5
"Be Prepared" Task List

Task	Preparation Time	Information or Resource Required
Basic demo	2 hours	Customer Web site
		Summary of business problem
Full-day demo	5 days	Detailed process flows
		Interview with customer
		Technical specifications
		Description of legacy systems
Basic RFP (50 pages)	1 day	
Long RFP (300 pages)	3 days	
RFP for new product	1 week or more	Involvement of product management
Sample product configuration	3 days	Description of current environment
		Expected transaction volumes for system
		Business service-level agreements
		Access to appropriate technical staff

people will begin to burn out, losing their edge and their desire to work. You can plan for the following three common issues to avert some of those negative consequences.

Negotiating Work Levels with Your Manager and the Sales Rep

Once you have established a common understanding of what your priorities are and how different tasks compare, you need to build an agreement with your manager regarding how long your workweek lasts. If you have more work than you can complete in that time, you should feel comfortable asking for help. If different project demands on your time conflict, try to resolve them using the structure provided in this chapter. If the sales rep disagrees, ask for your manager's advice. Let your manager intervene if you think a sales rep is being unreasonable or if two sales reps are fighting over your time.

On the other hand, if you can take the extra workload, go for it. You may make some extra commission and come out looking like a hero. This situation can become difficult when you are dealing with multiple sales reps who expect that you have infinite time to dedicate to their accounts. By being open about the demands on your time and your perceived priorities for those demands, you should be able to avoid many conflicts.

The one thing you should never do is act passive-aggressively when dealing with your sales rep. If you have a conflict and end up underpreparing for one of your meetings, you are undermining the effectiveness of your entire sales effort. If you end up being unable to renegotiate a task with the sales rep, at least he will understand the risk he is taking in continuing the previous problematic course of action.

Hint: Explain the Opportunity Cost to the Sales Rep

If a customer request will upset your schedule or lower the quality of your output, talk to the sales rep about it. Explain to him or her the cost of taking on additional tasks or meetings and ask which activities you should drop. Always remember to focus on the impact to the customer or to the sale.

Personal Commitments

Treat your personal commitments with the same level of professionalism that you treat your customer commitments. After all, keeping your spouse and friends happy is just as important for your long-term sanity and success as making your customers happy. If you find yourself being habitually late to social or personal engagements, you should either change your work schedule or make fewer personal commitments. Getting into the habit of treating personal commitments disrespectfully will undermine your reputation for dependability.

Working in Abusive Environments

You may encounter companies notorious for having unpleasant work conditions. If you go to work for one of these companies, you shouldn't be terribly surprised if it turns out you don't love your job. A single manager may make life difficult for you. Unfortunately, at times, all the discipline, hard work, and task management in the world cannot remedy such a situation. If you like the company, try getting reassigned to a different group that you might fit into better. If this isn't possible or doesn't resolve the situation, you should consider leaving the company. Some companies expect more of their employees than others. You will have the best chance for happiness and success if you find a company in which you can succeed by working a reasonable number of hours per week or, if you work more than that, in which you can do a superior job. If you have to work 80 hours a week just to stay afloat, you will probably have a difficult time meeting your personal and professional goals in the long term.

Summary

A clear time-management scheme has three primary goals. First, it should improve your efficiency because your prioritization scheme eliminates distractions from activities that are important but do not improve your sales. Second, your sales team will experience fewer misunderstandings and conflicts. The rules of engagement for customer and internal requests will be clear. You will jointly establish priorities and then gracefully accept any redirection on the part of your sales rep or sales management. Third, through effective time management, you should be able to lower the total number of hours worked as well as the variability in your workweek. Over time, this will lower the inherent stress and friction that can build up in a sales environment.

Skill Building

New SE	Build a structure and a strategy that makes sense to you. Find a planner or PDA that you can use to help you organize your time. Once you are comfortable, work with your managers to make sure you understand their criteria for prioritizing activities. Focus on establishing "be prepared" tactics. Try to keep in mind the challenges that the sales reps are facing. They are trying to juggle multiple customer and partner schedules, so to the extent that you can support them and not add additional turmoil to their lives, you will be helping them quite a bit.
Experienced SE	Work on your communications with the sales rep(s) you support. Make sure you use a common terminology for importance, impact, and timeliness. Many misunderstandings can result from differences in perceived or communicated levels in these areas. Some reps will be very understated, expecting you to pick up on their intent. Others will make even the most trivial activity seem like a deal breaker. Share your time-management methodology if appropriate. If you think the rep will not be receptive, just try talking to her about establishing "code words" representing different levels of urgency and impact.
SE Manager	Find a time-management methodology that works for you and popularize it among your SE team. The effort will pay off if you have SEs supporting multiple sales reps. The shared understanding will help you communicate more effectively and better understand their issues. Focus on helping your SEs lower their stress levels and improve the quality and consistency with which they deliver on customer commitments.

Chapter Goals

Introduce the concept of
organizing your time
according to measurable
metrics.

Discuss activities
suitable for tracking.

Discuss how a manager
can use this concept to
align activities across
your organization to
improve team
performance.

Managing by the Metrics

People and their managers are working so
hard to be sure things are done right that they
hardly have time to decide if they are doing
the right things.

Stephen Covey

Every day, employees are called upon to
decide how to allocate their time in order to
best achieve their objectives. *Managing by the
metrics* refers to the practice of identifying the
key activities that contribute to an organization's success and directing employees to prioritize those activities. Depending on the
organization, this can be either a simple or a
hard task. With call-center software, customer-support employees can directly track the
metrics by which their business is run. For a SE
pursuing a 6-month or longer sales cycle, deciding how to budget his or her time is one of the
most difficult challenges.

Individual contributors can use the techniques described in this chapter to prioritize
work and avoid "time-wasting" activities that
the company does not value. Managers can

employ the techniques to establish consistent expectations across a team. In addition, individual contributors and managers can use metrics to communicate with their management. In this chapter, we provide an introduction to management by metrics for individuals, discuss how a manager can utilize this methodology, and close with a discussion of pitfalls to avoid.

Managing by the Metrics for the Individual

As an individual contributor, you should read this chapter with an eye toward identifying activities that meet two criteria. First, they should advance your goals or those of your organization. Second, they should be within your control. Measuring your success based on whether or not your region achieves its quota may be within your control if you have the ability to pitch in and help others in their sales processes, provide training, and so forth. Measuring your success based on achieving worldwide sales is probably too lofty a goal for most individual contributors unless you are focused on a single product or perhaps a worldwide major account in which you can actually participate in a material portion of the sales activities that will result in those revenues.

Hint: Keep Your Metrics Relevant

If you are an individual contributor and your organization does not practice a metrics-driven approach, you can still use the tools in this chapter to guide your activities. Pick goals that meet one or both of the following criteria: accomplishments you would be pleased to have on your resume and information that would indicate to your VP of sales that you are a rock star.

Managing by the Metrics for the Manager

We recommend that you use a red-/yellow-/green-style traffic light scoreboard and focus on no more than a dozen clearly defined, easy-to-measure metrics. A slightly more sophisticated scorecard is shown in Figure 27.1, based on the Norton-Kaplan Balanced Scorecard methodology. This breaks the metrics down into four main categories: Learning and Growth, Process, Customers, and Finances. You will need to tailor the metrics and targets based on your organization's specific objectives and your infrastructure's current state. Set a numerical goal for each metric (by month, quarter, or year) and a range for the green, yellow, and red indicators. You should obtain agreement that you are measuring the correct metrics and

Mission Statement: "We lead, our customers succeed"
Grand Actionable Theme: "To be the #1 Sales Engineering Organization Within Our Company"
Psychological/Feel-good Variant: "To make Sales Engineering the most Respected Profession within our company"
The $$: "To over-achieve our revenue targets in each business unit"

Key
Green = met or exceeded goal
Yellow = 50% or greater achievement
Red = less than 50% achievement

Perspective	Objectives and Metrics	Score	Q2 Goal	Q2 Actual	Q1 Score	Q1 Goal	Q1 Actual	Initiatives
Learning and Growth Perspective	**Increase knowledge and thought leadership**							
	Actual Effective Training Hours/HC (lag)	115	20	23	70	20	14.0	Accumulate 80 hours per head count this year
	# of knowledge events (lag)	119	16	19	44	16	7	Q2; one for each of the 16 line managers and principal consultants or any combination to get to 16
	Enhance demo skills							
	% of customer-facing SE's with at least one certifications	95	40%	38%	N/A	Q2	Q2	Q2 Compile current list of certifications
	Retention (lag)	101	97%	97.8%	101	97%	97.8%	
	% presales staff who attend demo training	121	33%	40%	N/A	Q2	Q2	Conduct instructor-led "Perfect Pitch" training for eligible Presales individuals
	Increase feedback sharing between sales and presales							
	% of joint customer interactions with documented debrief	44	25%	11%	N/A	Q2	Q2	Q2 initiative
Process Perspective	**Focus on what we can and should sell**							
	% demos for key products	104	73%	76%	105	70%	73.5%	Publicize list of key products
	Import % for key products	70	5%	3.5%	135	5%	3.7%	Goal is less than 5%
	Total Headcount	98	145	142	94	143	134	
	Improve RFx qualification							
	Win rate RFPs	73	25%	18.3%	71	25%	17.6%	
	Success rate of Qual Scorecard (% of RFx which take recommended action)	75	100%	75%	71	100%	70.6%	
	Improve trial efficiency							
	Win rate Trials	97	60%	58%	N/A	60%	0/10 (all pending)	Analyze trials for each BU to identify what we are trialing and why; examine exceptions
	Trial cost as a % of the trial revenue	229	8%	3.5%	N/A		$199,618/0	Implement gold, silver, and bronze service levels
Customer Perspective	**Strengthen customer partnerships**							
	# of new references (key and beta products)	63	38	24	N/A	Q2	Q2	"Take a tech to lunch" initiative (start in Q2)
	# of business value stories (key and beta products)	116	38	44	50	4	2	Field Marketing Initiative
	"Likelihood to recommend" area average on a 10-pt scale (Satmetric)	99	6.8	6.71	105	6.5	6.81	
Financial Perspective	**Maintain status as #1 Presales Area in efficiency**							
	Revenue/customer-facing headcount	102	$784,737	$803,111	96	$411,000	$392,921	
	Overall Utilization (client-facing & client related)	107	60%	64%	110	60%	66%	
	Exceed NCV target for each business unit							
	% Revenue of acquisition products (<12 mo. and/or have overlay team); (lag)	83	28%	23%	74	28%	20.8%	
	% Revenue for key products (lag)	102	80%	0.812	93	80%	74.5%	
	Overall pipeline/quota coverage (lead)	82	3.00	2.45	49	3.00	1.47	

Figure 27.1

meaningful targets from your sales counterparts, human resources, marketing, and any other departments that may be impacted.

Hint: Why Red Is Actually Good

Beware of setting your goals too low, especially the first time through. Having a first scorecard with mainly green and a few yellow lights will call your credibility into question. Remember that this is not just a measurement tool but also a feedback tool for systematic improvement.

Learning and Growth metrics relate directly back to your staff and measure headcount, retention, and any type of internal, external, or on-the-job training and mentoring. Process metrics provide a linkage to win rates and execution statistics for RFPs, trials, and actual sales calls. They also usually measure the actual number of customer interactions, by type, for sales engineers, as well as the coverage efficiency (how often does a region or geography need to import and export technical assistance?). Customer metrics can measure the number of references obtained by the field, actual customer-satisfaction statistics, user-group attendance, and the like. Finally, the Finance section of the scorecard examines not only direct revenue attainment against quota but also revenue per sales engineer headcount, overall pipeline coverage, and revenue statistics for any overlay products.

Weighting the Metrics

A common approach to metrics-based management is to apply a weighting to certain categories, adding the total points within each category and then multiplying by the weighting. In the Balanced Scorecard example provided, perhaps a company would weight Learning and Development at 20% and Financial at 30%, while keeping the other components steady at 25%. Doing so highlights the relative focus an individual and an entire organization should place on each category.

Managing-by-Metrics Bonus Compensation Versus MBO

Many organizations use an MBO (management-by-objective) methodology, whereby an individual who completes certain goals receives a set bonus amount. These objectives can be revenue-related (such as helping win a certain number of new accounts in a new product line); more often, however, they are associated with the completion of major projects (e.g., creating and delivering a new training class or developing a new prototype). Because metrics-based management usually involves tracking several goals, it can be tied to compensation directly (achieving 87% of your objectives means you receive 87% of your base bonus); more frequently, the metrics represent a set of quantifiable guidelines that help the manager argue for a certain level of bonus compensation on a relative basis. By noting that an employee achieved 87% of the mutually agreed upon goals, a manager might decide that a certain proportion of the variable compensation (e.g., 80%) is warranted. In a situation where bonus money must be allocated among a group, these success levels can be useful to "stack-rank" employees. For example, the 87% achiever would be at the top, above 75% and 67% achievers. In such a force-ranked environment, each tier might receive a certain fixed percentage of the total bonus pool available (perhaps 40%, 35%, and 25%). In a more extreme performance-based environment, some companies institute a floor, where any MBO achievement under 70% counts as a zero when calculating overall achievement scores.

Rolling Out Metrics-Based Management to Your Organization

It is critical that all metrics defined at the top management level of the sales-engineering organization flow downhill to the rest of the technical-sales team. For example, if you decide to track the metrics at the regional level, you cannot have a mismatch between red and green lights for a metric between regions, countries, and the world. You also need to make a decision if a single red light on a metric at a regional level propagates upward by default to make the highest-level scorecard metric also red. For example, if the western U.S. region is red for RFP win rate and red for revenue attainment per headcount, does that automatically make the entire North American scorecard red for those metrics?

Items that support the overall organizational metrics should be included in the annual performance plans, development plans, and goals of individual contributors as well as first and second line managers. Items such as 12 days training per year or 60% utilization are good candidates for performance plans.

Avoiding the Pitfalls

Taken to an extreme, this methodology could lead an organization only to recognize time spent directly with customers. This would lead individuals to forgo training and to avoid helping other people internally, two activities critical to effectively selling, supporting customers, and driving revenues. As the previous example shows, participating in training classes can be identified as a key metric. Encouraging coordination, especially across groups, needs to be a component of your organizational culture. Managing by the metrics does not eliminate the need for softer organizational-management techniques and providing for sufficient discretionary activity on the part of individual contributors to achieve their goals (as defined by the metrics) as they see fit.

Another risk is defining objectives that are overly granular and require significant additional record keeping or management activity to implement. Once your metrics become sufficiently complex and impose an overhead upon overall productivity, you will find that individuals and managers will start to "game" the system in order to maximize their statistics—and possibly their compensation.

CASE STUDY: THE LAW OF UNINTENDED CONSEQUENCES

Our company instituted an MBO program that paid several thousand dollars every quarter if a sales engineer recorded more than 70% of his or her time in customer-facing activities. After the first quarter, the sales engineers learned what constituted customer-facing activity and what did not. Consequently, SE's were reluctant to travel to distant locations or build infrastructure, yet fought over assignments for traditional low-value activities such as trade shows and user groups.

Summary

Although none of us has the ability to define how we spend 100% of our time, we can use a metrics-driven approach to make sure our objectives align with how we are recognized (and likely paid) by the organization. Metrics provide a quantifiable way to track the precursor activities to revenue generation and avoid spending time on activities that the organization doesn't value.

Skill Building

New SE	1. Work with your manager to determine what metrics matter.
	2. Develop a list of quantifiable objectives, and use it to guide and motivate your behavior.
	3. Over the course of a few quarters, informally solicit feedback from experienced SEs, account reps, and others regarding what they believe moves the needle.
Experienced SE	1. Focus on spending your time on the higher value-add activities that improve win rates and drive revenues.
	2. Think about your output in terms of these metrics. Include a recitation of your successes in your performance reviews, and use them to define and support your leadership within the organization.

Final Words

I seldom end up where I wanted to go, but almost always end up where I need to be.

Douglas Adams

In sales, there is never really a conclusion. Certainly each quarter or year eventually ends and each sales cycle ends. But each ending provides a brief respite before you are thrown back into another deal. While reflecting on the material you have just read, always remember that you are going to be called on to do it again tomorrow. In this final chapter, we provide a few suggestions on how to integrate everything you have learned in a holistic fashion, enabling you to keep running the marathon that is sales.

Be Passionate

Out of the many people interviewed for this book, more than 80% identified passion as a key reason for, or indicator of, success in a salesperson. Customers are buying the chance to improve some aspect of their business, and if you are passionate about your company, your products, and their application to the customer's project, you are much more likely to get the deal. Passionate people also attract and inspire others.

Find products, companies, and customers that excite you. Use that passion to fuel your activities and to fire up your customers and coworkers. Balance this with an equal level of engagement in your personal relationships and life outside work. Pursuing your bliss outside the workplace makes you a more interesting and exciting person to be around in the workplace. If you become so dedicated to your career that you let your personal life falter, you will be on the path to burnout. This will benefit neither you nor your company. We have seen successful salespeople who have lost marriages or missed years of personal lives in pursuit of commission accelerators. This will lead to depression and a loss of the creative energy that allowed you to achieve those fabulous numbers in the first place.

By being a high-energy employee, you help to make your workplace invigorating for others. If you feel passionate about what you do, you are much more likely to enjoy your work.

Keep Work and Personal Lives in Balance

Keeping work and life in balance is particularly difficult for salespeople. But if you let your body decline, forget to feed your pets, and neglect your family, you will quickly find that you aren't able to focus on selling effectively. At the same time, you should share your career and revenue goals with your spouse. By doing so, you can jointly agree on the sacrifices you will make and the support you will have to give each other during the tough times.

Always keep your career and the results of the latest quarter in perspective. You are working for your manager (and by extension your company) for your mutual benefit. If you end up contributing less to the company than the company contributes to you, do not be surprised if you are asked to move on. If you feel that you are adding value beyond what you are being paid for, build a business case that will help your boss get you a promotion.

Consistently Outperform Expectations

If you are able to consistently deliver superior results to your company, customers, and coworkers, you will naturally find that revenue and career opportunities come your way. You will be the type of person with whom others want to associate and do business with. Much of this book describes the tactics associated with achieving superior performance. Consciously assess where your weaknesses are and work, using this book as well as any training resources offered by your company, to bring all of your skills to a level consistent with how you wish to be perceived.

Whenever you find yourself in a new position or a new work relationship, take the time to evaluate how you are adding value to the different people with whom you work. If you have different individuals or organizations supporting you, let them know (as appropriate) what you need to be successful. By properly communicating expectations, all parties are more likely to be able to outperform those expectations.

Most importantly, be sure you are personally adding unique value to your customers. If you are just doing demos and cashing checks, you may find yourself replaced by self-running videos and automated transfers! Certainly, this is an unlikely outcome, but you should establish yourself as a trusted—and necessary—business partner.

Keep performing for your customers and you will be in an excellent position to beat your quota. Making your revenue target is certainly the first and last metric that defines the successful salesperson.

Case Study: The Starbucks Lesson

> As well as being an impromptu meeting place for a large proportion of the world's sales engineers, Starbucks, that ubiquitous coffee house, serves as a poignant reminder of the power of listening to your customer, and the power of your personal brand. I recently had the opportunity to watch a new hire orientation session for Starbucks baristas. I expected the majority of the day to be spent teaching them how to work the coffee machines, but instead I witnessed a focused presentation on the importance of connecting with the customer. They were taught to always smile, look the customer in the eye, engage the customer in conversation, remember their name, and ask questions about what they were looking for in their choice of coffee so that they could sell them the right product and possibly up-sell other services. This is all for employees making $10/hour—contrast that with your take-home salary and draw your own conclusions about your talents and capabilities.

Build and Maintain Relationships

Always remember that the person you have control over today may have control over you tomorrow. If you are friendly, professional, and take an honest interest in advancing the goals of those around you, you will find that a network will naturally form to support you when you need help. By surrounding yourself with great people, you will naturally have opportunities to learn about the skills they use to be successful. You will also develop a great sense of personal satisfaction if you are able to give more to others than you receive in return.

Set and Achieve Goals

Apply the techniques described in the book to your personal life as well as your professional life. Over time, expand the scope of your goals to include every aspect of your life. We have used goal setting to improve many areas: career, quarterly revenue goals, personal development, financial, education, physical fitness, and personal relationships. We think you will find the simple goal-setting program we defined to be easily applicable to some of these "intangibles." We have personally experienced improved focus and success at work as a result of conscious personal development.

You will also find that you are better able to advance your career if you have crisply defined the specific criteria you need to achieve new levels of revenue growth or a new position within your company.

Continually Challenge Yourself

Continue to push yourself by benchmarking your skills against the competition. As you achieve your goals and master the skills you focus on, find new skills to improve or ask for additional responsibility at work. The best people and organizations we have worked for have remained at the top of their field by avoiding the complacency that can come with success. Always remember that coming in second counts for nothing, so each 1% of additional edge you can gain may be what makes you the winner.

This last bit of advice is a long time coming, but it is important: Smile and enjoy yourself! Sales engineering is an amazing profession and you truly have one of the best jobs in the world!

Please feel free to contact us at www.masteringtechnicalsales.com. Supplementary materials are available in electronic format. In addition, we welcome your comments and feedback.

About the Authors

John Care has been involved in high-technology sales for over 25 years, from both the vendor and customer viewpoints. He has created, hired, and led world-class sales-engineering teams at companies such as Oracle Corporation, Sybase Inc., Vantive/Peoplesoft, Clarify Inc., Hewlett-Packard, Computer Associates, and Business Objects. He is currently managing director of both Mastering Technical Sales, LLC, and Thanet Packers, Ltd. (U.K.), a British land-development company.

He has a B.Sc. (Eng.) with honors in chemical engineering from Imperial College, London, and is a contributing member of the M.B.A. advisory council for the Fox Business School of Temple University in Philadelphia, Pennsylvania. He has previously been published in periodicals such as *CIO*, *Infoworld*, *Touchline*, and the *Wall Street Journal*.

Aron Bohlig has built a career around staying at the forefront of evolving technologies and industries. His selling efforts have taken him to five continents, and he actively awaits an opportunity to visit those few that elude him. He is currently a vice president at Credit Suisse's Technology Investment Banking group.

He has a B.S. with a dual major in business technology and professional writing from the University of Puget Sound in Seattle, Washington, and an M.B.A. from the Wharton School of the University of Pennsylvania in Philadelphia.

Index

Recent Related Artech House Titles

Actionable Strategies Through Integrated Performance, Process, Project, and Risk Management, Stephen S. Bonham

GNSS Markets and Applications, Len Jacobson

Nanotechnology Applications and Markets, Lawrence D. Gasman

Preparing and Delivering Effective Technical Presentations, Second Edition, David Adamy

Successful Marketing Strategy for High-Tech Firms, Second Edition, Eric Viardot

Successful Proposal Strategies for Small Businesses: Using Knowledge Management to Win Government, Private Sector, and International Contracts, Fifth Edition, Robert S. Frey

For further information on these and other Artech House titles, including previously considered out-of-print books now available through our In-Print-Forever® (IPF®) program, contact:

Artech House
685 Canton Street
Norwood, MA 02062
Phone: 781-769-9750
Fax: 781-769-6334
e-mail: artech@artechhouse.com

Artech House
46 Gillingham Street
London SW1V 1AH UK
Phone: +44 (0)20 7596-8750
Fax: +44 (0)20 7630-0166
e-mail: artech-uk@artechhouse.com

Find us on the World Wide Web at: www.artechhouse.com